THE
Red
China
Papers

THE
Red China Papers

What Americans
Deserve to Know About
U.S.-Chinese Relations

ANTHONY KUBEK

ARLINGTON HOUSE·PUBLISHERS
NEW ROCHELLE, N. Y.

Library of Congress Catalog Card Number

ISBN 0-87000-

Manufactured in the United States of America

Library of Congress Cataloging in Publication Data

Kubek, Anthony, 1920-
  The Red China papers.

  Bibliography: p. 250
  Includes index.
  1. China--Foreign relations--United States.
2. United States--Foreign relations--China.
I. Title.
E183.8.C5K817   327.51'073   74-34222
ISBN 0-87000-261-9

To Chiang Kai-shek

For Fifty Years of Fighting for the Freedom of China, and Five Decades of Far-Sighted Wisdom and Warning to the Free World

Acknowledgments

Over the past decade a number of distinguished scholars have encouraged me in the research and writing that has resulted in this book. The following enumeration is not complete, but I wish to express particular gratitude to: Professor John A. Carroll, Texas Christian University; Father Raymond de Jaegher, New York City and Taipei; Professor C. T. Liang, Taipei; Father Daniel Lyons, S.J., New York; Professor David Nelson Rowe, Yale; Professor Paul K. T. Shih, St. John's University; Professor George Taylor, University of Washington; Karl Wittfogel, Professor Emeritus, University of Washington; Richard Yang, Washington University.

Anthony Kubek

September 1, 1974
Dallas, Texas

THE
Red
China
Papers

Contents

Preface

TRUE PROPHECY, so rare in history, is always worth recalling. At the turn of the twentieth century the scholarly American diplomat, John Hay, remarked, "The storm center of the world has gradually shifted to China." Most Westerners, including most citizens of the United States, did not finally awaken to the significance of the Far East until the afternoon of Sunday, December 7, 1941, when the Japanese attacked Pearl Harbor. During the four decades between Hay's statement and the Japanese attack, few Americans were really aware of what was transpiring across the Pacific. From an occasional newspaper or magazine, and then over the airwaves and in the "March of Time" at the movie house, Americans received only a trickle of information and commentary on the rising aggressiveness of Japan. In the novels of Pearl S. Buck and an occasional movie feature they obtained a slight glimpse of life inside China. Some philosophical writers were bold enough, as was the English savant Bertrand Russell in 1922, to suggest that the civilization of China was greatly superior to western civilization in all essentials. Despite such evils as poverty, disease and anarchy, Russell found that "the Chinese compensate by retaining a capacity for leisure and laughter . . . and philosophical discourse." Other serious writers were stressing that

China alone among the world's nations had managed to transmit its culture in uninterrupted continuity from prehistoric millenia to the twentieth century, adding their lament that Chinese cultural richness occupies so tiny and obscure a place in western educational and intellectual systems. At the same time Americans were being exposed to statistics which indicated that China was second only to Russia in geographical size, that its boundaries contained perhaps one fourth of the human race, and that more people around the world spoke Chinese than any other tongue. It was also generally known that since the turn of the century China had been the scene of one of the most convulsive revolutions in history, an extensive social and political upheaval that in its own way dwarfed the great revolutions of Europe and the Americas. And a few western scholars in the 1930s were even predicting that a shift of world politics from Europe to Asia would prove to be the major political fact of the century.

For all this, however, the American people did not know much, or think much, about China or East Asia until their proud Pacific fleet was in flames at Pearl Harbor. Perhaps most westerners regarded all stories from China to be tainted with the exaggerations of Marco Polo's pioneer account. Or perhaps they, and their teachers before them, had taken at face value the great historian Ranke's seminal pronouncement of 1880, in the preface of the first volume of his *History of the World*, that China was in a condition of "eternal standstill." But even then, though Ranke evidently did not see it, old China was hardly standing still. Already the Middle Kingdom was trembling with the first shock of a social and political earthquake which would shake down the ramshackle dynasty of the Manchus within a generation, and would shake the entire world in generations to follow.

The purpose of this historical "primer" is to acquaint the general reader with the central facts of the Chinese-American relationship over its extended history, and to highlight the several crises of the past three decades. To comprehend what has really happened to China since the close of World War II is, in fact, to understand much of what has happened to the entire world since 1945.

1

A Century of Chinese History [1841-1941]

AT THE TURN of the nineteenth century, China was like a giant plum tree in an unfenced orchard. She was simply there for the plucking. A decrepit dynasty of about a million Manchu mandarins had been ruling China's 300 million inhabitants for more than a century and a half when western visitors to the "Middle Kingdom" first began to appear in numbers in the 1790s. Maritime commerce with the port of Canton, on the south China coast, was economically important to enterprising seafarers from both England and America by 1800, as well as to the local *cho-hing* merchants, but the lucrative Canton trade was looked upon with increasing suspicion by the reigning mandarins in distant Peking. Soon the Manchu court, which traditionally regarded all foreigners as barbarians, was openly antagonistic to the British traders. The reason was opium.

Seeking profit, the Englishmen were bringing their India opium into China for purposes other than medicinal. So vast had the opium import become by the 1830s that it was rapidly draining away the silver bullion of the Celestial Empire, a fact which aggrieved the Manchus to the point that the Peking court issued a series of stern edicts against the traffic. When these edicts proved ineffective, the imperial government in 1839 installed an uncompromising official,

15

Lin Tse-hsu, as high commissioner at Canton to scrub and wash away the filth of opium.

Trouble was not long in coming. The Manchu commissioner's direct contention was with the resident superintendent of British trade, Captain Charles Elliott, who attempted to placate Lin by surrendering 20,000 chests of opium estimated to be worth the equivalent of six million dollars. Lin promptly ordered his police to pollute the opium with salt and lime and dump it into the sea. This was the first act of the Sino-British conflict known as the Opium War, a three-year debacle which brought western military might into China for the first time. The Treaty of Nanking, imposed upon the Manchus in 1842, ceded Hong Kong outright to Great Britain and opened the five ports of Canton, Amoy, Foochow, Ningpo, and Shanghai to foreign trade. Two years later the United States obtained its first treaty with China, and about the same time France gained the right to protect its Catholic missions in the Celestial Empire. As it proved, the acquiescence of the Manchus in these arrangements only whetted the exploitative appetites of the British and French who did not wait long before undertaking a second armed intervention—the so-called Arrow War—which yielded the Treaty of Tientsin in 1858.

The poor showing of the emperor's armies against the "barbarians," the forcible opening of the five ports, and the disastrous floods and famines of the late 1840s were portentous to the superstitious Chinese—and what followed was a great internal upheaval which very nearly toppled the Manchu dynasty. Possibly the Taiping uprising would have occurred in any event, but the sudden decline of imperial prestige was certainly a factor. In any case, the "Great Peace Rebellion" which erupted in 1851 proved to be the bloodiest convulsion in human history; some twenty million lives were lost before the Manchu authorities finally suppressed it thirteen years later.

The story of the Taipings is largely the biography of their fanatical and visionary leader, Hung Hsiu-chu'gn, an unsuccessful scholar who embraced the Christian Bible to the point where he came to regard himself as the younger brother of Christ. His revolt was pseudo-Christian but at the same time anti-Confucian, and herein lay the seed of its failure. Hung was never able to convert the Confucian gentry, and he made little effort to obtain support from either the foreigners in the treaty ports or the numerous anti-Manchu secret societies existing throughout China. His rebellion peaked in 1854 as the Taipings pressed to within a few miles of the Heavenly Gate at Peking, but thereafter it was downhill all the way to Hung's suicide a decade later. Meanwhile the imperial government had also to contend with the mounted, plundering Nien rebels on the north China plain for fifteen years before 1868, and with the blood-letting of fanatical

Chinese moslems until the middle '70s. All these troubles had the net effect of forcing the Manchus to shore up their leaky bark, and they thus became engrossed in what was called the Self-strengthening Movement.

The three decades which followed the liquidation of the Taiping rebellion in 1864 have been characterized by different historians in different ways. Some believe that the strenuous efforts of the Manchus toward dynastic revival, by way of the Self-strengthening Movement, was at least partially successful, and that there was an actual restoration of effective imperial rule at Peking. Certainly the maneuverings of the Empress Dowager, the iron-willed Tzu Hsi, and her shrewd co-regent Prince Kung did accomplish some of the declared objectives of the Movement. It was inspired by such remarkable scholar-statesmen as the ubiquitous Li Hung-chang, but it was hamstrung by certain basic shortcomings. For one thing, Li's leadership was sharply limited by his preoccupation with military modernization. Seeing China's immediate protective need for large guns and warships, he pushed through reforms leading to the establishment of an arsenal at Nanking, a military academy at Tintsien, and finally the pretentious Peiyan Fleet in 1888. But Li and his colleagues provided no important innovations of a political or diplomatic kind.

Some historians have concluded that the Empress Dowager's regime fell short in its self-strengthening goals largely because of her failure to cope with the internal and external realities of the "barbarian" problem. Whatever else may be said of the three decades following 1864, the attempted restoration of the dynasty was undertaken by the Manchus in the traditional Chinese way. The Middle Kingdom was still the absolute center of their universe; western ideas, other than a few that were strictly technological, had little place in it. Confucian China had always been the teacher, not the pupil, and the Mandarins were really willing to learn no more from the West than how to build a cannon foundry or a dockyard.

China's island neighbor, Japan, was meanwhile willing to learn much more. In the same decades that the mandarins of the Asian mainland were holding the West at arm's length, the Japanese were throwing their islands open to the full thrust of western civilization. It was happening so fast that the Chinese could scarcely have seen the extent of westernization in Japan even if the Empress Dowager and her advisers had been inclined to study the phenomenon. Commodore Perry's arrival in 1853 so fully awakened the ancient Land of the Rising Sun that within a generation Japanese feudalism had become almost an anachronism. Enthusiasm for things Occidental included a parliament, constitutions, and a streamlined bureaucracy—and, to China's great misfortune, a fervent expansionist urge.

What the Western powers had been able to wring so easily from China, in treaty ports and concessions, served as both example and incentive to the ambitious islanders nearby. Even though China's territorial losses to the West after 1860 were peripheral and largely ephemeral, such as Burma to the British and Indo-China to the French, the Japanese did not fail to note that the Manchus were vulnerable to every demand for the negotiation of a new treaty. Indeed, as early as 1871 Japan was seeking some treaty arrangement for herself as an equal nation. The scholar-statesman Li Hung-chang argued legalistically that such a treaty might be quite proper. Japan, he reasoned, had never really been a tributary of the Manchus even though the Ming dynasty had maintained suzerainty over the despised "dwarf nation." Li's advice prevailed, and the fateful pact was made. No sooner had Japan obtained China's recognition as an equal, however, than her leaders began to cast acquisitive glances at the jutting peninsula of Korea, whose Confucian king had reigned for centuries by Manchu consent. The Japanese decided in 1873 to challenge Manchu suzerainty in the "Hermit Kingdom," as Korea was known to the west, with the result that the status of Korea was in constant question for the next twenty years. Japanese statesmen became increasingly fearful that Korea might fall into the control of a strong hostile power such as Russia. Its proximity, they felt, would then make the peninsula a dagger pointed at the heart of Japan.

Meanwhile the military strength of Japan was increasing rapidly with the addition of westernized weapons and warships. In 1884 Chinese and Japanese forces clashed indecisively in Korea. This brief encounter cost Peking little in prestige, but ten years later Japan dealt China a stunning defeat which astonished the world and humiliated the Manchus as no incident had since the Opium war. The wooden junks of Li Hung-chang's esteemed Peiyang Fleet proved no match for the steamdriven, ironclad Japanese warships. Within six months the debacle was complete with the suicide of the Chinese admiral, and in desperation Prince Kung sued for peace. By the Treaty of Shimonoseki of April 17, 1895, China suffered drastically. The Manchu court was forced to recognize the total independence of Korea, to cede to Japan the large island of Formosa and the Pescadores, to pay a large indemnity in gold, to open four ports to trade, and to permit Japanese nationals to build and run factories in China.

The catastrophes of the Sino-Japanese War were quickly followed by additional humiliations. Recognizing the ramshackle condition of the Celestial Empire, the western powers did not hesitate to press for new concessions on the China coast. Germany found an excuse late in 1897 to squeeze the Manchus for special privileges in Shantung province, including a ninety-nine year lease on the port of Kiaochow.

Russia in turn obtained a lease at Port Arthur on the Liaotung peninsula, and Great Britain demanded and secured a similar arrangement at Weihaiwei.

By this time some younger Chinese intellectuals, feeling that the West could no longer be held at arm's length, had come to an important conclusion. The independence of China, they now thought, could be maintained only if certain basic reforms were undertaken and various features of western civilization adopted. On the other hand were those older mandarins who continued to believe that the "barbarians" could somehow be expelled and the classic isolation of the Middle Kingdom maintained. Prominent among the reformers were such officials and scholars as Kang Yu-wei, Chang Chih-tung, Liang Chi-chao, and a young physician from Canton named Sun Yat-sen.

Kang shocked the literati with his book *Confucius as a Reformer*, as did Chang with a little volume entitled *Learn*. But the reformers had no single recognized leader at this moment, and moreover they constituted only a tiny minority at court. Nonetheless their influence was such that the young Emperor was persuaded to issue, in the summer of 1898, a series of edicts that are remembered as the Hundred Days of Reform. These royal orders were intended to erect a modern system of government and simultaneously to alter such revered institutions as the imperial literary examination. Manchu officialdom, aghast at these measures, moved quickly to annul them. The Empress Dowager hastened out of retirement, allied herself with the military under General Yuan Shih-kai, declared herself regent, and resumed exclusive control of affairs. The hapless young Emperor was forced to rescind all his edicts and submit to palace confinement. His chief mentors fled abroad, and several of their associates were publicly executed in Peking.

The failure of the reformers of 1898 opened the way for action on the part of those Chinese traditionalists who believed that the salvation of the Middle Kingdom depended upon total expulsion of all "barbarians." The result was the spectacular Boxer Rebellion in 1900. Unlike the Taiping tumult of half a century before, this uprising was not opposed by the dynasty; instead the Empress Dowager more or less encouraged it. In its essence the movement was anti-foreign and anti-Christian rather than a crusade for internal change. The Boxers, as they were called by westerners because of their curious calisthenic exercises, comprised an assortment of secret societies such as the Chien Fists and Kam Fists. In 1899 these societies were loosely amalgamated as the "Righteous and Harmonious Fists" by the conservative governor of Shantung province. Wearing red insignia and employing charms and rituals, the Boxers drilled with swords and

19

lances but shunned firearms in the belief that their bodies would prove divinely immune to bullets in battle. Their purpose was simply to rid China of all "Hairy Men," by which they meant all foreign diplomats, missionaries and traders as well as all Chinese converts to Christianity or users of western trappings.

The Empress Dowager chose to regard the Boxers as local militia, and by the late spring of 1900 half of her imperial army had taken up the boxing craze. Fearing violence, the foreign diplomats at Peking called in their legation guards from the warships in Tientsin harbor. Within two weeks the uprising was ablaze throughout North China. The Empress Dowager finally decreed that the Boxers were I-Min, or the "Righteous Children of China," whose official mission was to exterminate all foreigners before breakfast. From mid-June to mid-August the Peking legations were besieged by the Boxers, and some 230 foreigners and many more Chinese Christians were killed.

It finally required an international expeditionary force of 18,000 soldiers to dispel the fanatic Boxers. On the day the foreign troops crashed into Peking, the Empress Dowager and her entourage fled westward to the city of Sian in disguise. This left the elder statesman Li Hung-chang, scapegoat of the Sino-Japanese War, to negotiate the Boxer Protocol and Indemnity a year later. Its terms were terribly humiliating to China. The legations of the eleven interested Powers became in sum a foreign fortress within the walls of the ancient Chinese capital, complete with armed garrisons to prevent a recurrence of native hostility. This was the price that the proud Chinese had to pay for one last decade under the Dragon Throne of the Manchus.

Had it not been for the firm stance of the United States at this moment, China would have had no reprieve at all. American interest in East Asia was more than a century old, of course, before the war with Spain catapulted the United States into a central role in Pacific affairs. The official attitude of the United States was embodied in Secretary of State John Hay's two Open Door notes of 1899 and 1900, which together established America's commitment to the principles of Chinese territorial and administrative integrity. Without Hay's diplomatic intervention, the powers would hardly have hesitated to carve out new and ever larger concessions on the China coast. There was, after all, little doubt in foreign capitals that the authority of the Manchus was crumbling. What would emerge in its place was uncertain, but foreign visitors to Peking came away convinced that the powerful personality of the Empress Dowager was the only glue holding the decrepit dynasty together.

The "Old Buddha" or "Imperial Woman," as Tzu Hsi was sometimes called, appears at last to have seen the need for a few props to uphold her disintegrating regime. Yet the reform program undertaken in her last years was hardly more than a blueprint. In 1905 the imperial literary examination for bureaucratic appointment, the revered Confucian "eight-legged essay," was actually abolished by her decree. But what is significant is that its demise occurred simultaneously with another stunning naval victory for Japan, and the Russo-Japanese War dramatically highlighted the fact that the Manchus had done nothing to modernize their own fleet in the decade since the Treaty of Shimonoseki. By 1908, the year that the Empress Dowager finally died, it was clear that Japan's foothold in Korea was so solid that the Manchus would never again be able to contest it.

The passing of the Empress opened the way for a full flowering of revolutionary activity on the part of the numerous anti-Manchu secret societies which had been forming throughout the country, especially south of the Yangtze, for a dozen years or more. The revolutionary ferment in South China was principally the work of Dr. Sun Yat-sen, the educated son of a Kwantung peasant tailor, whose unique combination of talents for abstract thinking and decisive action were to make him a legend in his own time. Following the death of the Empress Dowager the most powerful figure in North China was probably General Yuan Shih-kai, the governor of Chihli province. But easily the most influential person in the southern provinces was Dr. Sun, even though he had been out of the country during much of the past decade. His career as a revolutionary originated, in fact, among overseas Chinese and other devotees of the idea that the Manchu rule must be terminated and some form of western-style republican government established.

At the age of 28, after a brief medical practice in Hong Kong and Canton, Dr. Sun embarked in 1894 on his life's course. His first act was to organize a secret society in Honolulu, the *Hsing-Chung Hui* or "Revive China Society," with these objectives sworn in blood: "Drive out the Manchus, Restore the Chinese nation, Establish the Republic." His opening effort against the Manchus came at Canton the next year; it proved abortive, and ended with the execution of several of his cohorts. Throughout the next decade Dr. Sun was everywhere—Japan, England, the United States, Hawaii, Indo-China, Malaya—constantly on the move, enlisting whatever support he could find for his cause. He was in and out of China, usually in disguise and with forged credentials, and by 1905 he had more than forty chapters of his secret society in various Chinese cities. In that year he enunciated his famous "Three Principles of the People": People's Nationalism, People's Democracy, and People's Livelihood.

About this time Dr. Sun united his society with other secret revolutionary movements, the whole comprising the Tung Meng Hui. From

Japan he began to publish a monthly magazine, *Min-pas* (The People), two thousand copies of which were smuggled regularly to Canton and Shanghai. Among his recent recruits was a brilliant young Cantonese writer, Wang Ching-wei, who contributed to almost every issue of the magazine. In 1910 Wang made a spectacular attempt on the life of the Prince Regent in Peking, and was put into prison. The next spring another abortive revolutionary incident occurred at Canton. This was actually the tenth time that Dr. Sun had tried to launch the revolution; it ended with the execution of the "Seventy-two Martyrs." A few months later, while Dr. Sun was in the United States trying to raise fresh funds, still another revolutionary plot was uncovered by Manchu authorities at Hankow on the Yangtze. The result was the premature uprising at nearby Wuhan on October 10, 1911—the tenth day of the tenth month—which marks the "Double Tenth" as the beginning of the Chinese Revolution and the birthday of the Republic.

Once started, the uprising of 1911 sputtered along like a string of tiny firecrackers, each small explosion demonstrating the inability of local Manchu authorities to respond vigorously. There was little bloodshed, considering the fact that the population of the Middle Kingdom was then about 400 million, but there was sufficient shouting and burning and queue-cutting to cause nine provinces to declare their independence of the imperial government within a month. Dr. Sun, learning of the progress of the Revolution from a foreign newspaper story, hastened back to China in December and was welcomed with an ovation at Shanghai. On the first day of 1912 he took an oath in western fashion, before an assembly at Nanking, as provisional president of the Republic of China.

Meanwhile the Peking court in desperation had turned to its strong man, Yuan Shih-kai, commander of the only modernized army in the country. General Yuan was installed as premier with sweeping powers, but he chose not to try to confront the Revolution. Instead he opened negotiations with Dr. Sun and the provisional assembly at Nanking. It was obvious to both Dr. Sun and General Yuan, if not to the imperial officials in Peking, that a China divided between south and north would lie open helpless before the acquisitive eyes of both Japan and Russia. Dr. Sun promptly notified Yuan, therefore, that he was willing to relinquish the presidency in Yuan's favor if the six-year old emperor and the Prince Regent would consent to abdicate.

A month later General Yuan telegraphed his answer. The child emperor, he said, now recognized that the "Will of Heaven" favored a republic comprising a union of Chinese, Manchus, Mongols, Moslems, and Tibetans. "That in one leap we have passed from autocracy to republicanism," General Yuan declared, "is really the outcome of many years of strenuous efforts of you all, and is the greatest blessing to the people." On February 13, 1912 Dr. Sun submitted his resignation at Nanking, paying tribute to "the great exertion of General Yuan" in obtaining the Manchu abdication, and expressing confidence in the General's "political experience and constructive ability." Two days later Dr. Sun visited the tomb of the first Ming ruler outside the ancient city of Nanking, symbolically returning to the Chinese people the empire that the Manchus had taken from them almost three hundred years before. On the afternoon of the same day, Yuan Shih-kai was installed in absentia by the Nanking provisional assembly as president of the Republic of China.

Thus China began its career as a republic without the anguish of a long war and with apparent ease of transition. But the process had been deceptively simple, as events were soon to prove. President Yuan took the helm with full authority to plot the course of a new nation. A constitution of fifty-six articles was quickly promulgated, a parliament assembled, and a cabinet appointed. The form of government appeared western and democratic, but the president patently was neither. From the outset Yuan nurtured a dream of restoring monarchy in China with himself as the new emperor. A clue to his subsequent behavior was his refusal on a flimsy pretext to come down to Nanking for his inauguration. Instead, representatives from Nanking had to go north to that ancient seat of absolute power, the "Heavenly City" of Peking, for the ceremony.

Within a few months Yuan Shih-kai was negotiating with British, French and American financiers for a huge "reorganization" loan. It was the objection of Dr. Sun's disciples to the projected uses of this loan that caused Yuan to hoist his true colors. The national assembly at Nanking was filled with members of the Kuo-Min-Tang (Country-People-Party), the "National People's Party" organized by Dr. Sun in the summer of 1912; by the following summer General Yuan had his regiments marching south against the Kuomintang "rebels." This show of raw military force was enough to cause Dr. Sun and his personal staff to take refuge in Japan.

Early in 1914 Yuan Shih-kai dissolved the national assembly and began visible preparations for a monarchial restoration, which he optimistically scheduled for January 1, 1916. But World War I intervened to thwart his plans. The Allied Powers, notably Japan, counseled delay, and without their support Yuan was hesitant to fly in the face of southern provincial leaders whose anti-Manchu memories stiffened them against any idea of renewed monarchy. In the last month of 1915 a revolt flared in the southwestern province of Yunnan, and its spread forced Yuan to postpone the coronation. He renounced the throne and reinstated the republic, but his repentence was too late to satisfy his enemies. Broken in health and suffering loss of face, Yuan Shih-kai joined the spirits of his ancestors in June of 1916. His regime of four years had done little to establish a viable relationship between the Confucian heritage of China and the democratic technology of the West.

Although the arbitrariness of Yuan Shih-kai did much to undermine his regime, international conditions also played a part in weakening the new republic. The First World War gave Japan a fine opportunity to squeeze China once again. After driving the Germans out of Shantung Province in the early months of the war, the Japanese confronted the Peking government with the infamous "Twenty-One Demands" in the spring of 1915. Japan's allies were too busy on other fronts to take much notice; but the United States government, while momentarily embroiled in the *Lusitania* crisis, managed somewhat cautiously to warn Japan that her brazen attempt to obtain a protectorate over virtually all of China would be an intolerable violation of the Open Door concept. The upshot, however, was that the Japanese did plant themselves solidly in both Manchuria and Shantung, and when Yuan Shih-kai died a year later he left his nation an unhappy legacy which would bring China much trouble in subsequent years.

The passing of Yuan ushered Dr. Sun's Kuomintang back into political prominence, but only briefly. The republic was floundering so badly that in the summer of 1917 the monarchy was actually restored for a few weeks with the boy emperor, Henry Pu-yi, on the throne and supported by General Chang Hsun, a powerful commander in the Yangtze provinces. By this time the Peking government was technically at war with Germany, having joined the Allies in the same month that the United States entered the global conflict. But the real war for China was the internal struggle to hold together the fledgling republic.

Various military cliques were by now entrenched in the northern provinces, most notably in Manchuria under the warlord Chang Tso-lin and in Chihli, the home province of the Peking government. All of this militarism was terribly disheartening to Dr. Sun, who saw in it a flagrant violation of the constitution of 1912. At Canton late in 1917 he attempted to put together a new "revivalist" movement for the preservation of the constitution. Even though he held the title of generalissimo of the southern provinces, the actual power of command was in the hands of the local warlords. Early in 1918 he was forced to flee to Shanghai, where he settled down in disappointment and frustration to write an "Outline of National Reconstruction" and plan the reorganization of his Kuomintang.

Simultaneously a powerful intellectual movement, fired up by such factors as wartime industrialization in the coastal cities and patriotic fears of possible foreign intervention in the postwar period, was beginning to sweep the country. This new culturalism, unlike Dr. Sun's progressivism, was essentially pragmatic and anti-Confucian. Its principle activists were Chen Tu-hsiu, Hu Shih, and Tsai Yuan-pei.

A fervent French-educated promoter of western liberalism, Chen Tu-hsiu in 1915 founded a monthly magazine at Shanghai, *New Youth*, which aimed at destroying all vestiges of traditionalism among young Chinese. Hu Shih, a brilliant and extraordinarily facile Ph.D. from Columbia University and disciple of John Dewey, sought to make the *pai hua*, or "plain speech of the people," the accepted national literary form in place of the classic Confucian style of the old scholars. The oldest of the three, Tsai Yuan-pei, an early associate of Dr. Sun, had studied in both Germany and France before becoming chancellor of the National University of Peking in 1916. By the time the World War was ending, the intellectual revolt against conservatism in China had come to center at this university, commonly called *Pei-ta*, where Chen was now the dean and Dr. Hu a professor of literature.

In 1918 the Peking students launched a radical publication called "New Tide" as a frontal assault on Confucianism in all its facets. Writers in this magazine ridiculed such old customs as filial piety and the double standard of chastity, demanded a scientific reappraisal of the ancient Chinese classics, and urged such ideas as agnosticism and socialism. The next year Li Ta-chao, a Marxist-indoctrinated professor of history, became librarian at *Pei-ta*. His office was soon humorously known as the "Red Cell," and on his staff was a soft-featured young clerk named Mao Tse-tung.

Given the intellectual climate at *Pei-ta*, it is not surprising that some 5,000 students demonstrated wildly there on May 4, 1919. This was scarcely one week after the peacemakers at Versailles had decided the Shantung question in favor of Japan. The story of the failure of the Chinese delegation at Paris, headed by the American-educated Dr. Wellington Koo, must be told primarily in terms of President Wilson's desperate desire to bring Japan into the League of Nations. But it must be noted that President Wilson's high-minded innocence, and his idealistic conception of the modern world, were subtly played upon not only by the Japanese delegates but also by Britain's Lloyd George and Clemenceau of France, both of whom favored the Japanese claim to Shantung because they felt bound by their secret wartime diplomatic secret arrangements with Tokyo.

In any case, the Chinese delegation came home empty-handed from Paris. They had departed in protest without signing the Treaty of Versailles, and that left the Peking government out of the League of

Nations for the time being. China soon did gain a seat in the League by way of a separate treaty, but the damage had been done. The *Pei-ta* demonstrations of May 4 had reverberations throughout the country, and the entire Peking cabinet was finally forced to resign. This was the first time in the turbulent history of the new republic that the sweep of popular agitation had actually toppled a government. Moreover, the intellectual movement was broadened from its anti-Confucian base to include slashing attacks on what appeared to be the hypocrisy of western liberalism. Among young Chinese of all classes, and among many older intellectuals as well, the seeds of skepticism were deeply sown by the Shantung decision. Western versions of democracy and human values seemed to have played China false. As an alternative, some dissillusioned intellectuals now turned to the study of Marxist ideology just as that panacea was then being put into practice by the Bolsheviks in Soviet Russia.

Desperate for example and guidance, Chinese intellectuals were much impressed by a spectacular manifesto now issued by Lenin's deputy commissar for foreign affairs, Leo Karakhan. Only four thousand copies of the Karakhan manifesto were distributed by leaflet throughout China, but its effect was profound. By this pronouncement Soviet Russia became the first foreign power to forego extraterritoriality by renouncing the unequal treaties established under the Czars. "If the Chinese nation desires to become free like the Russian people," Karakhan declared, "it should understand that its only allies and brothers in the struggle for liberty are the Russian worker and peasant and the Red Army of Russia." Karakhan's generous gesture proved deceptive, of course, for the Soviets had no intention to relinquish anything. But the Russian stunt was timely in its contrast to Japanese rapacity and Western indifference. Many young Chinese, now looking upon the capitalistic West as mere preservers of the *status quo*, fell completely for it.

Lenin, in fact, had been watching China furtively for years. As early as 1912, soon after learning of the overthrow of the Manchus and the erection of the republic, he set pen to paper on the subject of China. He predicted in these writings that the Chinese revolutionary movement would ultimately be converted to the precepts of Marxism. The cause of international Communism, he thought, could somehow be served by the Chinese masses. A saying ascribed to Lenin was that Peking would prove to be the gateway to Paris—by which he meant that the East would bring Communism to the West. His cohort Joseph Stalin said essentially the same thing in one of his earliest writings, "Anyone who aspires for the victory of socialism cannot afford to forget the East."

Lenin was quick to grasp the fact that Dr. Sun Yat-sen, while not in power at Peking, held the key to the immediate future of China. He recognized clearly in 1918 that Communism in China could make ground only if it could be attached to Dr. Sun's revolutionary movement as then constituted in the Kuomintang. In contrast, Secretary of State Robert Lansing was advising President Wilson not to deal with Dr. Sun. "I doubt," Lansing wrote in 1918, "if he has any further real influence in China." As for Dr. Sun, he was duly impressed by the Bolshevik successes but did not fail to see the basic difference between Lenin's revolution and his own. The Marxist concept of class struggle, he thought, was basically alien to Chinese soil; the historic problem of China was national unification, not reconstruction of the social order. But now that Chinese national expectations had been shunted aside in favor of Japanese imperialistic demands at Paris, Dr. Sun's disappointment opened the door to possible contact with Lenin.

From Lenin's point of view, prospects were promising indeed. Early in 1920 he dispatched Gregori Voitinsky as his first agent to China. Voitinsky's assignment was specific: to launch a Communist movement there. To Lenin's great satisfaction Voitinsky reported that a Marxist study group already existed at the National University of Peking. Among the members of the *Pei-ta* cell were Professors Chen Tu-hsiu and Li Ta-chao, a radical student named Chang Kuo-tao, and the library clerk, Mao Tse-tung. (Professor Chen would come to be regarded as the grandfather of Chinese Communism, while Professor Li would be formally honored as the founder of the Chinese Communist Party.) Encouraged by Voitinsky, Professors Chen and Li and two other intellectuals, Li Han-chun and Shen Hsuan-lu, took the initiative and founded the Chinese Communist Party at Shanghai in May of 1920. Branches were quickly established at Peking and Canton and in the provinces of Hupei, Shantung, and Hunan. Despite the exertions of such skillful organizers as Chou En-Lai in Hunan, recruiting was slow. When the Chinese Communists met secretly for their first "national congress" at Shanghai in July, 1921, the twelve assembled delegates represented a total membership of not more than fifty-seven. The thirteenth delegate was an observer from Russia named Sneevliet alias Maring.

The Chinese Communist Party was creeping into China at a propitious moment. The country was in a state of almost complete anarchy and had been so since the death of Yuan Shih-kai. In the eyes of the world China was a republic and Peking was its capital, but in fact there was no effective government at Peking or anywhere else. Foreign nations dealt with Peking as if a stable government did exist there, and Peking reciprocated by sending one competent diplomat after another to represent China in capitals abroad. The actual situation, however, was that the Republic of China at this moment comprised nothing more than a collection of regional and provincial military regimes, each one of which was constantly at war with neighboring cliques. This condition presisted for a full decade following Yuan Shih-kai's death in 1916. By the summer of 1920, at the very moment that the first Communist cells were forming in China, control of the country was actually in the hands of ten or a dozen powerful military personalities, the storied warlords or *tuchuns*, who somehow had been able to recruit large private armies of coolies, peasants, beggars, and mercenaries.

Each warlord dominated the life of his district and fought to enlarge his domain. They were not of one mold on their origins, and a few were actually learned and sophisticated; but they were alike in that their obvious motive was personal aggrandizement, rather than the ideal of national unification set forth under the principles of the constitution of 1912. Each monopolized the opium traffic in his area, appointed all the local officials, imposed the taxes and squeezed the merchants who depended on the local regime for their very existence. Public projects, such as dams and roads, were badly neglected, symbolizing the deterioration of the young republic into disarray and chaos.

The *tuchuns* of the northern provinces were conspicuous during these years for the reason that each of them sought to control Peking itself. In 1920 several succeeded in driving out the shaky regime of the so-called *anfu* politicians, who had occupied office in the Heavenly City only briefly. These three chieftains then turned their armies against one another. The first winner was the scholarly and cultivated Wu Pei-fu. Marshal Wu liked to regard himself as a kind of George Washington who might unite China, but his selfish actions contradicted his intended public image. Wu's chief rival, who gained the upper hand briefly at Peking the next year, was the famous "Old Marshal" of Manchuria, Chang Tso-lin, a delicately-boned, soft-voiced man sometimes called the "Mukden Tiger" for his ferocity in war. Between these two, either as a pawn or a balanceweight, was the giant-sized "Christian general" of Hopei province, Marshal Feng Yu-hsiang, a gifted commander of rude stock whose troops were relatively well-disciplined, known for having baptized his troops with fire hoses. Still another provincial *tuchun* with great leverage in the north was the so-called model governor of Shansi, Marshal Yen Hsi-shan, whose domain was geographically isolated by mountains on the east, the Yellow River on the south and west, and the Great Wall partitioning Mongolia on the north.

Both central and south China were also largely dominated by warlords. Especially was this true of such important areas as the lower

Yangtze Valley, with its great cities of Nanking and Shanghai and the teeming Canton delta which was the prize sought by the Kwangsi clique as well as by the resident Kwangtung chieftains. In the Canton area, however, the contending *tuchuns* had to do battle with ideas as well as with enemy armies. These ideas were primarily the revolutionary principles of Dr. Sun Yat-sen, whose Kuomintang served as a magnet drawing together old constitutionalists, ex-parliamentarians from Peking, and miscellaneous idealists and local intellectuals.

By the summer of 1922 the Chinese Communist Party was officially one year old and had about one hundred members. Comrade Maring had been hard at work. A constitution formally linking the party to the Comintern had been adopted; and a proposal for a "united front" with the Kuomintang, against the "dual yoke of warlordism and foreign imperailism," had been issued. In June a second "national congress" of Communists met at Hangchow in Chekiang province. Just at this moment Dr. Sun was forced to flee from Canton by the rebellious troops of an erstwhile supporter, Chen Chiung-ming, who had broken with the Kuomintang because he opposed Sun Yat-sen's incipient plans for a military expedition against the northern warlords.

Circumstances had set the stage, and Maring made the most of these. In August, after a quick trip to Moscow, he again advised Professors Chen and Li of the decision of the Comintern: the Chinese Communists were to form a "united front" with the Kuomintang by joining Dr. Sun's party. On his part, Dr. Sun was by now thoroughly disenchanted with the West. The Washington Conference had proven to be a second Versailles. "Whose semi-colony is China?" Dr. Sun was asking his followers. "China is the colony of every nation that has made treaties with her . . . and we are not the slaves of one country but of all." Amid this climate, in the fall of 1922, one of Lenin's ablest negotiators, Adolf Joffe, a former professor of international law, arrived at Peking as the official Soviet envoy.

Lenin's instruction to Joffe was to establish formal diplomatic relations, if possible, with the existing warlord regime in Peking; otherwise Joffe was to deal directly with Dr. Sun wherever he could be found. Getting nowhere at Peking, Joffe met Dr. Sun in Shanghai at the end of the year and found the Kuomintang leader in a receptive mood. The moment had come. On January 26, 1923, the two issued a joint manifesto of profound importance which received wide publicity throughout China but was largely overlooked abroad:

Dr. Sun Yat-sen holds that the Communist order or even the Soviet system cannot actually be introduced into China, because there do not exist here the conditions for the successful establishment of either Communism or Sovietism. This view is entirely shared by Mr. Joffe, who is further of the opinion that China's paramount and most pressing problem is to achieve national unification and attain full national independence, and regarding this task he has assured Dr. Sun Yat-sen that China has the warmest sympathy of the Russian people and can count on the support of Russia.[1]

From Lenin's point of view, the Kuomintang-Communist entente of 1923 was very timely. The Comintern had actually designated China as its major objective for the five years between 1922 and 1927. From Dr. Sun's point of view, the joint manifesto was also timely. His followers had just regained control of Canton, and he needed all the support he could muster from any source at this moment if his revolutionary program was finally to succeed. He thought of the arrangement with Joffe as "purely a marriage of convenience" which would never really damage his Three Principles of the People. He scarcely imagined that a small number of individuals who were Communists could endanger the Kuomintang; rather he felt that the surest way to deter them from inciting class struggle was to absorb them as individuals in the Chinese Nationalist movement.

Moreover, Dr. Sun did believe that he might learn something in the way of techniques from a close study of Soviet methodology. What he wanted here were suitable tools with which to work out some of China's problems of unification; in no sense was he looking for philosophies of revolution based on the Marxian concept of class struggle. Just as Dr. Sun has been unfairly charged by some historians with "old-style warlordism" for his endeavors at national unification following the disappointment of Versailles, others have thoughtlessly criticized his entente with Joffe following the Washington Conference as a concession or sellout to Communism. Both accusations are blind to the critical situation confronting the father of the Chinese Revolution in these years. After a lifetime of effort, Dr. Sun was still trying to unify his country and still trusting those who seemed willing to help.

To implement the entente, Dr. Sun sent his bright and energetic chief of staff, the thirty-six-year-old Chiang Kai-shek, on an official visit to Moscow in August, 1923. Chiang carried letters of introduction to Lenin, Trotsky, and Chicherin, stayed four months, and returned to Canton with a generally unfavorable impression of Communism despite the warmth of his reception. He had seen at first hand the deep dissimilarities between the Russian situation and that in China. He clearly recognized that the revolution in Confucian China must be vastly different in its direction than the social experiment

[1]As in Warren Kuo, *Analytical History of the Chinese Communist Party* (Taipei: Institute of International Relations, 1966), I, 85.

in Bolshevik Russia. Chiang has described his reaction to the Soviets in these words:

Before I went to Russia I, too, had believed that the offer of the Russian Communist Party to help our National Revolution was motivated by a sincere desire to treat us as an equal and not with ulterior motives. As a result of my visit to Russia, however, I was completely disillusioned. I came to the conclusion that our policy of aligning with Russia and admitting Chinese Communists into our ranks, though it might prove to be useful in fighting Western colonialism for the time being, could not in the long run bring us to our goal of national independence and freedom. Furthermore, I felt that Soviet Russia's strategem and the objective of her World Revolution program were even more dangerous to national independence movements in the Orient than the old colonialism.[2]

During the same months that Chiang Kai-shek was in Moscow representing Dr. Sun, Lenin sent Leo Karakhan to China to negotiate a treaty with the Peking government. Karakhan's name was well known because of his famous manifesto of 1919 renouncing all Czarist claims and concessions in China. He was warmly received in August of 1923, but his impertinent questions on the status of Outer Mongolia and the ownership of the Chinese Eastern Railway impeded his discussions with Peking officials. It was becoming increasingly clear to the Soviets, therefore, that Dr. Sun's Kuomintang was indeed the key. In a personal letter to Dr. Sun, Karakhan informed the Kuomintang leader that a special Russian adviser, Michael M. Borodin, had been dispatched to Canton to be of assistance. Borodin, to whom Karakhan referred as "Comrade B", was an experienced Communist agent and "one of the oldest members of our Party . . . with whom you may talk as frankly as you would with me."

Borodin's name was an alias. A native of Russia whose actual name was Grusemberg, he had gone as a child with his parents to the United States and was educated in public schools in Chicago. Beginning his adult life under the the shortened name of Berg, he directed a business college for some time and became an insatiable reader of the works of Marx. It was on an assignment by the Comintern to carry the revolutionary doctrine to Mexico that he assumed the name of Borodin.

The versatile "Comrade B" reached Canton in the early autumn of 1923, and by the end of the year he had won the confidence of Dr. Sun with an elaborate plan for the reshaping of the Kuomintang. At the same time Dr. Sun was receiving encouragement by mail from Moscow. Chicheran and Karakhan were urging him to begin a pro-

[2]Chiang Kai-shek, *Soviet Russia in China* (New York: Farrar, Strauss & Cudahy, 1957), P. 24.

gram of land reform and to mobilize the support of the Chinese masses along Soviet lines. So far as techniques were concerned, Dr. Sun was willing to follow such advice. The Kuomintang simply had to be tightened and strengthened before it could become effective against the warlords.

Under Borodin's direction the Kuomintang was formally reorganized during the "First National Party Congress" at Canton in January, 1924, along the lines of the Communist Party of the Soviet Union. As in Mother Russia, direct control was to flow from central party headquarters down to the smallest units. Individual Communists, of whom there were still not many in China, were encouraged to join the Kuomintang with an oath of allegiance to Dr. Sun's Three Principles. Dr. Sun confidently hoped that the few scattered intellectuals who had embraced Marxism would now switch to the ideology of the Kuomintang. As the months went by, Dr. Sun became increasingly anxious to collaborate with Russia, and the influence of Borodin at Canton grew in proportion. At central party headquarters the most important positions fell into the hands of Communists such as Lin Tsu-han, who became Director of Peasant Affairs, and by the summer of 1924 the number of Communists in China increased to about 1,500.

Meanwhile Dr. Sun was giving a series of eighteen public lectures at the college in Canton on the subject of his Three Principles. In one of these lectures Dr. Sun spoke favorably on the socio-economic improvements which had taken place in the United States in recent decades, and at the same time he branded the Marxist class struggle "a kind of social disease." Borodin, who was present, became furious when Dr. Sun described Marx as a "social pathologist" rather than a "social physiologist." In lectures and press interviews throughout 1924, Dr. Sun reiterated his belief that the Three Principles of the People must never be confused by his Chinese followers with Marxism. By such statements he made it perfectly plain that he was categorically rejecting Communism, and accepting only those sophisticated techniques of organization which had proved useful to Lenin in Russia.

One such idea was to establish a military school to train officers for a national revolutionary army. In May, 1925, the Whampoa Military Academy was opened at Canton with some 500 cadets drawn from every region of China. General Chiang became its first superintendent. But then two Russian officers, Kisanko and Bluecher (alias Galen), arrived to offer their professional advice. As a result, the political department was soon under the chairmanship of a bright young Communist organizer from Hunan province. His name was Chou En-lai.

As early as the fall of 1924 Dr. Sun had determined to move at once against the northern warlords. He began preparations for a large expedition to be led by General Chiang, but in early November news came from Peking that Wu Pei-fu's regime had been suddenly over-turned in a local coup. Dr. Sun was suffering from a liver ailment, but he decided to go personally to the Heavenly City to negotiate with Wu's successors. Arriving on the last day of the year, he was immediately confined to a sick bed and was unable to open discussions. Meanwhile his old rival at Canton, Cheng Chiung-ming, made an attack on the city but was promptly repulsed by Chiang Kai-shek.

On March 12, 1925, Sun Yat-sen died in Peking at the age of 59 without seeing the fulfillment of his lifelong dream of the unification of the Chinese people under a republic. Sun wanted to bring China into the modern world and to gain for her an equal and honored place in the family of nations. Even during his long periods of exile, and his frustration and disappointment over lack of support from his own countrymen, his thoughts were always on China's future. He was first and foremost a Chinese nationalist. According to his will, which was read in public with great respect, the national revolution must be pursued until China achieved independence and equality. This became the sacred canon of the Kuomintang, and his Three Principles of the People the Nationalist bible.

The death of Dr. Sun posed the immediate problem of succession to the leadership of the Kuomintang. His will left a reminder that the work of the revolution had not yet been completed, but gave no clear indication as to which of the four of his closest associates should take up his mantle. These four were Liao Chung-kai, Hu Han-min, Wang Ching-wei, and Chiang Kai-shek.

Of the four, the most influential at the moment was the ultra-leftist Liao Chung-kai. He concurrently held thirteen different posts within the Kuomintang and was in intimate contact with Commissar Borodin, his close neighbor in the suburb of Canton. But the rightist Hu Han-min, a general who had once served as acting commander-in-chief for Dr. Sun, nourished the hope that the party leadership would descend upon him. A similar hope resided in the handsome and brilliant head of Dr. Sun's early disciple and secretary, Wang Ching-wei, who had taken down the Last Will and Testament and moreover enjoyed a kind of national reputation as a patriot because of his famous attempt to assasinate the Prince Regent in 1910. Borodin, despite a close association with Liao, actually favored Wang as Dr. Sun's successor because he seemed "ambitious and unprincipled" and "could well be used as a convenient tool." Perhaps least attractive to Borodin was the commandant of Whampoa, General Chiang Kai-shek, whose suspicion of Soviet intentions in China had been well known in the Kuomintang for more than a year.

While the leadership of the Kuomintang was thus unsettled at Canton, the Peking government was passing from one warlord to another—from the control of the "Christian general," Marshal Feng

Yu-hsiang, into the hands of the "Mukden tiger," Marshal Chang Tso-lin of Manchuria. Both had negotiated treaties with Lenin's deputy foreign minister, Karakhan, during the year 1924, but Chang was decidedly anti-Bolshevik in outlook where Feng was at least mildly pro-Russian. Feng's loss of control at Peking in 1925 made it imperative, therefore, that Soviet influence in the Kuomintang at Canton be enlarged by Borodin as quickly as possible.

Circumstances played into Borodin's hands. Scarcely more than two months after Dr. Sun's death, Shanghai was rocked by a violent anti-western, anti-Christian demonstration. It was staged by students expressing outrage over the death of a Chinese cotton-mill laborer and the subsequent shooting of eight agitators by British police in the international settlement. Repercussions of the "Shanghai Incident" of May 30, 1925 were felt throughout the summer, not only in Shanghai where a general strike paralyzed commerce and trade, but elsewhere as far inland as Chungking. Trouble of this kind was just what Borodin needed at the moment, and it was close at hand. At Canton more than a hundred Chinese were killed while demonstrating on the bund opposite the British and French concessions.

Then, late in August, a very serious disturbance occurred at the Kuomintang headquarters in Canton. The ultra-leftist Liao Chung-kai was shot in broad daylight as he entered the headquarters building. Liao died instantly, and his assassin was killed on the spot by guards, Borodin seized the opportunity to implicate Liao's rightist rival, Hu Han-min, in the assasination plot, thereby eliminating him as possible successor to Dr. Sun. Other important rightist Kuomintang members were forced, by various devices, to leave Canton in the next four months. The way now seemed open to Borodin for the seating of his favorite, the ruthless intellectual whom he hoped to use as a convenient tool, Wang Ching-wei.

But the conservative Kuomintang leaders who had fled Canton were not ready to surrender Dr. Sun's party to Borodin. Late in November of 1925 they gathered at the Western Hills, outside Peking, for a strategy conference in front of the coffin of Dr. Sun. In a strong statement they resolved to expel all Communists from the Kuomintang and to dismiss Borodin as adviser:

> Now that the Communists have disregarded all other considerations and gone ahead with a single purpose of promoting their own party interests, we are morally bound to protect the best interests of the Kuomintang and cannot permit the existence of a party within a party. It is, therefore, hereby resolved that all Communists who have joined our party be required to withdraw from the Kuomintang.[3]

[3]As in Chung-gi Kwei, *The Kuomintang-Communist Struggle in China, 1922-1949* (The Hague: Martinus Niehoff, 1970), 33.

Borodin's answer to this was to call a "national congress" of the Kuomintang into existence at Canton on January 1, 1926, with the purpose of asserting his control over the party. The Western Hills group then set up a separate headquarters in Shanghai. By this time Borodin had come to regard Chiang Kai-shek as the principal obstacle to his designs—and one figure to whom the Western Hills group might gravitate. Earlier the Soviet agent had attempted to embarrass General Chiang into resigning as director of Whampoa Academy, and now he tried something bolder.

In March of 1926 Borodin made an effort to trick Chiang Kai-shek aboard the gunboat *Chungshan* in the Yangtze. The thinly concealed purpose was to exile him into the custody of Russian authorities at Vladivostok. With Chiang out of the way, the Communists envisaged a general strike to be called by the labor unions in Canton and Hong Kong. Detecting the plot, Chiang took prompt action to thwart Borodin's schemes. He put Canton under martial law and moved decisively against the conspirators, increasing his own and the Kuomintang's prestige greatly by the action.

Chiang Kai-shek's position as a national leader was soon to be enhanced even more. Anxious to proceed with Dr. Sun's old plan for a sweeping campaign against the provincial warlords, Chiang felt it necessary to enlist the support of Borodin who by then controlled the Kuomintang leftwing. Borodin and the Chinese Communist had never been very enthusiastic about such an expedition. Violently antiwestern, they were convinced that a national military expedition against the warlords would stop short of their great goal—the total eradication of western influence and "extrality" in China. In his magazine, for example, Professor Chen Tu-hsiu predicted that in any such expedition the nationalist forces would end up by bargaining with the Western imperialists once they had reached the lower Yangtze valley.

As it turned out, Chiang Kai-shek obtained Communist support for his proposed expedition by way of a compromise. He dropped his investigation of the gunboat incident which might have revealed Soviet complicity at high levels, and accepted the expulsion of a single Soviet agent named Kisanko as sufficient retribution. Then, on June 6, 1926, Chiang was appointed commander-in-chief of the National Revolutionary Army and authorized to organize the memorable "Northern Expedition" against the provincial warlords. Within a month he had six armies in the field against the warlords, and he pressed the campaign with great energy in a dozen provinces throughout the rest of the year.

As Chiang Kai-shek's armies moved north from Canton, one warlord after another resisted, tried to bargain, and finally collapsed. With each victory the national enthusiasm mounted—and, as might be imagined, the Chinese Communists accompanying the expedition took advantage of its successes to propagandize and recruit everywhere among peasant and coolie classes. The tactics of the Communists were spectacular. Using various devices to attract attention, they harangued the peasants and coolies with anti-imperialist, anti-landlord slogans and catchwords, quickly creating mobs of followers who joined the vanguard of Chiang's armies.[4]

There is no question that the Chinese Communists, taking their instructions from Borodin, gave some impetus to the expedition. Moreover, the contribution of Soviet equipment and military advisers was doubtless of some value to Chiang Kai-shek. But Chiang's purpose was basically the original purpose of Dr. Sun; it was simply to unify the country by breaking the grip of the military despots who ruled the provinces for their own selfish purposes. The joint purpose of the Communists, on the other hand was to wipe out all western influence and overturn the Chinese class structure.

By November, 1926, the National Revolutionary Army had secured control of Hankow, but Communist agitators succeeded in exciting such anti-British fervor there that many foreigners had to flee for their lives to the shelter of the gunboats on the Yangtze. Elated, Comrade Borodin now insisted that the Kuomintang party headquarters and the government itself be moved from Canton to Hankow. No sooner was this done than Borodin became overt in his plan to discredit Chiang and install his scheming and unscrupulous favorite, Wang Ching-wei, in the general's place. At a dinner in Chiang's honor in December, Borodin boldly tried to provoke the commander-in-chief into resigning. Chiang remained calm, and the ploy did not work.

It was not long, however, before the Chinese Communists were trying another tack. They now determined to use Chiang Kai-shek's rapid penetration of the domain of the warlords as an opening wedge to make contact with the rural areas and organize the peasants along Leninist lines. At the same time they hoped to take advantage of Chiang's absence and preoccupation on the military front to build their influence among the coolie workers in the cities. The executive committee of the Comintern, meeting at Moscow in November, 1926, adopted a resolution declaring the enthusiastic response of the Chinese people to the Northward Expedition to be a third stage in the world revolution. It further resolved that the Chinese Communists should definitely remain with the Kuomintang fold, rather than break with the party, as a practical way to gain access to the peasants and coolies.

Toward the end of the important year of 1926 the Kuomintang cap-

[4]An excellent portrayal of this situation was given in the 1967 movie, *The Sandpebbles.*

ital was moved to Hankow. But this city was deep in the sphere of Communist influence, and the left-wing leaders there were obviously intent upon turning the national revolution into a Marxist proletarian revolution. Chiang Kai-shek meanwhile was attempting to consolidate the support of the middle class, and particularly that of the banking community of Shanghai. The Chinese Communists had solemnly promised to support the national program of the Kuomintang. They clearly broke that promise, and Chiang now courageously and wisely decided to sever all Kuomintang connection with the Russians.

In March, 1927, following the entry of Nationalist troops into Nanking, some soldiers became so excited by Communist anti-imperialist agitation that they senselessly attacked the residences of Americans and Europeans living in that city. Several lives were lost in this incident, and Chiang decided that the time had come for drastic measures. Accordingly, in April, he moved his offices to Nanking and away from the left-wing at Hankow, swiftly purged the Kuomintang of its Communist members and sympathizers, and by summer had broken the power of Comrade Borodin and forced his retirement from China.

The *entente cordiale* with the Soviets, lasting three years, had proven a complete failure. It was marked by endless Communist maneuvering for control of strategic positions within the Kuomintang structure and by secretive attempts to build up some popularity whereever possible. Chiang Kai-shek's housecleaning finally blasted the hopes of the Comintern to infiltrate the Kuomintang. Thus it was possible for the National Government of the Republic of China, as proclaimed at Nanking late in 1928, to be free of Russian interference and intrigue. In the words of Chiang Kai-shek, the defeat of the Soviet scheme in 1927 "had the effect of putting off Communist control of the Chinese mainland for twenty-three years."

But the efforts of the Communists to develop a separate base in China continued apace for the next decade. The years between the Kuomintang purge of 1927 and the outbreak of the Sino-Japanese war at the Marco Polo Bridge in 1937 comprise a very important, if not actually the most important, period in modern Chinese history. Throughout this pivotal decade, which brought economic chaos and the scourge of fascism to the west, China had to contend with the Japanese aggression in Manchuria as well as almost continuous civil war. Yet this has sometimes been called the "golden decade" because of the economic progress and the steps toward political consolidation south of the Great Wall, especially in the second half of the period, by the National Government.

Just as the extent and depth of the struggle between Chiang Kai-shek's Nationalists against the Communists was little understood outside the Orient at the time, except perhaps by a few alert statesmen and scholarly "China hands," the magnitude of this ten-year contest remains imperfectly understood by most westerners even today. Here was the critical period during which the Soviet seed fell on fertile ground in China. These were the years during which Communism began to spread its seductive poison among the millions of Chinese.

Chiang Kai-shek comprehended Communism. He knew it to be a religion in itself. Determined to thwart Communist ideology, he took strong measures to uproot it. Nonetheless Communism survived in this decade, spreading through the interior of China from the Yangtze to the Great Wall, always nourished by ideological encouragement from the Soviet Russia and growing gradually in direct proportion to the rising danger of aggression from Japan. History repeated itself here. The Marxist pattern of conquest in Russia was clear again in China. Just as Communism crept into Russia while the imperial government was facing the German threat in eastern Europe before and during World War I, so did Communism take hold in China while the National Government was preparing to meet the mainland thrust of the Japanese militarists. As before, and elsewhere ever since, Communism thrived on adversity in China in direct proportion to the problems facing the established government.

A few words on this decade are necessary to illustrate the points just made. Within a year of the cleansing of the Kuomintang, the National Government of the Republic of China was formally recognized by the United States—the first nation, incidentally, to do so. "The good will of the United States toward China is proverbial," declared Secretary of State Frank B. Kellogg, upon signing the treaty in July, 1928, "and the American government and people welcome every advance made by the Chinese in the direction of unity, peace, and progress."[5] But, while the years of the "golden decade" did witness some conspicuous progress in China, there was to be little unity or peace. Already the Chinese Communists were regrouping to oppose the Kuomintang, and the ensuing conflict between the armies of the two parties was soon marked by the bloody excesses characteristic of all such wars.

Briefly in 1929 Soviet Russia took a direct hand, encountering Chiang Kai-shek's forces in the skirmishes along the Manchurian border. But the major problem of the National Government was suppression of the Communist peasant forces—the bandits, as the Nationalist generals referred to them—who were gathering under Mao

[5]U. S. Department of State, *United States Relations with China* (Washington, D. C.: Government Printing Office, 1949), 12.

Tse-tung in the hills of Hunan and Kiangsi. Mao, then in his mid-thirties, was by now fast rising to prominence in the Chinese Communist movement.

Following the 1927 suppression, the titular leadership of the movement had passed from its founder, Professor Chen Tu-hsiu, to a Comintern favorite, Li Li-san, and the articulate Chou En-lai soon emerged under Li as an important spokesman. Li and Chou were intent upon a plan, formulated in Moscow, to use the 3,000,000 members of the trade unions to seize control of such large cities as Canton, Hankow, and Shanghai. This was in line with the Marxist concept of "proletarian hegemony," as contrasted with the idea of "peasant hegemony" which prevailed in the rural areas among the 10,000,000 members of the so-called peasant unions. But by 1930 Chou En-lai was frankly admitting that less than two percent of the party membership were factory workers. Scapegoat for the failure of the frustrated proletarian buildup was Li Li-san, who at the end of that year was recalled to Russia.

The new titular party chief at Shanghai was Wang Ming, but by this time the real power was gradually shifting into the capable hands of Mao Tse-tung. One time head of the so-called Peasant Department of the infiltrated Kuomintang, Mao had fled to the hills when Chiang's purge hit Hankow. His motley following of a thousand dissidents failed him in the "Autumn Crop" uprising of 1927, but three years later his several peasant armies in Kiangsi province contained most of the grand total of some 100,000 Chinese Communist Party members. Mao was now the most powerful Communist in the interior.

In December, 1930, President Chiang Kai-shek ordered the first of a series of "bandit suppression" campaigns intended to break up all Communist forces in China. The available Nationalist troops were superior in training and equipment, but the resistance of the Communists in Kiangsi proved stiff because of the effective employment of Mao's four principles of guerrilla warfare. He instructed his followers to retreat when the enemy advanced, to harass when the enemy halted, to attack when the enemy sought to avoid battle, and to pursue when the enemy retreated. They obeyed these orders and survived.

A second Nationalist campaign in February, 1931, was likewise unsuccessful, due largely to the failure of Chiang's Minister of war to coordinate the impressive assault of 100,000 troops, and the Communists managed to capture 10,000 rifles in May. Chiang personally took the field in a third campaign, launched a month later, which brought 200,000 or more Nationalist soldiers pouring into Kiangsi over three roads. Overwhelmed by sheer numbers, Mao hastily retreated as one after another of his districts was recovered by Chiang's columns. The successful end of this campaign seemed to be in sight when Japan suddenly attacked in Manchuria and unwittingly saved the Chinese Communists.

After the infamous Mukden Incident of September 18, 1931, Chiang Kai-shek had to rush back to his headquarters in Nanking to cope with the Japanese aggression in Manchuria. Many Nationalist divisions were now necessarily diverted to North China and to the coastal cities to prepare for the foreign emergency. As a result, the third "bandit suppression" campaign was abandoned and Chiang's anti-Communist program given pause at a critical juncture. Mao's followers quickly returned to reoccupy their districts in Kiangsi. Soon they had all but ten of the eighty-one counties of that province in their grasp.

Mao Tse-tung's moment was coming. Long dissatisfied with the titular party leadership of Wang Ming at Shanghai, he now cleverly used his leverage as an undefeated military chieftain to gain effective control of the entire Communist movement in China. Early in November the "First All-Chinese Congress of the Soviets" convened at Juichin, Mao's village headquarters in the hills of south Kiangsi. From the 290 delegates attending, an executive committee of sixty-one members was formed with Mao as chairman. He emerged also as head of the "Provincial Central Government of the Chinese Soviet Republic," which was proclaimed into existence with the hamlet of Juichin as capital.

All that remained was for Chairman Mao to engineer a transfer of the central executive committee of the Chinese Communist Party from Shanghai to Juichin. This he did within a few weeks by denouncing the "white terror" atmosphere of Shanghai and threatening to withold all party dues collected in Kiangsi. By the beginning of 1932, therefore, the erstwhile *Pei-ta* library clerk held the reins of Chinese Communism firmly in his hands. Mao's armies may have had no more than 150,000 troops, a third of whom still had no rifles. But he held unqualified control of his party, had a central headquarters deep in the interior, and enjoyed growing ties with the motherland of his Marxist ideals.

Mao Tse-tung's ties with Soviet Russia were greatly strengthened by the Japanese invasion of Manchuria. It was, in fact, this overt aggression by a foreign power which gave him a strong new rallying cry for his cause. In April, 1932, Mao's provisional government at Juichin formally declared war against Japan. The Chairman's avowed purpose was the expulsion of the Japanese from distant Manchuria. The actual purpose, however, was to exploit the tremendous anti-Japanese sentiment in Chiang Kai-shek's armies so as to divert the interest of Kuomintang troops from further anti-Communist campaigning.

Meanwhile the Communists were spreading into south Fukien, north Kwantung, and Shensi. On January 10, 1933, Mao grandly offered a "united front" to any armed unit in China that would join his Red armies in their declared war against Japan. This offer was in obedience to a directive of the executive committee of the Comintern, sent from Moscow four months earlier, which ordered Mao to "mobilize the masses under the slogan of the national revolutionary struggle against the Japanese and other imperialists."

Having easily overrun Manchuria, the Japanese were indeed entrenched on the Asian mainland. But Chiang Kai-shek's defense of Shanghai and Nanking had been successful, and he was now anxious to resume his struggle against the Communists. In April, 1933, amid loud cries for a formal declaration of war against Japan, the President made the choice to fight the interior enemy. He wished to cleanse China of Communism before committing his nation to a large-scale conflict with a powerful foreign foe. But the fourth "bandit suppression" campaign of the National Governmant, launched that spring under General Chen Cheng, broke down suddenly in Kiangsi. By the end of the summer Chiang was preparing still another campaign which he personally would command. But Mao's armies were growing daily in numbers and confidence. His five Red Army corps now totaled some 300,000 troops, and Communist Party membership was rising in proportion.

Chiang Kai-shek's program of anti-Communism reached a climax in October, 1933, with the opening of the fifth and largest campaign of suppression. A rebellion in Fukien held up the march briefly, but by the end of the year some 300,000 Nationalist troops were converging upon the principal Communist strongholds in Kiangsi and causing panic among Mao's generals and aides. This time the guerrilla tactics which they had used to good effect in the previous campaigns were insufficient, and the gradual tightening of the Kuomintang ring around their little capital could not be averted.

In January, 1934, the "Second All-China Congress of the Soviets" convened nervously at Juichin. The chief topic of discussion was evacuation to a new base. Then, as supplies ran low and the Nationalist pincers began to close, Chairman Mao, his cohorts, Chou En-lai and Lin Piao turned in desperation to their Soviet mentors for advice. Late in the summer the long-awaited word finally came from Moscow: pull out of Kiangsi province and seek safety somewhere else.

Accordingly, the "Long March" of the Red Army began in October, 1934. Exactly a year after the opening of Chiang's fifth campaign,

100,000 rag tag Communist troops broke through the Nationalist line one night. Their political chiefs with them, they retreated rapidly northward out of Kiangsi. It is hard to imagine that the people of Kiangsi were sorry to see the Communists go. In their seven years of political and military control in this province, its population had already declined by more than seven million.

The "Long March," which lasted a full year and took the Red Army 6,000 miles from South China to the Great Wall in the extreme northwest, is epic in the annals of Communism. On many days the distance travelled was forty miles, and some days it was even more. Nationalist forces were usually in hot pursuit, often using planes as was the case during the spectacular escape of the Reds on the old iron bridge over the Tatu River. Casualties in action, and deaths by starvation or exhaustion or disease, cost the Communists more than three-fourths of their effective strength. By October, 1935, Mao's forces were reduced to less than 25,000.

The easiest way to rebuild his numbers was to reiterate the attractive propaganda of a united front of the Chinese proletariat against Japan. This is what he did in the summer of 1935 while his decimated columns were resting in western Szechuan. On June 15, 1935, the Chairman issued an appeal for a "united people's front" against Japanese imperialism, but this time he specifically excluded its "accomplice Chiang Kai-shek with his terrorist bands of Blue Shirts." Only those troops who were ready to abandon Chiang were eligible to join, and Chiang Kai-shek himself was to be considered a traitor to China.

This aggressive line may have gratified Mao's lieutenants in China, but it was not consistent with the prevailing sentiment of Soviet policymakers at Moscow. The Seventh World Congress of the Comintern was presently meeting there, and it did not take the astute Chinese delegate Wang Ming very long to sense Stalin's mood. Unable to reach an accord with Hitler's Germany in 1934, Stalin was looking elsewhere for friends. If Germany should attack the Soviet Union simultaneously with Japan, Stalin knew that Mao's weakened Red Army could do little to deter the Japanese and prevent an invasion of Russia from the East. Only the armies of the National Government, he realized, could conceivably engage Japan on a sufficient scale to distract Tokyo's attention from the Soviet Union. Stalin decided, therefore, that the Chinese Communists should initiate the widest possible united front against the Japanese—one that would include, not exclude, the Kuomintang Party and Chiang's armies. Wang Ming accordingly urged this course on Mao, who had been out of touch with his Moscow masters for eight months, and on August 1 the chastened Chairman issued a new "Appeal to the Whole People of China to Resist Japan and Save the Country."

From his new capital in the Shensi village of Yenan, Mao in January and August, 1936, publicly offered a hand of friendship to Chiang Kai-shek if he would take up arms against Japan. Chiang, smelling a rat, made no reply but instead proceeded with plans for a sixth campaign of suppression. Though Mao's invitations did not impress the Kuomintang leadership, they had profound effect on the troops which Chiang had assigned to what he confidently expected to be the final campaign against the Communists.

At this point, late in 1936, Chiang Kai-shek made what was perhaps the worst blunder of his life. Feeling that the Nationalist government was only "five minutes away," as he later put it, from a complete victory over Communism in China, Chiang entrusted the mopping-up of Shensi province to the forces of the 'Young Marshal' of Manchuria, Chang Hsueh-liang. Chang was the son of the old warlord of Manchuria, and his soldiers tended to regard themselves as aliens in China proper. He and his followers despised the Japanese invaders of their northern homeland, but felt indifferently about the Chinese Communists.

In December, 1936, Chiang Kai-shek and his staff made a visit to Sian, capital of Shensi and headquarters of General Chang's Manchurian troops. His purpose was to map out the sixth anti-Communist campaign. But the perfidious marshal now boldly arrested Chiang and confronted him with a set of eight demands—seven of which were identical with points that Chang Hsueh-liang had discussed secretly with Mao Tse-tung and Chou En-lai some weeks earlier. These demands, corresponding almost exactly with a plan of "national salvation" publicly proclaimed by Chairman Mao on December 1, were presented in a crude effort to embarrass the Nationalist chief and substantiate a charge of treason against him.

At first the Chinese Communists were as elated as they were surprised by the Sian Incident. They thought they saw in this daring coup a rare opportunity to eliminate their arch foe Chiang Kai-shek by the simple expedient of a "people's trial" and execution. Within a fortnight, however, Moscow had intervened. The word from the Kremlin was that President Chiang was to be released in the interest of the United Front, which in the last month had suddenly become a Russian national imperative rather than merely a rallying cry of international Communism. It was the German-Japanese agreement, signed at Berlin in November, 1936, and commonly called the Anti-Comintern Pact, which saved the prisoner of Sian. More than ever the Soviet Union now needed Chiang, however temporarily, as a target for the rising militarism of Japan, which otherwise might strike at Stalin's bases in the far East.

The strategists of the Kremlin also realized that Chiang Kai-shek alone, of all the leaders in the Orient, could mobilize sufficient resistance on the Asian mainland to divert the attention and sap the energies of the Japanese militarists. Thus Chiang was spared, the United Front survived, and Communism in China survived with it. On Christmas day, 1936, the President flew back to Nanking, taking with him the hapless Chang Hsueh-liang to be court-martialed by the National Government in a face-saving gesture. General Chang was sentenced to prison for ten years, but was promptly pardoned as the curtain fell on the Sian farce and the first shots of the Sino-Japanese War sounded at Marco Polo Bridge in the summer of 1937.

With the erection of the United Front as official national policy at Nanking early in 1937, the ten-year civil war in China came abruptly to a close. A crucial period in modern Chinese history was past, and Communism had somehow lived through it. Clinging to the concept of the United Front as a single thread, the Communists systematically rewove their fabric for the next four years as the defensive war against Japan consumed the attention of Chiang Kai-shek and the National Government. After having vilified him for a full decade, the Communists began, in 1937, to refer politely to "Mr." Chiang Kai-shek. Soon they were addressing him reverently as "Generalissimo" and publicly acknowledging his indispensable wartime leadership.

The Japanese threat, of course was very real. Japan's ruthless seizure of Manchuria in 1931 had proven that point to the Chinese, and the angry exit of the Tokyo delegates from the League of Nations two years later had confirmed it to the world. Now, greatly worried by the economic progress being made in China south of the Great Wall, the Japanese military clique came to the fateful decision to strike again. The result of that decision was the Marco Polo Bridge incident near Peking on July 7, 1937, which served as Japan's flimsy pretext for launching a full-scale attack on China. So began the long, desperate, and costly war in the Pacific that was finally to involve the United States and to continue unabated until the atomic bombings of 1945 had obliterated the last dreams of the Japanese empire.

For the eight years that it lasted, the Pacific war was a pleasing spectacle to the Russian Communist Party. What side happened to be winning at a given moment was never so significant as the central, integral, and most important fact that the war was going on. The cause of international Communism was being served by the very existence of a struggle which, by forcing coexistence in China under the banner of a United Front against external aggression, gave Mao Tse-tung's followers the opportunity to sow their seed in ravaged soil. The early phase of Communist-Kuomintang cooperation, ending with the purge of 1927, had been all too brief to suit Soviet Russia. Now that a second phase of coexistence had begun, the war which brought it about should be extended as far as possible. By perpetuating the Pacific conflict, the Kremlin would be providing precious time for Communism to grow and spread on the mainland of Asia.

With this master plan as their guide, Stalin's strategists encouraged the Chinese resistance in every conceivable way. Even before the scrape at Marco Polo Bridge, Russian diplomats were negotiating with Chiang Kai-shek's government and promising practical assistance. In the early stage of the Sino-Japanese war, Soviet Russia was the only power which offered China material aid as well as moral support. The American President, in his famous "Quarantine Speech" of October, 1937, sharply denounced the Japanese aggressors, and similar words of condemnation fell from the lips of other statesmen in the chambers of the League of Nations. But only Stalin came through with the goods.

Within six months of the outbreak of hostilities, Russia had provided sufficient arms, equipment, and military instructors to outfit and train twenty-four army divisions for Chiang Kai-shek. Soon there were 500 new bombers and fighters in Chiang's air force, with Russian aviators and mechanics to get them into the air. Russian surveyors and engineers were everywhere to be seen in rural areas that lacked a usable road. All this material aid was charged against two large loans, amounting to $100 million, which Russia extended to China in 1938, and Chiang's agent was warmly received at Moscow when he came seeking a third loan of $150 million in the spring of 1939. Without such bountiful support, Chiang could not have held out six months against the Japanese—with it, China had just enough staying power to prolong the war indefinitely. This precisely, was what Soviet Russia wished to see happen in the Far East.

In setting up the loans to the Chinese government that made national survival possible in the face of severe external assault, Stalin's ministers shrewdly stipulated eventual payment. It was to be made in the form of shipments to the Soviet Union of large quantities of tea, wool, tungsten, and tin. But such raw materials were merely the technical price of Russian support; the actual price was Chiang Kai-shek's conciliation of Communism in China. After ten years as its arch-foe, the President was now forced to smile broadly at Communism with all his teeth.

The second *entente* between the Kuomintang and the Communists was never formalized by a written alliance. It rested instead on a series of parallel proclamations and manifestoes which were exchanged in the summer and fall of 1937. Both parties made sweeping promises in the name of the "All-China" front against Japan. The Kuomintang agreed to admit Mao Tse-tung, Chou En-lai, and others to its presidium and inner councils, and to permit the publication at Hankow of a Communist-controlled newspaper, the *New China Daily*. The Communists, on their part, consented to rename both their regime and their armies. The old "Chinese Soviet Republic" was now to be called the "Special Area Government." The Red Army in the northern provinces, comprising about 45,000 troops, was to be known as the "Eighth Route Army," a "New Fourth Army" of 10,000 men was to be fielded in Kiangsi and Fukien.

What the Soviet Union demanded and obtained, in exchange for Russian material aid, was Chiang Kai-shek's tacit acceptance of separate-but-equal recognition of the Chinese Communists. He still hated and feared the Communists, but co-existence was now a national imperative. Co-existence worked reasonably well for a time, particularly in the months immediately following the fall of Nanking to the Japanese in December, 1937, and the transfer of the principal offices and the National Government inland to Hankow where Communist influence long had been pervasive. When an important advisory committee, the People's Political Council, was established by the Kuomintang early in 1938, seven Communists obtained seats on it.

Not until October of 1938, when Hankow was taken by Japanese forces, did the Kuomintang-Communist *entente* begin to show signs of deterioration. Chiang Kai-shek now had to shift his headquarters still farther to the interior at Chungking, and the "Special Area Government" quickly moved itself out of the line of fire and northward to the Communist village of Yenan close to the Great Wall in Shensi province.

The departure of the Communist leaders for Yenan late in 1938, scarcely a year after the creation of the United Front, sharply illustrated an important fact. It revealed their policy to be more a cover for their subversive activities than a sincere, single-minded effort to resist the Japanese penetration. In later years Mao Tse-tung often fondly reminisced on the valiant exertions of his followers in the face of the Japanese onslaught. His idyllic interpretation of a gallant Communist soldiery in the front lines of defense is recognized today as the sheerest nonsense. In the early stages of the war the Communists not only avoided direct confrontation but were so invisible, as a matter of fact, that Japanese generals did not take them seriously. The result was that Chiang Kai-shek's armies, not the Communist armies, were the target and received the punishment. Even so sympathetic a writer as Theodore H. White, in his *Thunder Out of China*, has admitted that Mao Tse-tung's troops fought only "when they had an opportunity to surprise a very small group of the enemy," and that "during the significant campaigns it was the weary soldiers of the Central Government who took the shock, gnawed at the enemy, and died."

Meanwhile the Communists were busily recruiting behind the lines, in what they euphemistically called "areas of liberation," and their military strength naturally multiplied in the hills as Chiang's diminished on the battlefront. According to their official history, the Eighth Route Army is supposed to have expanded from 45,000 in 1937 to 400,000 by 1940, and the New Fourth Army from 15,000 to 100,000 in the same period. Such growth is believable when a contrast is made between the lofty United Front objectives of the Communists as publicly proclaimed, on the one hand, and two sets of secret instructions from Mao Tse-tung to his followers at the very outset of war. In the first of these, a message to his cadres entitled "The Strategic Lines of the Party," Chairman Mao explained exactly why the Communists were again collaborating with the Kuomintang:

> At the present juncture, when revolutionary sentiments are weak and low and our strength is limited and small, we must compromise with the Kuomintang in order that we may conserve and expand our power to strike. . . . Doubtless, the United Front is a compromise and is reformist in character. But it is only a temporary departure from the policy of overthrowing the existing institutions by revolutionary means. . . . The revolutionary makes uses of reformist methods to engage in revolutionary work in the open, to camouflage clandestine activities, and to foster the fighting strength of the masses, so that the bourgeoisie may be overthrown.[6]

The official Communist attitude on the prosecution of the war coincided, of course, with that of the Kuomintang as expressed in a position paper, "Program for Armed Resistance and National Reconstruction," drafted by the People's Political Council in the spring of 1938. But from the beginning of hostilities the Red Generals had as their secret policy the so-called "Principles of the Four Don'ts," which in effect directed Mao's field commanders not to fight at all. This is how he explained it:

> The Red Army does not fight for the sake of fighting. It fights in order that it may carry on propaganda among the masses, organize them, arm them, and set up Communist regimes for them. Without these objectives, fighting would be meaningless and the Red Army would have no justification for its existence.[7]

The myth of the United Front could not be sustained indefinitely under such conditions. As Mao Tse-tung's forces grew, the areas under

[6]As in Yah-kang Wan, *The Rise of Communism in China*, 1920-1950 (Hong Kong: Chung Shu Pub. Co., 1952) 48-49.
[7]*Ibid.*, 57.

Communist control became larger. Soon the Communist generals were dropping the pretense of cooperation with the National Government and ordering an active harrassment of Chiang Kai-shek's forces. They now adopted the treacherous tactic of attacking and absorbing government units that were fighting frontally against the Japanese or had been isolated in the rear of the enemy.

From the spring of 1939 to the end of 1940, many Nationalist troops were ambushed by the Communists at the same time that these troops were contesting the Japanese. Such conduct could hardly be tolerated in time of peace; it was intolerable when all the people of the nation were supposed to be resisting foreign aggression. In January, 1941, Chiang Kai-shek ordered the New Fourth Army, now swollen to more than 100,000, to move north of the Yangtze and to face the Japanese. Its commander, upon direct instructions from Mao Tsetung, turned south instead. His unmistakable purpose was to infiltrate or otherwise to hamstring Chiang's best armies.

When President Chiang now took steps to disarm and disband the New Fourth Army, a howl went up simultaneously from Yenan and from Moscow. Russian aid was suddenly cut short, and all ostensible cooperation between the Communists and the Kuomintang came to a halt. The "New Fourth Army Incident" marked the end of the second period of co-existence and the renewal of intense civil strife in China. Coming just eleven months before Pearl Harbor, it served significantly to stimulate the fantasies of the Japanese militarists in their dream of a "Greater East Asia Co-Prosperity Sphere." This in turn, of course, sped the fusion of the Pacific and European wars into a global conflict which the United States ultimately had to resolve.

What was happening on the Asian mainland was then of keen interest only to professional diplomats and dedicated "China watchers." The eyes of the world were focused elsewhere. As the uneasy *entente* between the Kuomintang and the Chinese Communists weakened and finally fell apart, larger international tensions commanded the news of the day. Yet China's changing tides were directly related to global currents because the future of international Communism was uniquely dependent upon the fate of Soviet Russia in a world at war.

For the first two years of Sino-Japanese hostilities, Russian statesmen and journalists vociferously denounced Japan as an imperial aggressor while praising Chiang Kai-shek loudly as a democratic champion of freedom. Until mid-1939 Japan was castigated as the gangster of the Far East because she had clasped hands with Nazi Germany in the despised Anti-Comitern Pact. Then came the spectacular agreement between Moscow and Berlin which made Stalin and Hitler partners in the plundering of Europe. Suddenly the official Soviet view of Japan began to soften, and Stalin's agents embarked upon a double game in the Far East.

Chiang Kai-shek was still to receive material aid and moral support for his resistance against the Japanese, but Moscow's propaganda campaign was abruptly ended. Tokyo was no longer to be insulted in the Moscow press or provoked by diplomatic hard talk. The Japanese militarists may have been surprised by this turnabout, but they were not inclined to scorn such Russian smiles. By the summer of 1940, after Hitler's panzers and Luftwaffe had rendered the Netherlands, France, and Great Britain incapable of defending their far-flung colonies, they were looking hungrily at the whole of southeast Asia.

Tokyo's dream of a "new order" in the Pacific was now quickly broadened so as to include new supplementary storehouses—the Dutch East Indies, Indo-China, Malaya, Burma, India, and even Australia and New Zealand—in the "co-prosperity sphere" which had Manchuria and China proper as its base. The Japanese saw clearly that only the two large neutral nations, the United States and Russia, could possibly block the realization of their dream. If the U.S. battle fleet should be sent to stop her, as might happen, Japan would need to be confident of the strict neutrality of her old foe, Russia, in the western Pacific. And Russian neutrality was now within reach.

As the bedazzled Japanese looked increasingly southward, Moscow had increasingly less to fear at her backdoor in northern Asia. By the spring of 1941 the Kremlin was far more worried about Germany than about Japan. As Stalin became apprehensive of an attack on his western front by the supremely confident Nazis, he decided to abandon Chiang Kai-shek altogether so that he might feel perfectly secure in the Far East. Accordingly, three months after the "New Fourth Army Incident" had shattered the fiction of cooperation between the Chinese Communists and the Kuomintang, the masters of Moscow accepted the overtures of Foreign Minister Matsuoka and signed a five-year treaty of non-aggression with Japan.

Chiang Kai-shek may have been shocked by the Russian reversal, but he could scarcely have been surprised. The Soviet-Japanese pact of April 13, 1941, was a shocking example of the perfidy of Communist regimes, a classic statement of the Communist style in the conduct of international relations. They had done it before, they did it now, and they would do it often again.

The invasion of the Ukraine which Stalin had been half-expecting from Hitler came like a thunderclap in June, 1941, abruptly ending the evil partnership that had plunged Europe into World War II. As Russia now joined Britain in the list of Germany's targets, the reaction of the United States government was immediately sympathetic. Washington policymakers, vigorously anti-German, chose to overlook the fact that Stalin had just pledged the Soviet Union not to make war on the Pacific member of the Axis, Japan, for at least five years. American lend-lease began its interminable flow to Russia, and Stalin had the satisfaction of knowing that he could use all of it against the Germans on the European front because Japan was not going to kick the Russian bear from the rear.

As Stalin figured it, so it happened. The eager Japanese, deluded by enlarged notions of a new order in the Far East, stepped up their program of military expansion. In midsummer of 1941 their armies occupied Indo-China, left defenseless by the fallen French. Within a few months their commitment to the illusion of a "Greater East Asia" would lead them irretrievably into a massive confrontation with the United States in the Pacific.

Chiang Kai-shek, meanwhile, was still struggling as usual, against the many well-equipped Japanese divisions on the Asian mainland, with the same old kit of simple tools. He had been at it for more than four years, and substantial help seemed finally to be at hand. When the United States declared war simultaneously on Japan and Germany in December, 1941, President Roosevelt acquired both Chiang Kai-shek's China and Stalin's Russia as allies. The difference was that Chiang was still fighting the Japanese, as he would ceaselessly until their capitulation, but Stalin had pledged by treaty that Russia would not do so.

The contractual commitment to Japan was to prove of immeasurable value to Stalin in his wartime bargaining with President Roosevelt and Prime Minister Churchill. It gave him, for instance, the ace card at Yalta. Once the usefulness of the 1941 non-aggression treaty was past, Stalin tossed it aside and ordered Soviet troops to descend upon the Japanese military remnant in Manchuria. That was on August 8, 1945, two days after the first atomic bomb had fallen at Hiroshima. The war had only a few days to go, but the Soviet-Japanese pact would not formally expire until the following April. This detail, while not historically important, is illustrative. Neither national honor nor posterity's verdict matter much to the Communist. All he ever seeks is the Marxist goal.

With the Japanese attack on Pearl Harbor, the diplomatic equation in the Pacific changed overnight. The United States, now a formal ally of China, was to make strong efforts to secure Chiang Kai-shek's full cooperation and collaboration in the waging of effective war against Japan. Behind these efforts was the hope that the National Government of the Republic of China, having been properly bolstered, would emerge as the principal stabilizing factor in postwar Asia. But the strengthening of Chiang Kai-shek was, of course, directly contrary to the aims and purposes of Marshal Stalin and Chairman Mao Tse-tung. Both Communist chiefs fully realized that their old objective of the sovietization of China would never be gained if the Kuomintang came out of the war with victor's laurels.

Stalin was determined to avert such an outcome. Correctly foreseeing that Japan had sealed her fate on December 7, 1941, Stalin now predicted that the Pacific war could and would be won without the participation of Chiang's armies. After Pearl Harbor, as Dr. Tien-fong Cheng has noted, Stalin no longer cared whether the Chinese continued the war against Japan, and the Soviet relations with China became exceedingly cool.

The attitude of Moscow was, in fact, more than cool. It was hostile. Almost from the day that the United States joined World War II and until its very end, Communists everywhere carried on an extensive propaganda campaign against the National Government of the Republic of China. The anti-Nationalist line emanated from Moscow and spread insidiously to every capital and principal city of the allied nations. It gave China the world's worst press at the close of her first turbulent century as a factor in modern history.

2

A Century of Sino-American Relations [1841-1941]

IMPERIOUS OLD John Bull may have been the pioneer in Sino-Western diplomacy, but bustling young "Brother Jonathan" was not far behind him. Shrewd American shipmasters from New England had been calling at Chinese ports since President Washington's time, and the fifty years of unofficial trade had built many a Yankee fortune. Such Boston firms as Bryant & Sturgis and Russell & Company had long maintained resident agents at Canton to conduct their unofficial business with the Hong Kong merchants. The sudden humiliation of China in the Opium War now convinced the acquisitive "Boston Men" that the moment was ripe to make it official.

Even before the ink was on the Treaty of Nanking, American traders were trying to climb on the China bandwagon. During the hostilities of 1841-42 the Anglophobic Washington government had watched with sympathy for the beleaguered Chinese, and at first the few American resident merchants at Canton were able to carry on their operations with larger profits than usual. When Commissioner Lin started his opium seizures, however, the Americans also had to surrender their share. They promptly called upon President Tyler for protection, and he responded by ordering the warships of Commodore Lawrence Kearny's East India Squadron into Chinese waters.

A tough old sailor, Commodore Kearny proved equal to his tricky task. He succeeded in persuading the Manchu officials at Canton to pay damages in the amount of several hundred dollars for injuries allegedly suffered by American citizens. More importantly, he requested and obtained assurances that henceforth the American traders would be placed on the same footing as those from England, that nation "most favored" under the Treaty of Nanking.

But the American merchants at Canton knew that someday Commodore Kearny would sail away, and they feared that then they would no longer enjoy the same commercial privileges that the British had extorted from the Chinese. Early in 1843 they asked President Tyler to appoint a resident commissioner in China to care for American commercial and diplomatic affairs. The President reacted by naming a shrewd lawyer and former Whig congressman from Newbury, Massachusetts, who had been a member of the House Committee on Foreign Affairs. Caleb Cushing thus beame the first official American representative to the Chinese empire.

Cushing's instructions were simply to obtain the same treaty priviliges, without using force, that Britain had obtained through war. Using indirect and intelligent pressure, he persuaded the Chinese to sign a treaty on July 3, 1844, at a village called Wanghia on the outskirts of Macao. By its terms Americans were permitted the same rights accruing to "most favored" nations with respect to trade, residence, and religious activity. The Wanghia concessions of 1844 provided the legal foundation for American dealings with China through the remainder of the nineteenth century.

Following Cushing's mission, however, the road ahead was rocky. One American commissioner after another found it difficult to widen contacts with Chinese officials. Humphrey Marshall's stay in China, for instance, was conspicuously short and his performance somewhat amateurish. Unable to achieve a working relationship with the emperor's "viceroy" at Canton, he bluntly asked for his passports, whereupon his Chinese host replied with Oriental obtuseness; "I avail myself of the occasion to present my compliments, and trust that, of late, your blessings have been increasingly tranquil." Succeeding Marshall in the spring of 1854 was Robert M. McLane, who remained at his post barely nine months. It was no wonder, since McLane proposed to the Chinese the frightening idea of a joint collection and administration of customs on the part of Great Britain, France, and the United States. He then with much audacity even recommended that China should open all her ports to American trade. Hearing nothing and discouraged over the evident failure of his plan, McLane sailed for home and was replaced by Dr. Peter Parker, an aggressive medical missionary with long experience as a "foreign devil."

Dr. Parker was talented in more ways than one, not the least of which was his extensive knowledge of the Mandarin language. But he had no more success than his predecessors in establishing diplomatic rapport with the Peking court. Very suspicious of British motives in China, he felt that the Queen's government evidently had "objects beyond those contemplated by the United States" and warned that "we ought not to be drawn along with it, however anxious it may be for our cooperation." Just as nervous over British designs was President Pierce's quite Anglophobic Secretary of State, Lewis Cass, who flatly rejected a memorandum outlining the Queen's goals in China and inviting American cooperation. "True wisdom," he told the British minister in Washington, "dictates moderation in attempts to open China to the trade of the world."

Meanwhile the next American agent, William B. Reed, was instructed to pursue peaceful cooperation with the Chinese since, as Secretary Cass reminded him, the United States was not at war with China, and only desired lawful commerce and the protection of its citizens. Like his predecessors, Reed found it difficult to secure an interview with the appropriate Chinese official. The entire year 1857 passed without a meeting. Finally, after much maneuvering and reaping the advantages of international pressures, Reed was able to report on June 18, 1858 that he had finally signed a paper. Known as the Treaty of Tientsin, this pact produced many changes in the relations between China and the United States. American consuls were vested with judicial powers for the trial of their own countrymen in China; direct correspondence with the highest authorities was permitted; and the American minister was granted the rare privilege of an annual visit to Peking on diplomatic business. The treaty also carried with it a subsequent convention under which the claims of American citizens against China were paid by the Manchus to the tune of almost three-quarters of a million dollars. Thus China was virtually stripped of all protection against foreign exploitation.

In executing his commission, Reed, who had been a professor in the University of Pennsylvania and who belonged, as we should say today, to the intelligentsia, discovered a distinct vein of idealism. His instructions from Secretary Cass consigned him to the distasteful role of beneficiary from the impositions on helpless China by other nations. He was personally ashamed of the clause providing extra-territoriality, or right of trial for accused Americans in their own consular courts, as this clause led to notorious abuses. English-speaking criminals of every sort claimed American citizenship because, even if convicted in American consular courts, they were immediately discharged for lack of jails to hold them. The United States government conveniently forgot this necessary corollary to criminal procedure, and the Chinese were forestalled by treaty from taking care of it themselves.

Then, too, Reed was wholly out of sympathy with Lord Elgin, the British minister, and resented that diplomat's determination to open up Chinese rivers to foreign traders. On no subject were Americans themselves more jealous, Reed knew, than on that of their monopoly in the trade of their own coast and rivers. On the opium question also Reed took an idealistic stand, though his wisdom in dealing with it is open to debate. Until 1858 the opium traffic had never been actually legal in China. The drug was imported on a huge scale, but its traffickers, both British and American, were technically smugglers. In the Treaty of Tientsin no reference was made to opium; but in negotiations undertaken shortly afterward for revision of the tariff, the subject was taken up. Thus Reed, who certainly was no friend of the opium trade, nevertheless played the key role in obtaining its legal recognition. As the early China scholar Tyler Dennett has observed, Reed simply debated the old, old question between high license and regulation on the one hand and ineffective prohibition on the other; and his error, if indeed he made one, was that of judgment only.

Reed did not remain in China for the ratification of his treaty. For what should have been a mere ceremony he was succeeded by John E. Ward, the Georgia politician who had presided over the Democratic convention of 1856 that nominated James Buchanan for the presidency. Ward naively expected to ratify the treaty at Peking, but of course Chinese prejudice opposed this. Finally the Chinese agreed to receive the British and French ministers on a similar errand. But on his journey to the imperial city, Ward, like Reed before him, became implicated to some extent in the combined French and British attack on the Taku forts which guarded the river approach to Peking. The aggressive commander of the U.S. Asiatic Squadron, believing blood to be thicker than water, unjudiciously had lent the British forces the aid of his American sailors. This was a breach of neutrality in flagrant opposition to America's chosen policy in China, and Ward wisely detached himself from the allied expedition and pursued an independent course toward the capital.

Ignorant of Chinese customs, however, Ward made the great mistake of allowing his hosts to specify his method of conveyance. He should have demanded a sedan chair—the established symbol of Western authority. Instead he was content with a yellow cart, which to the Chinese mind conveyed that he was no more than a Korean or some other petty tribute-bearer to the emperor. Once in Peking, he was kept almost a prisoner while negotiations were pending as to the manner of his reception at court. The Chinese demanded at least a modified kowtow to the emperor, but on this point Ward was cognizant of Western precedents. Declaring his willingness to 'bend the body and slightly crook the right knee,' he insisted that only to 'God and woman' would he actually kneel. No agreement being possible on what to Chinese sensibilities was so vital, Ward withdrew from Peking and the ratifications were exchanged instead at the coastal city of Pehtang on August 16, 1859.

Our entire Chinese policy in the 1850's, though superficially successful, witnessed a steady decline in real accomplishment. Reed and Ward were well-meaning and personally efficient, both somehow became embroiled in the Anglo-French pressure on China. This proved contrary to America's permanent interests and represented a distinct retrogression. American interest in the Orient, however, was growing rapidly. The Chinese treaties and Commodore Perry's celebrated voyage to Japan drew the attention of New England merchants and missionaries to the Far Pacific, and the recent acquisition of the Oregon country and California put many more Americans in perfect position to become deeply involved in the affairs of East Asia. But as traders and churchmen flocked to China, they found nothing but official contempt for Westerners in a land now torn by the turmoil of the great blood bath known in history as the Taiping Rebellion. Many Americans, particularly the missionaries, at first felt this uprising was truly a Christian movement which would break down official Chinese hostility to the West. The Americans soon discovered, however, that it was to their advantage to forego all sympathy for the Taipings and support instead the Manchu government that had given them most-favored-nation treatment in grade. Their hitchhiking methods had brought them privileges that both the British and the French had to fight to obtain, and they saw no good reason to bite the imperial hand that was feeding them.

American merchants ordinarily resided in the concessions held by other nations, but the missionaries often did not. Often posing as peddlers, these men braved the Chinese threat of death by strangulation to any "foreign devil" caught challenging Confucianism. At first they were rather crude in their relations, seldom learning to speak Chinese and working mostly among the *cho-hing* business class in the coastal cities. Later some of them did master the local dialects sufficiently to interpret for diplomatic officials, but not many churchmen ever manifested much respect for the Chinese social system. To them the Chinese were "benighted heathen" whom somehow they had to save. The missionaries actually made few converts. Their attitudes and methods antagonized most Chinese, and their belief in Christ was considered dangerously revolutionary by the Mandarins. More important than their religious fieldwork, really, was the role of the missionaries in interpreting China to the people of the United States. Through their interminable reports, numerous magazine articles, and occasional books they gave their fellow Americans, who were increasingly curious and anxious for the information, a larger awareness of the Orient and a corresponding deeper dimension in its affairs.

The advertising of Christianity, the fostering of trade, and the persistent dream of "civilizing" and democratizing the Chinese empire—these were the significant strands of American involvement in China in the second half of the nineteenth century. President Lincoln's Secretary of State, William H. Seward, adopted a policy of close cooperation with the other "treaty powers" in China. Seward wisely picked Anson Burlingame, like Caleb Cushing an ex-congressman from Massachusetts, to carry out that policy. Burlingame was technically the first American minister to China, and as such the first American official to reside in Peking. He had great personal charm and was extremely tactful in the ways of the Chinese. By working closely with the British, French, and Russian ministers, he helped to solidify American commercial interests and at the same time managed to prevent the powers from taking advantage of China's weakness.

Burlingame was so admired by the Chinese that when he retired in 1867 they asked him, in his private capacity as an American citizen, to serve as China's special representative abroad. Acting for the Manchu empress, therefore, Burlingame signed a treaty with Secretary of State Seward on July 28, 1868, that was mainly a cheap-labor deal providing coolies for the building of the first transcontinental railroad. Of the ten thousand construction workers on the Central Pacific, nine-tenths were Chinese. Without the help of the Chinese the line probably would not have been finished in time to receive the promised federal subsidies.

When railroad construction ended, the Chinese sought work wherever they could in a flooded market. Competing directly with native Americans for jobs, they proved so ubiquitous that a leading political slogan on the American frontier became "The Heathen Chinee Must Go." To attract votes from labor, both the Republicans and Democrats included demands for action against Chinese immigration in their national platforms. One of the most colorful of the orators specializing in anti-Chinese messages was the Irish-born political boss of San Francisco, Denis Kearny. After one meeting of some six thousand workingmen, hoodlums among them, invaded Chinatown, sacked fifteen laundries, burned buildings, and broke windows in the Methodist mission here.

Such outrages led Bret Harte to write in his famous obituary to Wan Lee: "Dead, my reverend friends, dead. Stoned to death in the streets of San Francisco, in the year of grace 1869, by a mob of half-grown boys and Christian school children." Californians demanded that Congress ban all Oriental immigration, but the main obstacle was the Burlingame treaty that allowed the Chinese to migrate freely to the United States. So many came, however, that in a surprisingly brief period the racial problem grew acute.

A matter clearly involving the foreign relations of the entire republic could not be left for California alone to settle. In 1876 a joint committee of both Houses of Congress visited the Pacific coast to study at firsthand the effects of oriental immigration. Under the chairmanship of Senator Oliver P. Morton of Indiana, the committee made an exhaustive investigation. The California businessmen who profited from Chinese labor told of their industry, efficiency, and general usefulness in building up the country. But spokesmen of labor were inclined to see Asian competition as more menacing than European; they argued the impossibility of white men competing industrially with the Chinese. California and indeed the entire West, they said, would soon be "Mongolian" unless a policy of exclusion was adopted. The professional classes, while less directly interested in the question, sided in the main with labor.

The Morton committee brought in a divided report. The chairman, with all the ardor of an old reformer, refused to face the considerable evidence that Pacific coast Chinese could not be easily assimilated. He was convinced that they, like the Southern Negroes and the Indians of the plains, would quickly adjust to the white man's way. He refused, therefore, to deprive the Chinese of the 'natural right' to settle where they pleased. But Senator Morton died before the Congress acted in the case. Had he lived, he doubtless would have used his influence to modify the decision that was made.

As it turned out, the majority report of the Morton committee urged restrictive legislation against a flood of coolie labor incapable of assimilation. But the report arrived on the floor just a week before the session ended, and action was postponed. Matters reached a crisis in 1879 when a state election in California threatened to turn in favor of the party that took the stronger anti-Chinese stand; the issue seemed, moreover, likely to influence the outcome of the next national election. Under much pressure, therefore, Congress passed a bill limiting to fifteen the number of Chinese that could enter on a single ship. President Hayes promptly vetoed it, and Congress responded by suspending immigration from Asia for twenty years. Again the President exercised his veto, but in 1880 finally he signed a compromise bill shutting off all Oriental immigration for ten years.

The whole immigration issue was influenced by complex economic and social factors in the United States. The yellow man knew what it meant to have "not a Chinaman's chance" in the United States, even though he had been recruited by American employers and had played an important part in the rapid industrialization of the nation. The issue became a serious irritant in Sino-American relations because it was so grossly one-sided. The Chinese had no recourse to the discrimination against them in America, but China was forced to admit foreigners to her shores and to permit foreign gunboats to patrol her inland waters. The Chinese imperial government had no gunboats to send to San Francisco or Seattle to protect its people.

By the Chinese Exclusion Act of 1882 it was further stipulated that no state court or federal court could admit Chinese to U.S. citizenship. As John Hay later put it, Congress had "done its work so well that even Confucius could not become an American though he should seek it with prayers and tears." The exclusion policy, subsequently renewed, lasted until 1943 when, under pressure of enthusiasm for World War II collaboration, China was granted an annual quota of 105 immigrants.

While America's direct relations with the Orient were almost as old as the nation itself, the importance of the relationship was not widely appreciated until the very end of the nineteenth century. The colonial programs of the major nations of Europe were in full bloom. After 1895, when the surprise Japanese victory revealed the dire weakness of the Manchu regime, four European governments scrambled for new economic and political concessions on the Asian mainland. The Russians acquired the right to construct a railway across Manchuria and procured a lease on Dairen and Port Arthur at the southern tip of the Liaotung Peninsula; the Germans extracted a 99-year lease on Kiaochow Bay and its port of Tsingtao, together with economic rights in Shantung; the British took a 99-year lease on Kowloon opposite Hong Kong; and the French obtained Kwangchow Bay in South China. "The various powers," the Dowager Empress is reputed to have said, "cast upon us looks of tiger-like voracity, hustling each other in their endeavors to be the first to seize upon our innermost territories."

The threatened partition of China was alarming to many Americans. With the rapid development of the west coast states, the purchase of Alaska, and the acquisition of Samoa, Guam, and the Hawaiian and the Philippine islands, the United States had reached the status of world power. But she arrived too late either to prevent or join the scramble for Asian concessions, and American entrepreneurs now feared the possibility of being deprived of the manifest opportunities beckoning in China.

Even though the Chinese trade had never exceeded three percent of America's total foreign commerce, it was easy to visualize a huge market of four hundred million people—more than five times as many potential customers as in the United States! Accustomed to follow European leads in the search for commerical privileges and benefitting by the "most-favored-nation" agreement with China, Americans could claim some economic rights. Not wishing to use European methods of force, and yet quite unwilling to abandon a growing trade to her hungry competitors, the United States government faced the important question: How to preserve American interests in China now that the Celestial Empire faced the threat of dismemberment?

The American answer to the battle for concessions was the famous doctrine of the "Open Door." This idea actually arose from the desire of the British to protect their predominant influence, which certainly would suffer if European imperialism should close the door of their sphere. About a month before the beginning of the Spanish-American War, Great Britain made overtures to the United States by asking, in effect, "Will you stand with us in our China policy?" President McKinley was too involved in imminent war with Spain to evince much interest. But pressures came from the writings and speeches of such individuals as Alfred Thayer Mahan, Henry Cabot Lodge, Theodore Roosevelt, and John Hay, each of whom fully understood the implications of the power struggle in the Far East.

Most important was the highly articulate John Hay, onetime ambassador to London and a thorough Anglophile, who believed strongly in cooperating with the British. He sympathized with the Queen in nearly all her ventures; England's enemies were automatically his. Hay became Secretary of State in 1899. His principal Far Eastern advisor was an old China hand, William W. Rockhill, who had spent many years in Asia. Deeply devoted to the welfare of the Chinese people, Rockhill was concerned that a partition of the Manchu empire would only worsen the lot of already downtrodden millions. He felt, moreover, that the collapse of the Manchus might intensify imperialistic competition and invite a world war. America, he thought, must now take the initiative; her mission was to become an Asiatic power.

The essence of Hay's effort was first aid to the injured. The tottering regime at Peking had all but collapsed in the 1894-95 war with Japan. The powers, regarding the Celestial Empire as practically dead, mustered round in ghoulish glee to gather the spoils; Hay's self-appointed task was to persuade the potential heirs to hold the estate intact. When he asked Rockhill to draft a statement on this subject, Rockhill sought the advice of an English friend from Peking, Alfred E. Hippisley, who worked in the British Commission of the Chinese Maritime Customs. Hippisley suggested that the time was ripe for the United States to announce a commercial policy for China. Rockhill submitted his memorandum to Secretary Hay and President McKinley, who approved it virtually without change.

On September 6, 1899, Hay sent his first Open Door note to Britain, Germany, and Russia, and two months later to Japan, France, and Italy. He asked the several powers to give guarantees that in their respective spheres of influence they would not interfere with the equal rights of other nationals in matters of tariffs, railroad charges, and harbor dues. In the absence of preponderant seapower, the Open Door Policy was only a suggestion—a sophisticated Yankee bluff. The replies to Hay's note were not very enthusiastic, the Russian reply being the most evasive of all. Nevertheless, the diplomatic language of the replies were such that Hay could quickly announce that the powers had given their assurances. The responses, he said, were "final and definitive."

Just as Secretary Hay announced his satisfaction with the replies to his first Open Door note, a violent anti-foreign uprising was set off in China by the secret society that Westerners called the Boxers. Armed with swords and spears, the Boxers laid siege to the foreign legations in Peking. The siege lasted about three long months. It took an international rescue force of some twenty thousand soldiers to lift it. The United States' contribution to the relief of the legations was 2,500 marines.

Secretary Hay feared that the powers would use the Boxer episode as a convenient reason for expending their spheres of influence. When the Boxers attacked some Russian business houses in Mukden, the Tsar's minister of war remarked, "This will give us an excuse for seizing Manchuria." Hay was prompted, therefore, to send another round of diplomatic notes. This time he did not ask for replies; instead he made a flat statement of American policy. In this second Open Door note, dated July 3, 1900, Hay announced boldly that the United States intended to preserve the territorial and administrative entity of China. In other words, the American government was taking a strong official stand against any further partitioning of the Manchu empire.

John Hay's two famous diplomatic notes reflected the pro-China views of W.W. Rockhill and his British friend Hippisley, both of whom saw in the Open Door a necessary expedient to bring about some stability in Asia. They scarcely dreamed that the concept would become the cardinal doctrine of twentieth-century American policy in the Orient. Secretary Hay had taken his nation into the uncharted waters of Far Eastern politics. His basic idea originated with the English, who certainly had far greater commercial investments in China than Americans did. Hay himself would have been glad to phrase a joint declaration with the London government, but the Anglophobia of Irish-Americans made this an impossibility.

The Open Door declaration did not avert the Boxer uprising. Nor did it prevent Russia and Japan from indulging their expansionist ambitions. Nevertheless, it committed the United States to defend the integrity and independence of a distant, vast, and uncertain country where American economic and political interests were not large or vital. Hay and Rockhill were convinced that the step they took had contributed importantly to the preservation of the Chinese empire. They believed that the further dismemberment of China could be prevented by simple self-denial on the part of the powers. They hoped that the Peking government might in time be able to modernize, improve its administrative techniques, and emerge as a stabilizing force in East Asia. But the tide of dynastic decline was by now too strong for any diplomatic effort to stem the flow.

The United States participated with the powers not only in the military expedition against the Boxers but also in the negotiations of a settlement after the rebellion had been put down. The Washington government joined in calling for an indemnity, punishment of the chief offenders, and restoration of order. But the American influence was exerted strongly in behalf of moderation. We refused to agree, for instance, to the exaction of an indemnity that would have the effect of making China a fiscal vassal for an indefinite period of time. By the protocol signed in 1901, China was required to pay to the powers an indemnity of about $330,000,000, of which the share of the United States was only about $24,000,000. But this sum was twice the total of the costs of the American contingent, and in 1908 Congress authorized the return to China of about $13,000,000. China showed her appreciation by setting aside this amount as a fund to be used in sending Chinese students to American universities.

The assassination of President McKinley in 1901 brought Theodore Roosevelt to the White House at a time when Russia and

Japan were heading for an inevitable clash over Manchuria. Economic interest in this area was of vital concern to both powers. To make certain that no major nation would support Russia in the event of war, Japan made an alliance with Great Britain in 1902 which became the cornerstone of the Tokyo foreign policy.

President Roosevelt was well aware of the Mikado's aspiration in Asia. He knew that Japan's bursting population could not be long limited to a land area about the size of California. He respected her westernization program and seemed convinced, in 1904, that her early success in the Russo-Japanese war was to America's best interests. At the same time he was realistic enough to see that a strong Japan might be too much for the United States to bear in the future. Therefore, as the war progressed, he hoped to see Russia at least survive as a factor in Asia in order to serve as a check on Japanese expansionism. In other words, he favored the idea of "balanced antagonisms." He even went so far as to warn both France and Germany that if they went to the aid of Russia he would support the Japanese.

Roosevelt finally offered to act as a go-between in peace talks. With typical decisiveness the President brought about a meeting of Japanese and Russian representatives at Portsmouth, New Hampshire, where both sides could get a close look at the biggest U.S. Navy yard. The treaty was signed on September 5, 1905. Russia withdrew from Korea and surrendered her special interest in southern Manchuria. The most serious obstacles to peace were Japan's demands for all of the island of Sakhalin and a large indemnity. The Russians said no to both, and threatened to renew hostilities. Roosevelt finally persuaded the Japanese to give up the idea of indemnity, and then arranged a compromise that gave only half of Sakhalin to Japan. Both sides praised Roosevelt for his skill in diplomacy, and the following year he received the Nobel Prize for his role at Portsmouth.

Two years later the U.S. government took a further step to protect Chinese territorial integrity. In a series of notes between Secretary of State Elihu Root and the Japanese ambassador in Washington, Tokyo formally subscribed to the American policy on China. By the Root-Takahira agreement of November 30, 1908, both nations promised to respect each other's possessions in the Pacific, to support the *status quo*, and to uphold the Open Door in China. This agreement seemed to indicate that the United States would not challenge Japan's newly created position in Manchuria; in turn, the Japanese promised they would not disturb the Philippines.

After Roosevelt's departure from the White House in 1909, his successor William Howard Taft turned U.S. Far Eastern policy in quite another direction. President Taft did not fully appreciate the power equation in Asia. A constitutional lawyer by training, he tried various legalistic maneuvers to promote American trade in Asia. In the end, his program of "Dollar Diplomacy" proved costly to American prestige in that part of the globe.

President Taft attempted to neutralize the foreign-owned railways in Manchuria with a plan devised by his Secretary of State, Philander C. Knox, also a lawyer of eminence. The crux of the idea was to arrange a large international loan for China to enable her to buy up all foreign railways in Manchuria. This presumably would strengthen the Open Door principle and at the same time discourage further penetrations of Manchuria by either Russia or Japan. By removing the Manchurian railroads from international politics, Secretary Knox thought that the menace to China's territorial integrity and political independence would be substantially reduced. But Knox was ignorant of local realities, and especially of the new friendship between Japanese and Russians in Manchuria. He overlooked the fact that the Manchurian railroads had great symbolic as well as physical worth. To ask Japan and Russia to neutralize their railway concessions was to ask them to retire from an area over which two wars had already been fought. Both powers gave their tacit approval to Knox's proposal, but nothing more. The Secretary soon discovered that his scheme was driving Russia and Japan into each other's arms, but he did not stop there. He set out on another program to finance currency reform and industrial development in Manchuria through an international consortium. But now China was faced with revolution, and Wall Street financiers were unwillingly to take the risk.

When Woodrow Wilson became President in 1913, he declined to support Taft's program of "Dollar Diplomacy" with government funds. He refused, he said, to be a party to international exploitation. But he insisted that his disapproval of the loan reflected no ill will toward the Chinese people:

> The Government of the United States is not only earnestly desirous of aiding the great Chinese people in every way that is consistent with their untrammeled development and its own immemorial principles. The awakening of the people of China to a consciousness of their possibilities under free government is the most significant if not the most momentous event of our generation. With this movement and aspiration the American people are in profound sympathy. They certainly wish to participate, and participate very generously,

in opening to the Chinese and to the use of the world the almost untouched and perhaps unrivaled resources of China.[1]

With the outbreak of the World War, the neutral United States could do little to avert the shameless "Twenty-One Demands" imposed on China by Great Britain's ally, Japan. These were patently designed to reduce China to a vassal state of the Japanese— an ironic reversal, to say the least. Secretary of State Bryan notified both Tokyo and Peking on May 11, 1915, that the United States would not recognize any agreement that might impair the political or territorial integrity of the Republic of China, or the international policy relative to China commonly known as the Open Door Policy. His strong note had little effect on the determined Japanese, but it did announce the important principle of non-recognition that the United States would use again in its tenuous relations with Japan.

In 1917, the tension was reduced temporarily as the Japanese and the Americans found themselves on the same side in the war. Japan promptly seized the diplomatic initiative, and that summer an extraordinary delegation under Viscount Ishii came to the United States. Ishii's purpose was to test the extent to which President Wilson would accept Tokyo's contention that it was entitled to a special position in China. Secretary of State Lansing cautiously exchanged views with the Japanese diplomat. Ishii wanted recognition of Japan's special interest in China, but Lansing specifically denied that "special" meant "paramount." In this difficult atmosphere the two signed a somewhat ambiguous statement on November 2, 1917 which admitted that "territorial propinquity creates special relations between countries." Hence the United States government recognized that Japan indeed had special interests in China, particularly in the part to which her possessions are contiguous.

The Lansing-Ishii agreement really did no more than to leave each power to interpret it to suit its own purposes. Ishii said in his memoirs that he and Secretary Lansing were only performing the act of photographers of Japan's paramount situation in the Far East. Believing the United States had betrayed them, the Chinese protested the agreement. But in 1917 something had to be yielded in the interest of allied unity, and China was earmarked as the sacrifical victim.

This is the explanation of William E. Dodd in his biography of President Wilson. Some of Wilson's friends deeply regretted the

[1]Department of State, *Foreign Relations of the United States: Diplomatic Paper, 1913* (Washington, D.C.: Government Printing Office, 1920) 171.

Lansing-Ishii agreement, and Wilson himself knew that the surrender of Shantung province to exploitation by the Japanese violated his entire liberal philosophy as well as the cherished principle of self-determination. He chose to consider it a temporary concession that would allieviate allied tensions during the war. Early in the war the Japanese had seized the German leasehold in Kiaochow Bay; subsequently they extended their control over the entire Shantung peninsula. The Japanese had promised to restore Chinese sovereignty in Shantung, but then they managed by such wartime finagling as the Lansing-Ishii pact to obtain allied recognition of their dominant position in Shantung.

At the Paris Peace Conference in 1919 the Chinese demanded the return of the German leasehold. At first the American and Chinese delegations worked closely together as President Wilson hoped to free China from all restrictions on her sovereignty. But Japan had secret treaties with her European allies that bound them to support her claims to the occupied German concessions. Moreover, the Chinese had reluctantly accepted the Twenty-One Demands in 1915, and had also agreed to abide by any German-Japanese decision as to the disposition of the German concessions.

China's hope and Wilson's efforts on China's behalf were tragically unsuccessful. When the Japanese threatened to quit the peace conference rather than yield, Wilson accepted a clause in the treaty draft by which Germany renounced in favor of Japan all its rights to Shantung. The Chinese thereupon refused to sign the Treaty of Versailles.

The controversy was not resolved during the following years. At the Washington Naval Disarmament Conference in 1922 the Chinese and Japanese delegates met with British and American officials to consider again the problem of Shantung. As a result of these direct negotiations, Japan and China signed a treaty on February 4, 1922; it provided for the restoration of Shantung in full sovereignty to China. The reassertion of sovereignty over Shantung, achieved with American assistance, was a considerable victory for the Chinese. They thought they saw a chance to redeem the failure at Versailles.

At the Washington conference there was a great deal of enthusiasm to check Japanese imperialism, but China was still troubled with disunity and chaotic conditions. The Chinese government was in no position to assert itself. In fact, a number of Chinese nonpolitical organizations sent their own observers to witness the participating nations sign the Nine-Power Pact. By this treaty the United States, Britain, Japan, France, Italy, Portugal, the Netherlands, and Belgium agreed not to interfere in the internal affairs of China and to allow the Chinese to solve their domestic problems. Essentially the participating Powers agreed to the Open Door idea: to respect the sovereignty, the independence, and the territorial and administrative integrity in China.

The Nine-Power Pact looked good on paper. But it did not fulfill the hopes of the Chinese delegation. There was no enforcement machinery whatever; the treaty required no one to defend the principles of the Open Door but merely to "respect" these; its only sanction was the good faith of the signatories. What China had surrendered in previous years, remained unrecovered. The Chinese wanted to set their own tariff rates, but the powers offered a five percent increase on imports and promised to carry on further discussions. Nothing was accomplished to end extra-territoriality nor to answer the Chinese demand that foreign troops be removed from Chinese soil.

China was told, in so many words, that she must put her house in order and develop a capacity to govern herself according to western standards. The 1922 treaty went as far as the signatories were willing to go at the time. None was willing to pledge force to defend the abstract principles of the Open Door. The reaction in China was adverse. At Shanghai 20,000 demonstrators staged their opposition to its results.

The United States government continued to sympathize with the efforts of the Chinese to achieve those political institutions which would best meet their needs in the modern world. When Chiang Kai-shek's armies were driving northward through the Yangtze Valley in an effort to unite the country, Secretary of State Frank B. Kellogg restated America's agreement with the aims of the Kuomintang and the American policy of non-interference in the internal affairs of China. "The United States has watched with sympathetic interest the nationalistic awakening of China," he declared on January 27, 1927, "and welcomes every advance made by the Chinese people toward reorganizing their system of government." When a level of unification was finally achieved, the United States promptly recognized the National Government of the Republic of China. The date was July 25, 1928. Secretary Kellogg expressed the American attitude: "The good will of the United States towards China is proverbial, and the American Government and people welcome every advance made by the Chinese in the direction of unity, peace, and progress."

But peace and progress in China soon were Russia's new encroachments into Manchuria. Having recently co-signed the Kellogg-Briand Treaty renouncing war as an instrument of national policy, China and Russia now appeared ready to fight just as the celebrated treaty was being proclaimed and praised around the world. The pact of 1928 proved ultimately as meaningless as an agreement not to raise umbrellas except in rainy weather. No one was legally obligated to redeem it. But Secretary Kellogg's successor, Henry L. Stimson, considered it in the interest of the United States to do so. Stimson assumed and maintained throughout President Hoover's term, a strong stance of world leadership. He attempted to turn the lifeless phrases of the Kellogg-Briand Treaty into specific rules of international conduct. Much as John Hay had deliberately construed the nebulous replies to his Open Door notes as unanimous and wholehearted approval, Stimon read into the Pact of Paris exactly what he wanted to see in it. To him, it was more than a mere group of unilateral statements made by the signatories, declaring pious purposes on the part of each, of which the signatory was to be the sole judge and executor, and for a violation of which no other signatory could call him to account. Stimson was certain that the pact actually conferred benefits to be denied to violators, that it rested upon the sanction of public opinion, and that it carried with it the implication of consultation.

In Secretary Stimson's hands the Kellogg-Briand Treaty became the bridge to a more active American co-operation with the League of Nations than Woodrow Wilson, in his hour of defeat, might have imagined possible. Stimson in 1929 boldly reminded both China and Russia of their obligation as signatories. The Soviets paid no attention. Russian forces invaded Manchuria and overcame the Chinese defenders. Maxim Litvinov, the Soviet Foreign Commissar, indignantly informed Stimson that the Kellogg-Briand Treaty does not give to any single state the function of protector. He regarded Stimson's intereference as unwarranted and one-sided since the United States had recognized the Chinese government but not his own.

The aggressive Stimson, a Long Island squire who had served as Secretary of War under President Taft, was somewhat inclined to make quick judgments. The Japanese watched his performance with suspicious eyes. They knew there was no effective machinery behind his one-man effort to dislodge the Soviets from Manchuria. Over the years the Japanese had built a formidable financial stake in northern China which they considered absolutely essential to the welfare of their island nation. But China, now more than ever, considered Manchuria as hers to control. And the United States seemed to be standing up for the Chinese.

Anti-Japanese feeling in Manchuria became so bitter in 1931 that numerous clashes occurred. One such incident gave Japan a convenient excuse to rush in with armed force. On the night of September 18, 1931, the Mikado's soldiers struck without warning at the Chinese garrison outside Mukden. Few informed observers doubted that the Japanese had moved according to a preconceived plan.

Several days after the Mukden Incident, the Chinese government formally appealed to the League of Nations. While the United States was not formally represented at Geneva, the Chinese hoped to draw the American government into some decisive action. They reasoned that Secretary Stimson would again be on their side, as he had been during the difficulties with the Russians; and they knew President Hoover to be an old friend who had spent his early career in China. But Hoover was preoccupied with the domestic problems of the depression. He felt that the United States ought not at this point to play favorites in Asia, but of course he sympathized with the underdog China and felt that the Japanese were grossly violating their treaties. This view was strongly expressed by the chairman of Foreign Relations Committee, Senator William E. Borah, who found no justification at all for Japan's use of force in Manchuria.

Indignation among leaders of American opinion led to private endorsement of some form of economic sanction against Japan. Precisely such co-operation was presaged in a giant petition drafted by President A. Lawrence Lowell, of Harvard University, and hastily signed by many professors and others. As the Japanese expanded their activities in Manchuria, Secretary Stimson began to stiffen. He began speaking of "firm ground" for an "aggressive stand" in defense of Chinese rights.

President Hoover would not go as far as his Secretary of State. He opposed both economic and military sanctions, feeling that either could lead to war. The mobilization of public opinion was about as far as the President would go. He agreed that an American official should sit as an observer in the debates of the League of Nations on the Manchurian question. When the Japanese defied a League resolution calling on them to evacuate the territory they had seized, a special commission headed by Lord Lytton of Great Britain was selected to go to the Far East to investigate on the spot. One American, Frank F. McCoy, went with Lytton's group.

As the Japanese army extended its domain in Manchuria, Secretary Stimson became increasingly angry. He finally got

President Hoover to approve a doctrine of "non-recognition" as the pivot of American policy toward Japan. On January 7, 1932, Stimson sent identical notes to Japan and China saying that the United States would simply not recognize any agreement or situation impairing American rights under the Open Door policy, or any gains made in violation of the Kellogg-Briand Pact. To strengthen his statement Stimson tried to secure the support of the British, but the London government would not associate itself with his doctrine.

The Japanese refused to be deterred by Stimson's dramatic move. Their warships attacked Shanghai and their planes bombed Chinese refugees on the roads out of the city. This evoked very strong anti-Japanese sentiment in America, and President Hoover hastily ordered more ships of the Asiatic Fleet into Shanghai harbor and landed more U.S. marines. On February 18 the puppet state of Manchukuo was proclaimed by Tokyo. The full impact of Stimson's efforts was now felt as the League of Nations adopted a resolution containing the non-recognition principle. This meant that most League members would refuse to recognize Manchukuo as independent from China.

On October 1, 1932 the League of Nations released the report of the Lytton Commission on conditions in Manchuria. The commission had interviewed many government leaders and other individuals in China, Manchuria, and Japan. Its report was written largely by two American assistants to the commission, George H. Blakeslee of Clark University and C. Walter Young of Johns Hopkins. The report roundly condemned Japanese actions in Manchuria, but was also critical of China's behavior under the affair. It recommended an independent Manchuria under the political control of China, but Japanese interests were to be protected.

When the League of Nations voted to adopt the Lytton report, the Japanese delegates walked out of the chamber. Manchuria had gone the way of Korea. The combined efforts of Washington, London, and Geneva to restrain Japan—to arrest a process of Far Eastern imperialism of which Great Britain and France were two of the principal originators, and in which they were still silent partners—had proved a total failure. The chief Japanese delegate at Geneva, Yosuke Matsuoka, arose dramatically and told the assembled delegates that as Christ had been crucified on the cross, so was Japan being crucified by the member nations of the League. Privately Matsuoka complained that the powers had taught Japan the game of poker, but when the Japanese had acquired most of the chips they pronounced the game immoral and took up contract bridge.

Japan's action in Manchuria was the first great test of the League of Nations. The Japanese kept their troops there, and this of course meant effective control. The western world was in the throes of the Great Depression, and Manchuria was simply too remote to command much real attention. On the other hand, Manchuria was next door to Japan—and the Japanese were determined and bold. Mere words, without the show or threat of force, were insufficient to deter them.

Secretary Stimson should be credited for his attempt to mobilize global opinion against overt militarism in Asia. In violating the League Covenant, the Nine-Power Pact, and the Kellogg-Briand Treaty the Japanese were clearly threatening the structure of world peace. Stimson had tried to persuade President Hoover to urge the League to punish Japan with strict economic sanctions. But Hoover, a profoundly peaceful man, would not go quite this far. It took the attuned ear of the newly elected Franklin D. Roosevelt to appreciate Stimson's effort to stabilize the situation in the Far East. Stimson hoped to persuade Roosevelt to make a very strong stand. On January 9, 1933, he had an all-day conference with the president-elect.

During these early days of the administration of Franklin D. Roosevelt, the American people were thinking primarily in terms of the Great Depression and its effect on their own individual lives. Despite a romantic sympathy for China, they were hardly in a mood for serious involvement in foreign affairs. Yet President Roosevelt had given a vague assurance to Stimson that he would maintain the policy of non-recognition of Japanese conquests. "I have always had the deepest sympathy for the Chinese," he told his Democratic advisers. "How could you expect me not to go along with Stimson on Japan?"

The new Secretary of State, Cordell Hull was trained in the fundamentalist politics of Tennessee backwoods, and as such he held some highly moralistic convictions on international behavior. Hull felt simply that nations should play by the rules of the game. Violation of agreements and double-faced diplomacy were as aggravating to him as naked aggression. Like his predecessors, he fully believed that the United States had a definite interest in maintaining the integrity of China and in preventing any one nation from gaining the upper hand in East Asia. As he entered the State Department, Hull wrote in his memoirs, he had two ideas on the Far East definitely in mind. One was the interest his country had in maintaining the independence of China and in preventing Japan from gaining overlordship of the entire Far East. The other was the equally definite conviction that Japan had no intention whatever of abiding by treaties but would regu-

71

late her conduct by the opportunities of the moment. The Japanese puppet state of Machukuo, therefore, remained unrecognized by the United States.

When Japan then copied a page from American diplomatic history and announced her "Monroe Doctrine" for the Orient—i.e., Asia for Asians, but under Japanese hegemony—Secretary Hull could never accept it. The United States would not assent to the Japanese "hands off" policy. But in Tokyo the American ambassador, Joseph C. Grew, was worried. A veteran diplomat adept at getting inside information, Grew was not hesitant to speculate on the future course Japan would take. In a dispatch late in 1934 he warned his superiors at the State Department that the Japanese intended to gain economic and then political control of China, the Philippines, the Straits Settlements, Siam, the Dutch East Indies, and the Russian maritime provinces. Japan would try to get them by bluff if possible but by war if necessary, Grew predicted, and the United States would be "reprehensibly somnolent" in trusting to the imagined security of restraints or international comity.

What Ambassador Grew prophesied was already being carried out in Manchuria. The puppet regime there had established an official monopoly, called the Manchurian Petroleum Company, to control the distribution of oil products. Secretary Hull protested this action as a violation of the Nine-Power Treaty, but the Japanese persisted in penetrating deeper into China. Late in 1935 they attempted to combine the five northern provinces of Hopei, Chahar, Suijuan, Shansi, and Shantung into a single autonomous area. In a statement to the press Secretary Hull reiterated that the United States had faith in the fundamental principles of its traditional policy, by which he meant the policy of the Open Door, and since the American government adhered strictly to the provisions of all treaties to which it was a party, it expected other signatories to do the same.

But mere words alone were scarcely enough to deter the Japanese from their plans to dominate China. On July 7, 1937, another convenient incident occurred at the Marco Polo Bridge outside Peking, and three weeks later Japanese armies invaded China in force. The war in the Pacific had begun. Japan did not formally declare war, choosing to refer instead to the "China Incident," but the number of lives it cost soon shocked the western world. Literally thousands of Chinese civilians were murdered on the roads out of Shanghai. Catholic and Protestant missionaries stationed in China brought the picture of such atrocities home to the American people, and with it came a tide of sympathy for the beleaguered Chinese.

Most Americans, of course, clearly favored China from the start.

President Roosevelt certainly did, and Secretary Hull issued platitudinous statements which indirectly warned Japan to renounce the use of force. Hoping to bring about a quick settlement, he even suggested American territory as neutral ground where Japanese and Chinese representatives might meet to negotiate. Tokyo flatly rejected the idea, and President Roosevelt was outraged. On the technical ground that there had been no declaration of war, the President refused to apply the Neutrality Act to the Far Eastern conflict. He therefore made possible the shipment of munitions to China. "We have not put into effect the neutrality proclamation," he explained, "for the very simple reason that if we could find a way of not doing it, we would be more neutral than if we did."

As Japanese military operations increased in intensity, it became evident that Tokyo was bent upon settling the 'China Incident' by brute force. President Roosevelt now decided that the American public was ready for some positive statement. In an address delivered at Chicago on October 5, 1937, without mentioning any nation by name, he sharply condemned "the present reign of terror and international lawlessness." "When an epidemic of physical disease starts to spread," he said, "the community joins in a quarantine of the patients in order to protect the health of the community against the spread of the disease." So it must be with the present epidemic of world lawlessness. The reaction to the Quarantine Speech was mixed. Those who favored some form of collective security cheered the President's remarks, but the vast majority of Americans still preferred a strict isolationist position. The President was rather surprised at the public indifference to his warning—which included a lack of support from leading members of his own party. "It's a terrible thing," "to look over your shoulder when you are trying to lead, and to find no one there."

As the Asian war deepened, the United States found numerous occasions to protest officially against Japanese violations of its treaty rights in China. Secretary Hull insisted upon full protection of all
· American missionaries in the war zone as well as any Americans engaged in commercial activity. But the Japanese frequently violated mission property either by outright seizure or by bombing and shelling. It appeared that Japan was deliberately trying to eradicate all western cultural influence in China. American mission stations in the interior were always conspicuously marked with flags, but the Japanese usually disregarded such identification. Hull's protests brought few explanations and little satisfaction. Meanwhile the British initiated a conference at Brussels for the purpose of discussing the implications of the Pacific war and its effect on the other signatories of the Nine-Power Treaty. The meetings opened inauspiciously. Germany declined

73

to be present, assigning the reason that she was not a signatory of the 1922 agreement. Italy sent a delegate, but only to treat the conference with scorn and to support the case of Japan. Significantly, on the fourth day of the conference Mussolini's government officially joined Germany and Japan in the Anti-Comintern Pact.

The Japanese, of course, flatly rejected the invitation to Brussels, complaining that the League and the United States had already condemned them without a hearing. When the conferees inquired whether the Japanese would meet for consultation with representatives of a smaller group of powers, that proposal also was declined. Nor was the United States ready to do anything. Isolationism was still too strong. The American delegate was instructed to 'observe closely the trend of public opinion in the United States and take full account of it.' Without American cooperation, the effort at collective security against Japanese encroachments proved fruitless. The conference ended in failure.

During the first year of the Sino-Japanese war, the Far Eastern policy of the Roosevelt administration rested on two contradictory principles—protection of American nationals and legal rights in China, and maintenance of some degree of military presence in the Western Pacific. One-third of the small U. S. Asiatic Fleet of forty-five vessels was ostentatiously concentrated in Shangai harbor, but there were also 2,555 U. S. marines ashore there as well as about 500 more at Peking as well as some 800 infantry at Tientsin. Secretary Hull several times took occasion to express the desire and intention of the Washington government to remove these land troops as soon as their function of protection was no longer needed. The eventual withdrawal of the marines from Shanghai and the infantry detachment from Tientsin attested to the sincerity of this pledge.

As Japanese armies penetrated deeper into China proper, U. S. officials began hastily evacuating American nationals and withdrawing the legation guards and Yangtze River gunboats long stationed in China. In this kind of tense atmosphere there was always the risk of another incident. It came on December 12, 1937, when Japanese aviators in broad daylight bombed, strafed, and sank the plainly marked United States gunboat *Panay* which was assisting in the evacuation of American personnel and escorting American tankers down the Yangtze. Two American sailors were killed, and others suffered wounds. The Tokyo government immediately made a profuse apology and offered reparations to the wounded and to families of those killed. This prompt response on the part of the Japanese seemed to calm American emotions.

As the war dragged on, Japanese troops ventured further into the Chinese countryside after consolidating their control of large coastal cities. But Tokyo could not bring the China Incident to an end either by political maneuver or naked force. As Japanese planes bombed the crowded Chinese cities, American schools and churches were destroyed and business establishments ruined. Occasionally an American life was lost, and the image of Japan grew increasingly sinister in American eyes. But the people of the United States were still largely apathetic. Speaking before the National Press Club early in 1938, Secretary Hull rehearsed his familiar moralistic line and reiterated the President's reluctance to retire completely from China. To let the Far Eastern position of the United States go by default, he said, would merely encourage Japanese wrongdoing and "thus contribute to the inevitable spread of anarchy throughout the world." But such words did not convince very many. According to a Gallup survey, seventy percent of the American people were by now favoring a complete withdrawal from China.

Administration officials seemed to be moving in one direction and the American people in another. There had long been a popular fear of a possible repetition of the World War involvement. American thinking against involvement was stimulated by such anti-interventionist tracts as C. Hartley Grattan's *Why We Fought* and Walter Millis' *Road to War*. Even more important were the investigations of the Senate Committee headed by Gerald P. Nye of North Dakota which "proved"—at least to those who believed it in the first place— that bankers and munitions-makers, the "merchants of death," had been responsible for America's entanglement in the Great War. Widespread support developed across the country in 1935 for a proposed constitutional amendment, introduced by Congressman Ludlow of Indiana, that would require a popular referendum before war could be declared. But strong statements from the President and the Secretary of State were enough to thwart this move, and in a clever countermove the administration sponsored a bill to "allow" the President to halt arms shipments to one or all belligerents in future wars. On August 31, 1935 this bill became law as the First Neutrality Act.

By invoking the neutrality laws in 1937 President Roosevelt would have shut off munitions to both Japan and China. Japan did not need them, but China did. The neutrality legislation, if brought into play, would have hampered the victim of aggression more than the aggressor. The effect on Chinese morale would have been disastrous. Realizing this, the President refused to put the embargo into effect. China received American arms, and America moved a step closer to ultimate involvement in the Asian war.

As the months sped by, the great debate between isolationists and internationalists raged on. The latter gained ground, but when war erupted in Europe in 1939 the neutrality laws were still in effect. On November 4 of that year the President signed the "Cash and Carry" bill, a joint resolution of the Congress that permitted belligerents to come to the United States and purchase what they wished—provided that they carry the purchases away in their own ships. This made it almost impossible for China to get any further help from the United States. Her isolation was virtually complete. Tokyo took full advantage of every sign of American vascillation. In increasingly caustic statements the Japanese replied cavalierly to each of Secretary Hull's moralistic defenses of treaty right in China. They were especially critical of Hull's constant harping on the Open Door. To them the concept was outmoded, not applicable to conditions of today and tomorrow. This was a diplomatic way of saying that no official U. S. policy, however venerable, would be allowed to stand in the way of Japanese plans in the Far East.

Once the Washington government realized that Tokyo's course was unalterably set, a loan of $25,000,000 was arranged through the Export-Import Bank to bolster China's economy. Some American officials still toyed with hope that anti-military Japanese leaders might recover some influence in their government, but the militarists easily kept the initiative as they moved from one goal to another. Japan next seized the large Chinese island of Hainan, thus menacing both the coast of Indo-China and the sea route between Hong Kong and Singapore. This was followed by the annexation of the Spratley Islands, a tiny but strategically important group about four hundred miles southwest of the Philippines. The Japanese were now poised to threaten American possessions as well as those of the French, Dutch, and British. Secretary Hull's protests did nothing to deter their intense ambitions, and in the first half of 1939 the bombings of American property in China continued on the average of one every three days.

Many Americans were now demanding an embargo on all war supplies going to Japan. The Washington government was somewhat hindered by the commercial treaty of 1911 which stipulated that no trade could be forbidden to the Japanese unless similar prohibitions were applied to all other nations. But on July 26, 1939, the State Department abruptly gave the required six-month notice necessary to cancel the old treaty. This action was a heavy blow to the national pride of the Japanese and gave warning that American patience was running thin. Ambassador Grew emphasized this in a luncheon address in Tokyo when he told the American-Japanese Society that public opinion in the United States was very nearly unanimous in opposition to Japan's abrasive actions.

According to a wide sampling reported in August, eighty-two per-

76

cent of the American people wanted to prohibit the sale of all war material to Japan. Taking note of this trend, important interventionist groups now made a strong effort to skake the American people out of their complacency. Henry L. Stimson, as chairman of the Committee for Non-Participation in Japanese Aggressions, published a long letter in the *New York Times* arguing for anti-Japanese embargo legislation. Reprints of his letter received wide circulation.

By now the war in Europe had begun. As the months went by, Japan displayed less intention than ever of mending her ways. The militarists were in solid control. Each new Japanese cabinet on taking office announced "settlement of the China Incident" as its first and foremost objective. Progress toward that end, however, had been limited by the fact that the Chinese National government under President Chiang Kai-shek steadfastly refused to entertain all terms acceptable to Japan. Japanese armies had secured control of practically all of China's seaports and had overrun her richest provinces. Yet the Nationalists showed no inclination to abandon the struggle.

A Tokyo paper complained that since the Chinese were accustomed to "a lower strata of life," there was no vital spot in China whose capture would end the will or capacity to resist. Suffering untold hardships, the Chinese people simply would not crack. Their morale got a boost when Secretary Hull denounced Tokyo's move to set up a puppet regime in the coastal provinces. He declared that the United States would continue to recognize President Chiang's government whose capital was now a thousand miles inland at Chungking.

That city was the most bombed place in the world until the new record was set at London in 1941. Raids were concentrated in the summer, and the almost constant haze from September to April led to the saying that in Chungking the dogs barked only at the sun. The city was honeycombed with caves that could accommodate the larger part of the population. The warning system was probably the best in the world at the time. Spies with radios near enemy bases, spotting the movements of enemy planes, would report the size and the direction of every flight. Chiang Kai-shek's headquarters in the threatened city would then send out the warning by flag signals and sirens. People who could not take shelter had time to disperse to the countryside. The morale in Chungking was high, despite terrible losses, at this moment of the war. The Nipponese planes had a way of stirring up the people to angry determination to resist. The clean-up, fire-control, and repair services were likewise admirable. Yet there was a limit to the punishment that people could take, and there was danger that they might come to view the future as hopeless unless China could find some means to check the bombings.

As Chungking was being put to the test, the war in Europe was breaking out. The infamous non-aggression pact between Hitler and Stalin made it possible, of course, and Tokyo was as surprised as London, Paris, or Washington. President Roosevelt quickly proclaimed a limited national emergency and ordered a small increase in the armed forces. At the same time he solemnly promised the American people that he would keep ships and citizens out of dangerous areas. The President was still watching the Far Eastern situation very closely. His Secretary of Treasury and confidante, Henry Morgenthau wasted no time in acting on a request from the Chinese ambassador, Hu Shih, for another life-saving injection in the form of a loan, to sustain morale. Roosevelt instructed Morgenthau to "do everything for him [the Ambassador] that we can get away with."

Secretary Morgenthau's ubiquitous assistant, Dr. Harry Dexter White, took a special interest in the 1939 loan and in other current projects to aid China. Such measures, he told Morgenthau, would materially strengthen her staying power against Japan and would decrease China's dependence upon Russian assistance. His apparent sympathy with Chiang Kai-shek's cause at this time is interesting in view of his later behavior. It was White who delayed the gold shipments to China which Congress voted immediately after Pearl Harbor, and in 1948 he was finally charged in Congressional hearings not only with adhering to the Communist party-line but also with spying for the Soviet Union. In 1939, of course, Stalin was aiding President Chiang; the Soviet line changed to strong criticism only after the American entry into the Pacific War. And the views and efforts of Harry Dexter White, and too many of the junior officials whom he brought to Washington, also shifted accordingly.

Step by step the American government began to drape an economic noose around the neck of the Japanese. In July, 1940, Congress passed a bill placing certain strategic exports under strict license. Tokyo protested vehemently when President Roosevelt now ordered aviation gasoline, lubricating oils, and high-grade iron and steel scrap to be included under the licensing device. But the President in fact had imposed only a partial embargo on strategic exports to Japan; he feared that more stringent economic sanctions might actually provoke the mercurial Japanese to some act of war. He was convinced that Germany presented a greater danger to the United States than did Japan, and he would do nothing that might diminish or detract from his efforts to hamstring Hitler. Yet the new policy, even though it proved ineffectual, was the first strand in a web of economic sanctions that would eventually threaten to strangle Tokyo. Foreign Minister Toyoda gravely warned Ambassador Grew that the peace of the Pacific might be involved, and Grew wrote in his diary that it would now be hard to stop "the momentum of the downgrade movement in our relations . . . . the obvious conclusion is eventual war."

Hitler's resounding victories of the spring and summer of 1940 stirred the Japanese expansionists as nothing before. Their campaigns in the interior of China had not forced President Chiang Kai-shek into submission, and there was little prospect of subduing the Chinese so long as Soviet Russia and the United States continued to provide aid to the Chungking government. As against the dreary outlook deep in China, the Japanese now saw alluring vistas before them in the open waters of the southwestern Pacific. The French, beaten in Europe, were still technically in possession of the rich rice bowl of Indo-China, while the vanquished Dutch still held the East Indies from which Japan might hope to secure oil and other much-needed strategic materials.

To many Japanese leaders it seemed almost criminal to let slip this golden opportunity to assure the present and future needs of the national economy. Britain was under the blitzkrieg and hardly in a position to obstruct Tokyo's grand plan for a 'Greater East Asia Co-Prosperity Sphere'—and there was doubt whether the United States would, in the long run, offer determined opposition. But of course the Germans, as victors over France and the Netherlands, would clearly have something to say with respect to French and Dutch colonial possessions. This was all the more reason for the Japanese militants to seek an arrangement with the master of Europe, Adolf Hitler.

By the military alliance with Germany and Italy, formally known as the Tripartite Pact, Japan now recognized Hitler's "new order" in Europe and Germany and Italy accepted Japan's "sphere" in Eastern Asia. The most significant part of the treaty, Article 3, was directed specifically against the United States. If the United States should become engaged in hostilities against any one of the signatories, the other two promised to assist the third party.

Little by little, American economic pressure on Japan was becoming a tense issue in Tokyo. Ambassador Grew, closely watching reactions, warned that the program of economic sanctions, once fully developed, might conceivably lead to eventual war. In mid-1940 President Roosevelt invited into his cabinet the veteran Republican statesman who had convinced him of the efficacy of sanctions back in 1933. With the appointment of Henry L. Stimson as Secretary of War, the administration began systematically to tighten the economic pincers on Japan. This made Ambassador Grew's diplomatic work doubly difficult. As he had predicted, the Japanese soon were formulating new policies to accelerate their expansion southward. They were eager for those areas that could supply the vital resources of oil, rubber, and rice.

In the same month the Tripartite Pact was signed, Japanese armies overwhelmed Indo-China in a two-day campaign (September 22-24, 1940) which saw a remnant of 800 French colonial troops die in futility. The governor's small command at Saigon had been totally written off by the Vichy Government of Marshal Pétain, who in fact had made a formal agreement with the Japanese permitting them to occupy a vast ricebowl of 285,000 square miles. In response to Japan's sudden southward thrust, Washington stiffened immediately. On September 25 the United States announced a huge new loan to China, and the following day Secretary Hull declared an embargo on all shipments of iron and steel scrap. "This is a direct hit at Japan," Secretary of War Stimson recorded in his diary, "a point which I have hoped we would hit for a long time."

For four and a half years preceding Pearl Harbor, a period longer than World War I, Chiang Kai-shek's armies fought the Japanese alone. Foreign assistance in these years was, generally speaking, either too little or too late—and not always of a kind best suited to strengthen President Chiang's posture or add to China's chance of survival as a free nation. American efforts on behalf of Chiang in this period call to mind the Chinese saying: "There is much noise on the stairs, but no one enters the room." Considering the magnitude of his problems, American assistance was indeed as meager as it was slow. Despite all assurances of sympathy and interest, the arms and munitions sent from the United States during the entire year of 1940 amounted in value to only nine million dollars. It should be added, however, that the will to do better was not lacking. The American public had long held China in real affection, and the government had never wavered in its policy of supporting the Chinese against Japanese aggression. The obstacles to effective material aid were almost altogether of a practical nature. On the one hand there were problems of transportation, and on the other the tremendous demands made on American industry by the requirements of beleaguered Britain.

The famous Lend-Lease Act, designed primarily to extend effective aid to Britain, also applied to China. Secretary Hull, presenting an argument in support of the bill to the House Foreign Affairs Committee on January 15, 1941, stated:

> It has been clear throughout that Japan has been actuated from the start by broad and ambitious plans for establishing herself in a dominant position in the entire region of the Western Pacific. Her leaders have openly declared their determination to achieve and maintain that position by force of arms and thus to make themselves master of an area containing almost one-half of the entire population of the world. As a consequence, they would have arbitrary control of the sea and trade routes in that region.[2]

Secretary Hull failed to note an important angle which should have been obvious at that moment. While American aid to the Chinese would

[2]*Department of State Bulletin*, January 18, 1941, 85, 88.

weaken Japan in the western Pacific, the weakening of Japan would strengthen the position of the Soviet Union in the Far East—and Stalin was still Hitler's partner at the time. Hull should have made clear, if indeed he understood it, that Stalin would welcome American aid to China—up to a certain point. But American assistance, to the point of consolidating Chiang's Nationalists against the Chinese Communists, would never be welcomed in Moscow.

The Lend-Lease bill became law on March 11, 1941. Four days later President Roosevelt, in a speech to the White House press corps, mentioned "the magnificent will of millions of plain people" as expressed "through the Generalissimo" and added: "America has said that China shall have our help." Words were one thing, but action was another. The relative meagerness of American aid to China in 1941—$26,000,000 compared with $1,500,000,000 to Britain and Russia—reflected the President's "Europe First" outlook and policy. Hitler's containment and ultimate defeat was his prior strategic aim. American political leaders and opinion-makers were oriented toward Europe, and at the start lend-lease was mostly thought of as "aid to England." Some strongly favored helping the Chinese, of course, but to others China was so remote as to be almost unreal. And certain important individuals, especially in the War Department, were actually opposed to China aid. They figured that scarce military items would do more good in Europe or in rearming the United States.

In March of 1941, as if to counterbalance lend-lease, Japan's new ambassador, the affable, poker-playing Admiral Nomura, began informal conversations with Secretary Hull. Their talks were aimed at some kind of understanding that might repair relations between Washington and Tokyo. Held in Hull's apartment over a period of several months, these conversations resulted in six proposals—three by the Japanese (April 9, May 12, and June 15) and three by the Americans (May 16, May 31, and June 21). Three major questions stood out: how to interpret the Tripartite Pact, how to settle the "China Incident," and how to assess Japanese economic expansion in the Western Pacific. The United States urged Japan to withdraw from the Axis alliance—and the Japanese flatly refused. Japan asked the United States to stop aiding Chiang Kai-shek and allow Tokyo to deal with the Chinese without outside interference—and the American reply was a restatement of the principle of the Open Door. In the Western Pacific the United States insisted on specific Japanese pledges against military expansion of any kind, and Japan answered by insisting that her plans for expansion in that area were strictly economic rather than military. The Japanese then tacked on the gratuitous suggestion that the Americans renounce any intention to build up their own military posture in Eastern Asia. The United States refused to make such a promise.

By the middle of June it was clear that Washington was determined to convert the Japanese to the principle of the Open Door, and equally clear that Tokyo was determined to apply its own version of the Monroe Doctrine in East Asia. The United States sought a solution based on a forty year-old principle, and Japan sought an excuse to preserve all the gains made in the past decade. The cordial conversations between Secretary Hull and Ambassador Nomura brought no agreement because there could be no retreat by either side. They were stalemated.

Within a month the Japanese had tightened their hold on Indo-China and the die was cast. President Roosevelt and Prime Minister Churchill held their historic first meeting off the coast of Newfoundland in mid-August of 1941. The epochal Atlantic conference provided Churchill with a charter of sufficiently strong assurances of American military support in the Far East to enable him to structure some very important decisions on those assurances. But the Atlantic Charter was not necessarily cheered in Chungking. The Chinese felt that they had been pointedly ignored in a vital negotiation. In a radio address Madame Chiang Kai-shek explained the Chinese view:

> We feel that we have earned the equality of status with the other democracies, but we do not want it granted to us in charity . . . . We have an indispensable right to be consulted and to make our voice heard when others deliberate about Asia and the Pacific. We are the senior nation in the stand against aggression, therefore we ought not to be treated as a junior in the common council of the anti-aggression nations . . . . We cannot rest secure until you unreservedly recognize our right to take our full share of responsibility in planning a world order that will prevent future aggression.[3]

China was also suspicious, of course, of any rumor of new negotiation between the Americans and the Japanese. Late in the summer Prime Minister Konoye, realizing that the Pacific situation was worsening, made a proposal to meet personally with President Roosevelt at Honolulu. Ambassador Grew was so deeply impressed with the sincerity of Konoye's suggestion that he sent an urgent message to Secretary Hull. Grew pleaded with Hull to use all the force at his command to keep the Japanese proposal from being turned aside. "The opportunity is here presented," Grew said, ". . . for an act of the highest statesmanship . . . with the possible overcoming thereby of apparently insurmountable obstacles to peace hereafter in the Pacific." Secretary Hull instantly rejected the idea of a Konoye-Roosevelt summit. To Ambassador Nomura he declared flatly that there could be no such meeting without a prior agreement on basic principles. He fully realized by this time, of course, that no such agreement was possible. In other circumstances, Hull's reason for rejection might have had

[3]*U. S. Foreign Relations,* 1941, IV, 395.

some validity. In the unique circumstances of the Konoye proposal, it had none. The meat of the Konoye suggestion was in the implication that Emperior Hirohito was now personally ready and anxious to take necessary action to avert a conflict with the United States. Hull somehow missed this point altogether.

Historians may long debate what might have happened had President Roosevelt consented to meet with Prime Minister Konoye in September of 1941. Ambassador Grew and his counselor at the Tokyo embassy, Eugene Doonan, had a sense that the refusal was a tragic error. To them it seemed that the Washington government had missed its great chance to lead Japan back to peaceful ways. Prince Konoye, they thought, was perfectly honest in his own acceptance of those codes of international conduct for which the United States stood, and with the support of the Emperor he would have been able to sustain his pledges. After the fall of Konoye's cabinet, the power structure in Japan shifted dramatically and finally into the full control of the military. A veteran of the Machurian invasion, General Hideki Tojo, called "Razor Brain" by his colleagues, now became prime minister, and he ordered Admiral Yamomoto to proceed with certain preparations. The diplomatic dualing intensified between Tokyo and Washington, but some officials in both capitals still grasped at the straws of peace. Finally, in early November, Ambassador Nomura was instructed to offer a *modus vivendi*, or ninety-day diplomatic truce, to Secretary Hull. At first this idea was welcomed by Hull, who even went ahead and drafted his own version of the plan. President Roosevelt regarded it a fair proposition, but was not very hopeful of its success. The proposed *modus vivendi* provided for a period of three months during which neither the United States nor Japan would advance by "force or threat of force" anywhere in East Asia or in the southern or northern Pacific. The Japanese would agree to withdraw their troops from Indo-China and to relax their export restrictions, permitting the resumption of trade in embargoed articles. The United States would modify its trade restrictions in the same way. But the Japanese matched their moves in the diplomatic chessboard by enlarging their military potential. President Roosevelt and his key advisors in Washington were fully aware of this. In the summer of 1940, almost a year and a half before the Pearl Harbor attack, the Army Signal Corps had broken the basic Japanese diplomatic code. American officials were thus able to decipher all "Purple" messages between Tokyo and Japanese embassies around the world, including Nomura's in Washington. It is a major historical mystery why a Purple deciphering machine was not made available to the U. S. military command in Hawaii—and even a bigger mystery why the senior American commanders in the Pacific were kept in total ignorance of the fact that the Japanese code had been cracked. The concentration of eight of America's eleven battleships in Hawaiian waters, and the designation of Pearl Harbor as headquarters of the U. S. Pacific Fleet early in 1941, would seem to make a decoding office desirable if not indispensable from the viewpoint of security.

At noon on November 25, 1941, Secretaries Stimson of War and Knox of the Navy came to the White House with their uniformed chiefs, General Marshall and Admiral Stark, for a meeting with Secretary Hull and the President. The discussion dealt mainly with an intercepted Japanese message fixing November 29 as the deadline for negotiations. The President, Stimson wrote in his diary, brought up the possibility that something would happen before the deadline, because the Japanese were notorious for making an attack without warning. The main question was "how we should maneuver them into the position of firing the first shot without allowing too much danger to ourselves." The next day, the 26th, Hull told Stimson over the telephone that he had been with the President that morning and they had decided against the *modus vivendi*. Hull was ready, he said, to tell Nomura that the United States had no counter proposal at all. This would, of course, "kick the whole thing over" diplomatically and leave only a military solution possible. Hull later explained that he dropped the *modus vivendi* scheme largely because the Chinese government had violently opposed the idea. The conclusion of any such arrangement with Tokyo would have been a major blow to Chungking. Hull saw in it a serious risk of collapse of Chinese morale and resistance, and even of disintegration of China. What actually happened is that the special U. S. adviser to the Chungking government, Professor Owen Lattimore of Johns Hopkins University, had sent an urgent cable on November 25 to his friend in the White House, the presidential assistant, Lauchlin Currie, strongly arguing against any accommodation between the United States and Japan. The question arises here as to whether President Chaing Kai-shek did indeed resist the idea of a ninety-day *modus vivendi*. The Chinese ambassador later denied that his government was opposed to any temporary arrangement that might afford a cooling-down in the Far Eastern situation. It cannot be denied, however, that the Chinese felt hurt at again having been ignored in diplomatic discussions that would vitally affect the future of their nation.

The curious role played by individuals associated with the influential Institute of Pacific Relations must always be taken into account when analyzing Secretary Hull's rejection of the *modus vivendi* of November, 1941. On the 25th, the very day that the Lattimore cable was received at the White House, Dr. Harry Dexter White of the Treasury Department sent a telegram marked "urgent" to the New

York office of Edward C. Carter, secretary-general of the Institute of Pacific Relations, asking him to come immediately to Washington. When Carter arrived the next morning, White was able to assure him that everything was now "okay" and that "every friend of China could be satisfied." At that very hour Secretary Hull was with the President, and the two of them were deciding to "Kick the whole thing over" because Chiang Kai-shek supposedly had opposed the *modus vivendi* proposal.

Dr. Lauchlin Currie, the White House aide who was the President's special assistant on Far Eastern Affairs, seems to have been a key figure in the rejection of a diplomatic truce with the Japanese. He is reported to have been highly agitated over the *modus vivendi* proposal. But on November 28, when Currie lunched with Edward C. Carter, he was no longer worried. In place of the *modus vivendi*, Secretary Hull had submitted to the Japanese a list of ten conditions which Tokyo would certainly find too stiff a price. Conflict was now inevitable. "I should think," Carter wrote on November 29, "that Currie probably had a terribly anxious time for the past week. For a few days it looked as though Hull was in danger of selling China and America and Britain down the river."

On the afternoon of the 26th, having abandoned all thought of a *modus vivendi*, Secretary Hull put into final form his ten-point statement. The Japanese diplomats, Ambassador Nomura and special envoy Kurusu, were then summoned to Hull's office for a reading. Japan, the Secretary said, must withdraw all military, naval, air, and police forces from both China and Indo-China. This was not diplomatic language; it was nothing less than a flat demand. Nomura and Kurusu were aghast. General Marshall and Admiral Stark, aware of the exposed U. S. military position in the Pacific, had advised against any ultimatum being delivered in this manner to the mercurial Japanese. But Hull went ahead with it. As he told Secretary of War Stimson, "I have washed my hands of it and it is now in the hands of you and Knox—the Army and the Navy." It is a curious and highly significant fact—and a fact that is seldom mentioned in history texts or college classes—that the ultimatum presented by Hull to the Japanese on November 26, 1941, was almost identical to a memorandum drafted in the Department of the Treasury a week earlier. The author of that memorandum was none other than Dr. Harry Dexter White, Secretary Morgenthau's expert on international monetary policy and everything else relating to foreign affairs. Back in May of 1941 Dr. White had prepared a long paper on the Far Eastern situation, and after Hitler attacked the Russians in June, the little doctor became even more interested. On November 18 Secretary Morgenthau sent along to Hull a lengthy memorandum, drafted by White, which suggested the exact terms that should be presented to Japan. The next day Maxwell Hamilton, chief of the Far Eastern Division of the State Department, reviewed the White memorandum. He found the paper the most constructive one he had yet seen. Secretary Hull had both the White memorandum and Maxwell's minor revision of it before him when he worded his fateful statement of November 26. It is important to note that eight of White's drastic demands found a place in Hull's text. The terms embodied in the memorandum drafted by Dr. White were so harsh that even Secretary Morgenthau, who himself knew almost nothing about Asia, must have realized that Japan could never accept them. Certainly Dr. White realized it. He appears, therefore, to have been anxious for war between Japan and the United States—and his reason perhaps was that such a conflict would naturally reduce Japanese pressure on Russia's Far Eastern flank. The Soviet Union had over 200,000 men facing Japan in the Far East, and these troops were now desperately needed in the defensive struggle against the Germans. Congressional testimony in 1948 pointed conclusively to the intimate connection between Dr. White and secret agents of the Soviet Union. In other words, Harry Dexter White may very well have been consciously serving the interests of Soviet Russia when he recommended an uncompromising attitude toward Japan late in 1941. War between the United States and Japan was, after all, a primary aim of Soviet policy at that time.

On December 4 Army Intelligence made available to the highest officials in Washington a most important intercepted dispatch from the Tokyo government to its embassies in Washington and in Havana. This dispatch ordered the immediate destruction of certain code machines. According to Admiral Richmond R. Turner, who was then the chief war-plans officer of the Navy, such an instruction could have only one meaning: war was imminent! Sharing this opinion was Rear Admiral John R. Beardall, naval aide at the White House, who personally discussed the intercepted message with President Roosevelt. In Congressional testimony Admiral Beardall revealed the gist of their conversation: "I said, Mr. President, this is a very significant dispatch, which he read very carefully, and he said, Well, when do you think it will happen? I said, Most any time." Yet no hint of the imminence of war was relayed to the American commanders in Hawaii. Another important interception that should have given the Washington officials a sharp warning was the detailed report of the Japanese consul in Honolulu on the exact location of all U. S. carriers, battleships, and cruisers in Pearl Harbor. As the diplomatic situation grew more tense during the fall, Tokyo's interest in the condition of the U. S. Pacific Fleet naturally intensified and the Japanese consul increased the frequency of his ships-in-harbor report to two a week.

Not the slightest reference to the activities of the Japanese consul was sent to the Hawaiian commanders. "Had I learned (of) . . . the ships-in-harbor messages," wrote Rear Admiral Husband E. Kimmel in his memoirs, "I would have gone to sea with the fleet." Generations of Americans have the right to ask why the commander of the U. S. Pacific Fleet, of all people, was not made aware of what was known in Washington concerning Japanese interest in his anchorages.

Another strange circumstance in the Pearl Harbor debacle was the so-called "Winds signal" intercepted on December 4 by the naval intelligence station at Cheltenham, Maryland. The Japanese government had set up a secret code system for the specific purpose of notifying its diplomatic representatives around the world of the exact moment of the outbreak of war against the United States. But the U. S. Navy cipher experts at Cheltenham had unwound the code. The war signal was to be a false weather report, "East Wind Rain." The Cheltenham team was on high alert for such a message. As soon as it was decoded, Lieutenant-Commander A. D. Kramer handed it to his senior colleague, Captain Laurance F. Safford, with the telling remark: "This is it." In his Congressional testimony Captain Safford insisted that he put the "Winds" message into the proper channels that would take it to the White House, but somehow the word never reached the American military commanders in Hawaii. At 2:00 P.M. on Sunday, December 6, Army Intelligence intercepted a message from the Japanese foreign minister to Ambassador Nomura stating that the formal reply to Secretary Hull's ultimatum of November 26 would be sent shortly in thirteen parts—and that a fourteenth part would inform the ambassador as to the exact time the reply should be handed to Secretary Hull. This pilot message was available to Hull, Stimson, and various other officials by 3:00, and the thirteen-part intercept was on the way to the White House that evening. About 9:00 President Roosevelt was handed the thirteen-part intercept. He turned to Harry Hopkins and exclaimed: "This means war!" The President then tried to get in touch with Admiral Stark, the Chief of Naval Operations, who was at the National Theatre. Unable to establish contact, the President told Hopkins that he would reach Stark later since he did not want to risk public alarm by having the Admiral paged. Everything thus pointed toward a Japanese surprise attack of some sort—and the American battle fleet was riding at anchor in Pearl Harbor. There was ample time in which a warning could have been sent to the Hawaiian commanders. The fourteenth part, fixing 1:00 P.M. on Sunday, the 7th as the hour for delivery of the Japanese reply to Secretary Hull, was intercepted and decoded at the Cheltenham station at 7:00 A.M., which was 1:30 A.M. Hawaiian time. This was nearly six and a half hours before the attack. In the three decades since the Pearl Harbor disaster, this lapse of time has not been explained satisfactorily by a single apologist for President Roosevelt's administration.

Another mysterious element in the Pearl Harbor equation was the last minute behavior of General George C. Marshall, the Army Chief of Staff. When Colonel Rufus S. Bratton saw the fourteenth part of the Japanese message, he immediately tried to contact Marshall but was unable to do so. The general had left his office on Saturday afternoon, the 6th, soon after learning of the pilot message but before the thirteen parts of the Japanese reply had come in. He did not return to his office until 11:25 A.M. on Sunday. His explanation to a Congressional committee was that he had been riding his horse that morning in Rock Creek Park, as was his habit.

When General Marshall finally arrived at his office, he began a close reading of the entire Japanese intercept which lay decoded in fourteen parts on his desk. Colonel Bratton tried desperately to show him the significance of the last part, the time-of-delivery instruction, but the General insisted on reading the entire text. Fifteen minutes later, when he finally came to the last part of the message he agreed with Colonel Bratton and the other officers present that it indicated a Japanese surprise attack upon American forces somewhere in the Pacific at or about 1:00 P.M. Washington time. General Marshall then wrote out in longhand a warning to the several Pacific commanders in the Hawaiian and Philippine Islands. It was ready for encoding at 11:55 A.M., which still left ample time to contact Honolulu. But the General chose not to use the scrambler telephone on his desk, or the Navy radio, or the FBI radio—any one of which could have reached both Admiral Kimmel and the Army commander, General Walter C. Short, thirty or forty minutes before the attack began. Instead, the message was sent by Western Union to San Francisco and then by RCA commercial radio to Honolulu—not even marked "Priority." It reached Short's headquarters six hours after the attack, and Kimmel got it two hours later.

Did General Marshall deliberately hold up his warning message and send it by means he knew would get it there too late? The Army Pearl Harbor Board could find no reason for his delay. The investigators concluded: "We find no justification for a failure to send this message by multiple secret means either through the Navy radio or the FBI radio or the scrambler telephone or all three." There has never been a satisfactory explanation why, even on the very morning of December 7, Washington officialdom failed to send a single word of warning to Hawaii in time to anticipate a Japanese attack. It is difficult to conclude that any official could commit so grave an error of omission and retain his post unless he were acting under orders. Such orders could have only come from the President. Admiral Kimmel has summed it up in these words:

> When the information available in Washington prior to the attack was finally disclosed to me, I was appalled. Nothing in my experience of nearly forty-two years' service in the Navy had prepared me for the actions of the highest officials in our government which denied this vital information to the Pearl Harbor commanders. If those in authority wished to engage in power politics, the least they should have done was to advise their naval and military commanders what they were endeavoring to accomplish. To utilize the Pacific Fleet and the Army forces at Pearl Harbor as a lure for a Japanese attack without advising the commander-in-chief of the fleet and the commander of the Army base at Hawaii is something I am wholly unable to comprehend.[4]

What do these details on the Pearl Harbor disaster have to do with China? The answer is inclusive: everything. President Roosevelt's "back door to war" proved to be Stalin's "open door" to the Communist conquest of China. The Japanese had struck for the third time in sixty years without warning. China and Russia, in 1894 and 1904, had in turn suffered similar "surprise" attacks. The sneak tactic, adapted to the age of airpower, sufficed again. "Have those Americans," asked a Japanese pilot in his diary, "never heard of Port Arthur?" But while the United States Navy lost most of its battleship fleet in the smoke and flames of Pearl Harbor, its four Pacific-based carriers were fortuitously at sea. Fuel and repair facilities at the naval base were left largely intact, and throughout America there was suddenly an unprecedented unity. The American people at last were ready, as a result of the "treachery" of the Japanese, to commit themselves fully to the same cause for which Chiang Kai-shek's beleaguered Nationalists had been fighting for years. That cause was a free China.

[4]Husband E. Kimmel, *Admiral Kimmel's Story* (Chicago: Regnery, 1955).

3

The Pivotal Period
[1942-1945]

WHAT HAPPENED inside China in the hundred years between the
Opium War and Pearl Harbor, and what occurred simultaneously in
the Sino-American relationship, are matters of straight historical record. Because temptations to depart from what is called "historical
objectivity" are few, the story of this long century in Eastern Asia is
nearly the same regardless of who is telling it. The prejudices of particular authors may be evident in some shadings here and there, but
there is really very little in these hundred years of Eastern Asian history upon which serious scholars can disagree fundamentally. The
historiographical honeymoon ends here, however. Figuratively speaking, the bombs that fell in Hawaii on December 7, 1941, tore apart all
such pleasant unanimity of interpretation. The Japanese attack
made the United States a formal ally of the Republic of China, and for
more than three decades this connection has been the subject of the
most intense historical as well as political controversy. Indeed, from
Pearl Harbor Sunday to the present, the whole subject of Far Eastern
affairs has been debated by adherents of two schools of interpretation
that are in diametrical conflict.

The one side, with an impressive collection of university professors and other "China experts" in its lineup, has been uniformly critical of the political and economic behavior of the Chinese Nationalists

and correspondingly generous in its interpretation of the activities of the Chinese Communists. The other side, with fewer professional scholars but perhaps a larger number of public spokesmen, has been sympathetic in its view of the Chinese Nationalists and correspondingly critical of the Chinese Communists. The two schools can thus be identified without the use of Pavlovian labels. It is just as wrong to brand the latter "the China lobby" as it is to tag the former "the Red China lobby."

The historiographical debate on the China Question opens abruptly with opposing interpretations of the pivotal World War II period. Both schools have carefully assessed the events of the critical years between 1942 and 1945, and both schools have put various documented accounts into print. But seldom indeed are the conflicting interpretations of the War years mentioned in the same breath—or even included in the same bibliography! The beginning reader has usually been a captive, therefore, of the particular book or article that comes first, most forcibly, or most appetizingly to attention. Its viewpoint has become instant gospel in the absence of conflicting viewpoints, which exist in print but are kept conveniently out of sight. The other side simply succumbs to silence.

This sorry state of affairs is perhaps understandable in light of the vociferous political debate that has swirled on the China Question for the past generation. But it is nonetheless a sad situation for anyone seriously trying to understand the recent past in the Far East. It is, in fact, reminiscent of the historiographical blackout that prevailed in educational institutions of both the North and South for many decades following the American Civil War. In this way are books burned without bonfires.

Anti-Kuomintang interpretations of the World War II years fill the pages of a long shelf of books, many of them from the most prestigious publishing houses of the United States. These sophisticated writings by distinguished academics and acknowledged "China experts" began to appear at the end of the war, with such volumes as Owen Lattimore's *Solution in Asia* (1945), and they became increasingly potent over the next few years as Chiang Kai-shek's government lost ground to the Communists. Prime examples of anti-Nationalist summation in this crucial period were Theodore D. White's *Thunder Out of China* (1948), and that beloved bible of Chiang's American detractors, *The United States and China* (1949) by Professor John K. Fairbank of Harvard, the high priest of Asian academicians in the United States.

The stream of anti-Kuomintang literature slowed to a trickle during the Korean War, with the carefully constructed *China Tangle* (1952) of Herbert Feis, an interesting specimen of measured scholarship, and there were comparatively few important criticisms of the

Nationalist Chinese on the American publishing scene in the anti-Communist atmosphere of the '50s. But the flow of persuasive print started up again in the Kennedy years, as evidenced by such tomes as Professor Tang Tsou's *America's Failure in China* (1963), and it was soon coming on readily in rhythm with the Vietnam War protests. By the time the Johnson Administration had fallen, such strident Kuomintang critics as the World War II diplomats O. Edmund Clubb and John P. Davies, Jr., were finally published authors. The flood of anti-Nationalist assessment did not crest, however, until Peking's ping-pong diplomacy and President Nixon's celebrated visit to the Chinese Communist capital. Then it hit like high tide on the Yangtze. Today the bookstalls are loaded with literally dozens of impressive new publications which tell the World War II story in terms terribly unsympathetic to Chiang Kai-shek and his party. Conspicuous among them is Barbara W. Tuchman's prize-winning blockbuster, *Stilwell and the American Experience in China* (1971)—a book sufficiently strong and bustle and engrossing to convince almost anyone who has not done his own researching, that wartime China had the world's worst leadership and levels of corruption unexcelled even in Al Capone's Chicago. Another example—noteworthy for its single-sidedness but even more for the fact that the author happens to be a senior and very distinguished diplomatic historian rather than a "China hand"—is Richard W. Vanalystine's *The United States and East Asia* (1973). According to this writer, no one in Chungking between 1942 and 1945 was interested in fighting the Japanese except General Stilwell and the Chinese Communist resident agent Chou En-lai.

It will be clear by now that the purpose of this chapter is not to recount World War II happenings in China. The reader who wants that story can easily get it elsewhere. Instead the purpose here is to call attention to those significant details which the anti-Nationalist interpretators have seen fit to mention only in passing to dismiss with ridicule, or to omit altogether. These neglected points, when properly understood, throw quite different light on the whole Chinese horizon in the pivotal 1942-1945 period. If the anti-Kuomintang writers had not censored these details, it would be unnecessary to highlight them here. But the blackout has been almost perfect in the anti-Nationalist literature. It is time to penetrate the curtain on such subjects.

How best to ventilate these partially concealed subjects? A convenient way might be to discuss them in the framework of five major interpretive themes that have been advanced, in one fashion or another, by the anti-Kuomintang writers. The five themes are the following:

1. The *Real China* theme, which underscores differences between the mental picture that most Americans (including President Roosevelt) had

of the Republic of China as an ally in 1942, and the supposed realities of the situation at Chungking.

2. The *China Aid* theme, which strongly presents one side of the large question of lend-lease material and wartime loans but always omits a most important detail—the incredible delays of the Treasury Department in the shipment of gold. |

3. The *Fighting Joe* theme, which emphasizes the soldierly skills and determination of the senior American officer in China, Lieutenant General Joseph W. Stilwell, by taking at face value every vitriolic opinion set down by "Vinegar Joe" in his personal diary.

4. The *Field Reports* theme, which accepts as biblical truth practically every judgment made between 1942 and 1944 by General Stilwell's political advisors, the several junior U.S. diplomatic officers on station in China, without taking into account the integal most important fact that their well-intentioned young men simply did not, under wartime strain, have a clear view of the vital difference between ideologies.

5. The *Big Wind* theme, which deprecates the abilities and questions the integrity of President Roosevelt's trouble-shooter, Patrick J. Hurley, who came to China in 1944 as Stilwell was leaving and stayed for a bitterly frustrating year as the U.S. Ambassador.

Anti-Nationalist interpreters have a high time with the "Real China" theme. They go to considerable pains to prove that after 1937 the American public was given a very sympathetic portrait of Chiang Kai-shek fighting alone against the Japanese invaders. For this supposedly too favorable image they blame, most of all, the China-born and Yale-educated magnate of *Time* and *Life* magazines, Henry R. Luce, whose publications often called attention to Chiang Kai-shek's conversion to Christianity and his happy marriage to Mayling Soong. The fact is, however, that the General's government did contest the Japanese virtually alone—with a few supplies from the Russians and a little encouragement from the United States, but without much practical help from the theory-spouting Chinese Communists—for most of the four years preceding Pearl Harbor. He therefore fully deserved the good press he got in America as a resister of aggression in a world of appeasers. His administration at Chungking was neither as experienced with representative government nor as democratic as Roosevelt's in Washington—and it was perhaps overpraised occassionally in this regard—but it was certainly "democratic" in any comparison with the government of its mortal enemy, Japan. This was the China which became America's ally after Pearl Harbor, and any differences between reality and fiction were largely semantic. Accordingly, the Washington government was not much disturbed in December, 1941 by negative reports on Chiang coming in from the senior "China hand" of the U.S. diplomatic corps, Ambassador Clarence E. Gauss, or from its recently assigned military inspector, Brigador General John A. Magruder. These watchdogs were expected to find fault, which is what they dutifully did, but such carpings were quite beside the point in the larger strategic and psychological exigencies of the moment.

When President Roosevelt welcomed the Chinese foreign minister, Mayling's brother, T. V. Soong, to the White House on New Year's Day, 1942, as the representative of an equal ally, he knew exactly what he was doing. He well knew why Prime Minister Churchill of Britain and Ambassador Litvinov of the Soviet Union did not really wish to acknowledge Chinese equality. They were wholly dependent on the United States for lend-lease, as now China would also be. By giving the Chinese full-fledged membership in the Big Four, the American president won their unqualified respect and admiration—and at the same time he put the British and the Russians in their proper diplomatic place as supplicants. But this part of it has been conveniently ignored by the anti-Nationalist writers, who have said simply that President Roosevelt was taken in by Kuomintang propaganda emanating from Dr. Soong's office.

On the subject of China, the President had not been taken in by anyone—not as yet, at least. He was ready to acknowledge Chiang Kai-shek's government as a full-fledged ally for two very practical reasons. First, as a politician he had to remain reasonably plausible in the eyes of the American press and public. The United States was catapulted into World War II by the Japanese attack at Pearl Harbor, and after all the Japanese had attacked not because they were crazy or suicidal or especially treacherous—but rather because the Washington government had unsparingly applied Open Door principles to the crisis in the Far East. In other words, the American people were now at war because of China; and to deny that the Chinese were allies worth fighting with, as well as for, would be a psycho-political blunder of the clumsiest kind. Secondly, the President clearly recognized at the outset that the Pacific war was a twentieth-century war in all aspects. It was necessarily total, and therefore American policy objectives were necessarily unlimited: the total defeat of Japan, and the removal of the totalitarian Tokyo government as an effective factor in East Asian affairs. To replace Tokyo with a democratic stabilizer in the Pacific balance of the postwar world, the President saw only one viable candidate. That was the Chinese Nationalist government of Chiang Kai-shek. To imagine that a master politician like Franklin Roosevelt was unconscious of these considerations, and therefore a mere dupe of propagandists, is both a convenient anti-Nationalist interpretation and sheer nonsense.

In one hour at Pearl Harbor, the Japanese navy delivered to the

United States fleet the most serious blow in her history. Yet in so doing, the warlords of Tokyo totally misread the chemistry of the American people. Instead of paralyzing the national will and giving greater vent to isolationist sentiment, the "Day of Infamy" had the effect of uniting a divided, hesitant people who were psychologically unready for participation in any foreign war. If the Japanese had chosen simply to ignore the American military presence in the Pacific and had continued to push southward, it is possible that the Washington government ultimately would have found some excuse to declare war. It is improbable, however, that the public opinion could have been successfully mobilized at any early date for vigorous support of the war effort. By their dramatic strike the Japanese did what the American president had been unable to do. As Admiral Yamamoto is reported to have said upon receiving the details of the damage at Pearl Harbor, "What we have done is to awaken a sleeping giant, and to fill him with a terrible resolve." Indeed, Tokyo's act had rallied the whole American nation behind President Roosevelt's twin foreign policy objectives: one, to save England from Hitler; the other, to save China for the Chinese.

Which of these two objectives deserved precedence in the days and weeks following Pearl Harbor? In Washington, D.C., the question of White House priority was on everyone's lips. Would the President decide to "get Hitler" first, or would he want to "save China" first? The present plight of Great Britain was obvious, but Pearl Harbor had the inevitable effect of dramatizing the Pacific side of the war. No one would deny that it was important to strengthen, in all ways possible, the British and Russian resistance against the Germans in Europe, but the United States had been attacked in the Pacific, not in the Atlantic, and certainly the Chinese now deserved to be bolstered in major ways after their decade-old resistance against Japan. Indeed, it seemed to many sophisticated observers that a united, nationalized China was finally within the orbit of democratic influence. If Japan's aggression in East Asia had any effect that could be described as long-range, it was to make of the Chinese peasant one of the most assertive exponents of nationalism in the world. After ten years of struggle against stiff odds, the huge human mass of China was seen by many to be ready at last to be molded into solid national form and energized with democratic ideals. To ascend to such a role in the postwar world, China would have to be helped while the war lasted. She was due a reasonable share of the aid, in material and in money, that the United States was now prepared to dispense. Anti-Nationalist writers leave the impression that Chiang Kai-shek's government obtained a great deal of aid and then either frittered away or hoarded it. But in the years 1941 and 1942 Chungking received only about one and one-half percent of the total of U.S. lend-lease shipments, in 1943 and 1944 only about a half of one percent, and in the last year of the war only about four percent. As Secretary of War Stimson later explained, "In Anglo-American grand strategy the war against Germany came first. Second . . . the Japanese island empire. The China-Burma-India theater was a poor third. . . ."

From the outset, as it proved, there was evidence of both smallness and slowness in lend-lease shipments to China. The first supplies to Chungking were on their way a few weeks after Pearl Harbor, but some of their shipments were suddenly and inexplicably recalled. Thereafter, much of the military equipment earmarked for Chungking was either diverted to another theatre or siphoned off at receiving stations in India and elsewhere. Amphibious craft that had been assembled for the promised landing in Burma, for example, were whisked away to the Mediterranean, and badly needed cargo planes were diverted to Alaska. Stanley K. Hornbeck, chief of the Far Eastern division in the State Department, kept reminding the Lend-Lease managers that the President had solemnly promised full aid to China. The whole Far East, he warned, might be irretrievably turned against the West "in absence of, and for want of, a little more effort on our part to convince the Chinese that we mean what we say when we praise China for the fight she has made." But conscientious officials like Hornbeck could only urge action; someone else had to take it. Decisive action was necessary if Chungking was to get a fair share of the planes, trucks, and field guns, that the American government was funneling to its allies. But such action was not taken effectively until the very last months of the war—not until, in fact, the final collapse of Germany in 1945. As long as Germany remained in the war, Britain and Russia had prior claims on all war material from the United States. China, though recognized by the American President and Congress as an equal ally, received only the table crumbs of American lend-lease.

In the estimation of certain key officials in the Washington bureaucracy, it was apparently important to give the Chinese enough help to keep them fighting—but not enough to allow them to win. American decisions on Lend-Lease took little account of the need to sustain China's morale. The Chinese leaders accepted with fairly good grace the idea that the defeat of Germany was the first allied priority. But they resented a degree of emphasis on the European theatre that denied to China the military supplies which were vital to effective field operations. They figured that they had already proven themselves in battle, and they were increasingly annoyed by the implication that they needed to prove it over and over again in order to justify additional supplies. As Ambassador Gauss himself admitted in 1944, the lessening of the Chinese military effort was not the result of any lack of will to resist the Japanese but rather a result of the lack of munitions and replacement parts.

Equally as serious in the war years, and ultimately far more so, was the failure of the Washington bureaucracy to provide the Chungking government with adequate financial assistance. But seldom mentioned in books on the Pacific war is the curious behavior of the U. S. Treasury Department in the matter of what was known as the China Loan. We are told simply that soon after Pearl Harbor the Chinese applied for, and were granted, credits of $1,000,000,000 by the United States and Great Britain on an equal-share basis. The Chinese did make such a request, but the British were hardly in a position to comply since they were already borrowing heavily from the United States. President Roosevelt, however, was anxious to help. In February, 1942, he asked Congress to approve a loan of $500,000,000—two-fifths of it in gold—to Chiang Kai-shek's government for purposes of internal economic stabilization. The loan was voted through, and Treasury Secretary Morgenthau was given the responsibility of arranging the details. Like his friend the President, Secretary Morgenthau understood the problem of economic stabilization and sincerely wanted to help. But Morgenthau's principal aides in the Treasury Department felt differently. The central figure in the Treasury at this time was Dr. Harry Dexter White, chief of the international monetary division and special assistant to the Secretary on foreign policy matters. Dr. White and his associates had it in their power to stabilize the Chinese currency and preserve the Chinese government—or to debauch the currency and encourage a collapse of that government—and they took the latter course. Only approximately $29 million out of the $200 million in gold, earmarked by Congress and the President early in 1942 to combat inflation in China, reached Chinese shores before the capitulation of Japan in 1945. Dr. Arthur N. Young, financial advisor to President Chiang Kai-shek, correctly suspected "skullduggery," and Secretary Morgenthau finally chastised his people for putting him in "an absolutely dishonorable position." But Dr. White was confirmed as Assistant Secretary of the Treasury before the war was over. Subsequently, J. Edgar Hoover identified White's involvement in the Communist apparatus from more than thirty sources, but he died mysteriously in 1948 before the full impact of his disservice to the United States was understood.

Potent as they have proven, the "Red China" and "China Aid" concepts have not had quite the dramatic import of a third anti-National theme—the "Fighting Joe Stilwell" idea. Central to all anti-Chiang Kai-shek interpretations of the World War II period is a part-truth which rests on the experience of Lieutenant General

Joseph W. Stilwell as the senior U.S. military officer in China from early 1942, to the fall of 1944. According to almost every anti-National writer, the historical facts are as simple as this: General Stilwell wanted to fight the Japanese, but General Chiang wanted only to get another crack at the Chinese Communists. But this is not the whole truth, or even half of it.

In the first few months of the enlarged Pacific war, the Japanese were able to make phenomenal advances. Tokyo's grand strategy was to quickly expel the Americans while the British were engrossed in the European war and before the United States could muster her huge might. A tight economic blockade of China was foremost in the battle plan. General Sugijame, the Japanese chief of staff, gave particular emphasis to the importance of destroying China's supply line from the outside world by cutting the all-weather highway between the city of Kunming, in the southwestern province of Yunnan, and the British towns in Burma. Hundreds of thousands of Chinese laborers had toiled for two years to build the Burma Road through the southern spur of the Himalayas. The Japanese now moved swiftly against Burma. When General Stilwell arrived at Chungking in February, 1942, his first order of business was the defense of Burma. British, Indian, Chinese, and some American troops were committed to the Burma campaign. It soon became a mishmash of suspicions, countermeasures, and personality conflicts on the part of the British officials, Chinese generals, and American personnel which played to the ultimate advantage of the Japanese. Anglo-Chinese relations were cool from the beginning of the campaign. This was partly because the American president had decided on his own that Chiang Kai-shek should be recognized as supreme commander in the China theatre, and partly because Chiang had then requested an American officer rather than a Britisher as chief-of-staff. Stilwell, a veteran of two earlier tours in China, was selected for the assignment.

But Stilwell wore too many caps when he arrived in China. He was simultaneously chief-of-staff to General Chiang, commander of all U.S. Army forces, and supervisor of Lend-Lease. A brave and aggressive field commander, Stilwell regarded a success in Burma almost as an end in itself. He was determined to prove what every career soldier desires to prove—that he could lead troops to victory. General Chiang, on the other hand, felt that his best armies must not be sacrificed in the Burma jungles. The original purpose of sending the Chinese 5th and 6th Armies to Burma was to help in the defense of Rangoon. But Rangoon was lost to the Japanese on the very day Stilwell arrived at Chungking. If Stilwell had not been so hasty in exercising his authority, those Chinese forces stationed in Burma could have been gradually moved north from Mandalay. Instead of assessing the larger strategical situation, he hurried off to the battle area and ordered thousands of Chiang's soldiers into combat. His imprudence and thirst for success did not win the confidence of Chinese generals at the front, and of course he found them inadequate by his West Point standards.

The Japanese employed ten infantry divisions and two armored battalions in the Burma campaign. With superior air power and a unified strategy, they easily overcame the allied remnants and cut off the road to China in one swoop. Stilwell was forced to walk out of the jungle with 25 Americans, 16 Chinese, 13 Britons, and a few Burmese. They covered 140 miles on foot, then flew to New Delhi where Stilwell boldly pledged to recover Burma. From that day forward General Chiang had little respect for Stilwell's judgment, and his faith in his chief-of-staff began to crumble. General Chennault was just as critical. "If Stilwell had been a company, battalion, or regimental commander whose primary responsibility was for the troops in his immediate command," Chennault wrote, "his walkout would certainly have been commendable. But for a man with the tremendous burden of the ranking American officer in Asian and chief of staff of the Chinese Republic, it was a startling exhibition of his ignorance or disregard for the larger responsibilities."

Because Stilwell did not like Tu Yu-ming, the commander of Chiang's 5th Army, he did not order General Chennault's planes to the assistance of Tu. As a result, tens of thousands of Chinese troops were left in the severe cold without food. But Stilwell placed much of the blame for his fiasco in Burma on the shoulders of Chiang Kai-shek, frequently complaining to his superiors in Washington that General Chiang would not 'co-operate' with him. To such charges Generalissimo Chiang replied that he had willingly placed Chinese armies under American command and had been ready to support American policies. "What a contrast this is," he noted, "to the attitude of the British and Russians who, whenever it concerns their own interests, will not make concessions to the general interest." Chiang was unwilling to invest additional divisions in what he considered a futile fight against superior forces, and Stilwell castigated him as "bigoted and selfish," suffering from megalomania. "The cure of China's troubles," he wrote, "is the elimination of Chiang Kai-shek. . . ."

In one message to General Marshall, Stilwell proposed a *quid pro quo* approach in all future dealings with the Chinese government. Marshall relayed this suggestion to the White House only to find the President highly displeased. "I have read this letter with a good deal of care," Roosevelt replied, "and Stilwell has exactly the wrong approach in dealing with Generalissimo Chiang, who, after all, cannot be expected, as a Chinese, to use the same methods that we do." Stilwell's chemistry was simply not up to the challenge of his assignment. Because he was determined to make up for what he regarded as a personal defeat, he came to conclude that the recovery of Burma was the fundamental purpose of China's war of resistance against Japan. The British also opposed Stilwell's plans, but the more opposition he encountered the more obsessed he became with the idea that the reconquest of Burma was the only important and feasible military objective in the entire Asiatic war. He became increasingly bitter toward the British for not taking a second campaign seriously, and he grumbled against his superiors in Washington for not ordering America's allies to agree with him. As the loss of Burma remained unavenged in 1943 and 1944, the cynical diary of "Vinegar Joe" revealed his pathological conviction that everybody in Chungking, London, and Washington was an ignorant S.O.B. except Joseph W. Stilwell. This was the "Fighting Joe" who is still the darling of the anti-nationalist interpreters of the war years in China.

Anti-Nationalist writers have stressed the clashes between Stilwell and Chiang as rooted in the larger question of strategy involving a theoretical debate on ground war versus air war. Practically, however, it was a confrontation between Stilwell and Claire L. Chennault. Retired from U.S. Army Air Corps for reasons of poor health, Chennault joined the Chinese Army in 1937 to train pilots for Chiang. Upon the creation of the American Volunteer Group in 1941, Chiang appointed him commander with the rank of colonel in the Chinese service. Chennault's Flying Tigers amassed a remarkable record against the Japanese. In the dogfights over Burma between March 24 and April 20, 1942, for example, his pilots shot down thirty-three planes against the loss of one. His performance won international acclaim, including President Roosevelt's personal commendation. In the Spring of 1943 Chennault received a presidential appointment as brigadier general commanding the Fourteenth U.S. Air Force, which put him second only to Stilwell among American officers in the China theatre and left him virtually autonomous. Stilwell and Chennault could not agree. Where Stilwell was thinking of liberating Burma from the Japanese, Chennault thought primarily of attacking the Japanese strongholds in the Chinese coastal provinces. Stilwell kept talking about reopening the Burma Road, which meant a ground defensive, but Chennault favored an enlargement of the Hump air shipments. Like Chiang, Chennault did not consider a Burma campaign as urgent in any sense.

The year 1943 began with some important gestures and decisions.

In mid-January, the Secretary of State signed a treaty relinquishing American rights of extraterritoriality in China, and the British offered a similar concession the same day. Meanwhile, President Roosevelt and Prime Minister Churchill were meeting at the Moroccan port of Casablanca and making decisions on global strategy. They discussed ways to increase the strength of allied air power in the China-India area, and selected ANAKIM as the code name for a plan to retake Rangoon. But the Far East was not paramount in anybody's mind. What was really significant at Casablanca was President Roosevelt's sudden announcement of "unconditional surrender" as the allied objective for both Germany and Japan. The announcement came as a total surprise to Secretary Hull, and Churchill himself was caught unprepared. Present at the time was Elliott Roosevelt, who claims that his father decided to use Grant's famous phrase one day at lunch. "Of course," sucking his tooth, "it's just the thing for the Russians. Uncle Joe might have made it up himself." The implications of this decision were profound. It enabled Hitler to convince the majority of Germans that they now had to fight to the bitter end, win or lose, and it hardened the resolve of fanatical Japanese to continue the struggle. Roosevelt's announcement meant prolongation of the war, and probably caused unnecessary loss of American lives. The only nation to benefit by this formula was Soviet Russia.

Soon after the Casablanca conference, Chiang Kai-shek prevailed on Roosevelt to call Chennault to Washington to hear his arguments for air action in China. At the same time, however, General Marshall instructed Stilwell to return to give his side of the story for a new Burma ground offensive. As both men arrived in Washington on the same plane at the end of April, 1943, views varied among White House staffers and the military chiefs. Harry Hopkins, special assistant to the President, and Dr. Lauchlin Currie, his resident expert on Far Eastern affairs, were inclined toward air power and therefore sided with Chennault. Marshall and Stimson regarded ground forces to be of greater importance and supported Stilwell. In the presence of Roosevelt and Churchill and at meetings of the staff chiefs, Stilwell twice crudely ridiculed Chiang Kai-shek, to whom he was at least technically responsible. By these actions alone he betrayed the trust placed in him. When Roosevelt summoned Chennault for a long prepared talk before his departure, and then gave permission for Chennault to report directly to the White House, Stilwell was beside himself with anger. Marshall had warned Roosevelt that it would be embarrassing for Stilwell to return to his post in China if Chennault were given "all the Hump tonnage." Roosevelt's response of "So what?" was well known among members of the Presidential staff. Stilwell may have learned of it, considering his close relationship with Marshall. "After this," Harry Hopkins told T. V. Soong, "Stilwell should be aware of the President's high respect for the Generalissimo. Even with the backing of Stimson and Marshall, he could not move the President one bit. . . . He will not dare to be arrogant as before. In case another dispute develops, it would take only a message from the Generalissimo to have him transferred."[1]

In the wake of the Washington visit, Stilwell's sole responsibility was to train and equip thirty Chinese divisions. Now a major general, Chennault was given the singular mission of bombing Japanese supply lines. The Fourteenth Air Force was made independent of the Tenth Air Force. Now that Stilwell and Chennault had exclusive commands, the friction between them should have dissipated. But this was not to happen. Their differences had roots in competing claims to Hump shipments, and both would continue to fight for priority and a bigger share of India-China air deliveries. Stilwell wanted more arms to equip his Chinese divisions, and Chennault demanded gasoline and spare parts for his planes. Monthly capacity over the Hump was then a mere 4,000 tons. Stilwell thought that 1,500 tons should be enough for Chennault, but after the Washington visit the tables were turned and "Vinegar Joe" started getting the short end. Chennault and Chiang, of course, were old friends, and Stilwell's diary entries amply reflected their comradeship.

As the war progressed, the importance of China as a combatant was steadily diminished by American policy makers. Early in the war, on orders from the White House, some assessments were made in Washington on the possible role of the Soviet Union in the Pacific strategy of the allies. In the summer of 1942 Major General James H. Burns of the Army Ordinance Department, who had an important role in the Lend-Lease program, prepared a confidential memorandum for Harry Hopkins which forshadowed later decisions. Burns wrote: "We not only need Russia as a powerful fighting ally in order to defeat Japan. . . . We [also] need her as a real friend and customer in the post-war world." He went on to suggest that the President would do well to "establish the general policy, throughout all U.S. departments and agencies, that Russia must be considered as a real friend and be treated accordingly." A year later, at the Quebec Conference, Hopkins presented parts of this same memorandum as a guideline for upcoming strategy in the Pacific:

The most important factor the United States has to consider in relation

[1]Chin-tung Liang, *General Stilwell in China, 1942-44: The Full Story* (New York: St. John's University Press, 1972) 122.

to Russia is the prosecution of the war in the Pacific. With Russia as an ally in the war against Japan, the war can be terminated in less time and at less expense in life and resources than if the reverse were the case. Should the war in the Pacific have to be carried on with an unfriendly or a negative attitude on the part of Russia, the difficulties will be immeasurably increased and operations might become abortive.[2]

Hopkins' biographer, Robert Sherwood, understood the implications of the Burns memorandum, but few other writers have noticed it at all. What it meant, of course, was that China was no longer to be regarded as important in the winning of the Pacific war—unless, that is, the Soviet Union desired the Chinese to play a role. And there could be no doubt which Chinese the Soviets would endorse.

The Chinese Nationalists were not invited to send a representative to the Quebec meetings of the allied chiefs of staff. Nor was China given an opportunity for preliminary consultation on decisions regarding the distribution of Lend-Lease supplies from India. Such lack of respect greatly irritated the face-conscious Chinese. China was being treated not as an equal ally but patently as a ward. Until now President Roosevelt had shown himself to be a consistent friend, and the Chinese had been loyally responsive. But Chiang Kai-shek now felt himself entirely out of touch with large strategical decisions which would profoundly affect his country's future. Chiang's protestations through diplomatic channels finally caused the President to do something dramatic. He suggested a summit conference with Chiang at Cairo.

Late November, 1943, Roosevelt and Churchill met Chiang at Cairo and promised him that "all the territories Japan has stolen from the Chinese, such as Manchuria, Formosa and the Pescadores, shall be restored to the Republic of China" This pledge to the Republic of China is sometimes forgotten today as Mao Tse-tung claims to be the sole representative of the Chinese people. At the same conference the American President also set the tone for what was later to result in one of the major controversies of the last three decades. He notified Chiang that Mao Tse-tung's Communists would have to be integrated into the Chungking government. "I'd told him it was hardly the modern democracy that ideally it should be," Roosevelt explained to his son Elliot. "I'd told him he would have to form a unity government, while the war was being fought, with the Communists in Yenan." To Chiang Kai-shek the realities of "unity" meant a possible repetition of the situation of the late twenties when the Communists attempted to move the Kuomintang toward class struggle and away from Dr. Sun Yat-sen's princi-

[2]Robert E. Sherwood, *Roosevelt & Hopkins, An Intimate History* (New York: Harper, 1950), 748-49.

ples. Nevertheless, though Chiang had strong reservations about any such coalition with Mao's forces, he had every reason to believe that the American President would honor the pledge to restore to the Republic of China all territory seized by the Japanese.

Roosevelt's promise at Cairo, however sincere it may have been, was revised a few days later at Teheran. Chiang had gone home, and Stalin was coming to the summit. Eager to please Stalin in their first face-to-face exchange, the President sought a strong assurance of full Soviet participation in the Pacific war after the defeat of Germany. He therefore went very far to gain the Marshal's good will. He also wanted Stalin's co-operation in a postwar United Nations organization. After the Teheran summit Roosevelt and Churchill got together again at Cairo to assess their decisions. The prime minister was dead set against another Burma venture. "In the face of Marshal Stalin's promise that Russia will come into the war," he said, "operations in the Southeast Asia Command have lost a good deal of their value." Roosevelt was inclined to agree. He felt it would be best, therefore, to give the Chinese Nationalists a minimum of encouragement in the months ahead, despite his personal promises to Chiang, and instead to concentrate on the Soviet potential in the Pacific war. This was a fatal decision that would have vast repercussions in the postwar period. It made the Russians, and subsequently their clients the Chinese Communists, a dominant factor on the Asian mainland. But President Roosevelt did not see this. He ended his travels and meetings in 1943 with the feeling that somehow he had sold "Uncle Joe" on the idea that, as a good ally, the Soviet Union should endorse and support the central government of China.

Another favorite refrain of the anti-National school has been the *Field Reports* theme. During the war years a small but influential number of China specialists from the Far Eastern Division of the State Department found it possible to use General Stilwell's personal antipathy to Chiang Kai-shek as a lever to advance thier own antipathy to the Kuomintang. So that Stilwell might have his own liaison and consultative staff to help the irascible general in his dealings with local authorities, the State Department assigned a team of junior Foreign Service officers as political advisers to the military headquarters in Chungking. The chief of this group was John Paton Davies, Jr., whom Stilwill requested because of his unique "China background." Davies, the son of missionary parents, brought with him to Chungking three others of similar background and experience—John S. Service, John K. Emmerson, and Raymond P. Ludden. Each one was, like Davies, a professional U. S. diplomat whose idealistic interest in the success of the Chinese Revolution and deep concern for the welfare of the Asian peasant could be traced back to childhood. These youthful "old China hands" had in common a conviction that the Kuomintang was oligarchic, inefficient, and corrupt. The found it easy to blame President Chiang Kai-shek for everything that went amiss. Stilwell's obsession with the reconquest of Burma, coupled with his profound distaste for administrative detail, made it a simple matter for the young careerists on his staff to feed him an undiluted diet of their prejudices. The reports written by them soon obtained a wide circulation. Copies went to the State and War departments, and a select few even got to the White House by way of the Treasury, the Office of War Information, or the Office of Strategic Services. It became a common joke in Chungking that Stilwell's office was developing its own private foreign policy with John P. Davies, Jr., as Secretary of State. The constant line was that the Chinese central government was autocratic and incorrigible—and that, up north in the hills around Yenan, another more democratic government of agrarian reformers was quite ready to assume a role of national leadership.

In his memoirs General Chennault describes what happened when, in the spring of 1944, a team of military observers was sent by Stilwell to visit the Communist base at Yenan. The American mission to Yenan was hardly established, he writes, before Stilwell's political advisers began to "proclaim loudly the superiority of the Communist regime over the Chungking government." Reports from the Yenan mission, classified as confidential, were freely discussed over the dinner table by Stilwell's staffers, who openly expressed their admiration for the peasant reform programs of Mao Tse-tung's followers and declared them to be "more like New Dealers than Communists." Mao Tse-tung and his associates, moreover, made a great impression on Stilwell by "shrewdly letting it be known that they would be delighted to have him command their armies." This was a notion, Chennault thought, that tempted Stilwell to the very last day he spent in China. And the young diplomats on his staff understood its appeal. They assiduously plied the old soldier with the fantastic prospect of Mao's legions behind him into battle on all fronts against the Japanese.

While zealous reports of the Foreign Service enjoyed a wide circulation, it is of course difficult to guess just how much immediate influence their words had on policy decisions in Washington, Nevertheless, their constant denunciations of the Kuomintang were certainly persuasive in the cumulative sense. "The main effect of their reporting," writes the historian Herbert Feis, was to "weaken faith in the power of the Generalissimo and his group to govern China." A recurring note was that Chiang's armies were doing very little fighting, and that Chiang expected the United States to beat the Japanese and later on permit him to hoard his men and supplies to fight the Communists. On the other hand, the young diplomats were always quick to praise the guerrilla tactics of Communist troops. and they had no qualms about complimenting the "progressivism" of "agrarian reformers" at Yenan.

At first General Stilwell's political advisers were not overtly pro-Maoist; they were simply anti-Kuomintang. But in the end it was hardly possible to be the one without the other. As Chiang's dealings with Mao's agent Chou En-Lai grew increasingly difficult and the precarious relationship between the National government at Chungking and the Communist regime at Yenan came under new strains, the career diplomats surrounding General Stilwell took full advantage of their general's distaste for Generalissimo Chiang. By the early spring of 1944 rumors were flying furiously throughout Washington officialdom that Chiang's troops were no longer fighting the Japanese anywhere but instead were wholly engaged in circumscribing Mao's Eigth Route Army. Such reports were reaching the ear of President Roosevelt most often via his administration assistant for Far Eastern affairs, Dr. Lauchlin B. Currie—or via the American Communist Party leader, Earl Browder's personal representative to the White House, Miss Josephine Truslow Adams, who during the war had no less than forty private conversations with the President.

Roosevelt was alarmed. Something had to be done. Late in the spring. Vice President Henry A. Wallace was chosen to make a visit to China. Secretary of State Hull was not consulted on the advisability of this special mission. He was merely informed that Wallace was going. The ultra-leftist inclinations of Wallace were already so well advertised that it was rumored he would be dropped from the Democratic ticket in the upcoming election. But meanwhile he could perform one last task for his old chief. He could get the Chinese to cooperate with one another and with General Stilwell.

"When I see the people that this department is sending to China, I shake in my shoes." This remark has been attributed to Dr. Stanley K. Hornbec, the veteran Asian specialist who was then assigned to Secretary Hull's office as a special adviser. He had good reason to shake. The Wallace entourage included two of the most vociferous critics of the Chinese Nationalist government, John Carter Vincent and Owen Lattimore. Vincent at that time was heading the Office of Chinese Affairs in the Division of Far Eastern Affairs at the State Department. Professor Lattimore, as deputy director of Pacific Operations in the Office of War Information, was that agency's principal spokesman on the Orient. Coming by way of Soviet

Central Asia, where they were fêted by the local Russian authorities in a mocked-up "Potemkin village" which just a few days before had been a slave labor camp. Sergei Godlize, head of the Soviet executive committee in Siberia and an intimate friend of Stalin, offered a dinner toast to Lattimore and Vincent as the men "on whom rests great responsibility for China's future."

The American party arrived in Chungking late in June, and conversations with Chinese Nationalist officials began at once. Wallace, whose career had been devoted largely to agrarian problems, was not much impressed by President Chiang's military bearing and political opinions. Chiang kept insisting that the Chinese Communists were the political puppets of Moscow rather than the simple agriculture reformers that had been described to Wallace by his China experts. Generalissimo Chiang repeatedly expressed his strong hope that the United States would maintain official 'aloofness' toward Mao Tse-tung's clique at Yenan. Wallace could not quite understand Chiang's attitude. Communists in the United States, he said, seemed to have a "patriotic point of view." Generalissimo Chiang pointed out this basic difference; Earl Browder's people could see no possibility of seizing the reins of government in Washington, but Mao Tse-tung's people expected to do just that on the Asian mainland. Following a suggestion by Vincent, Wallace now insisted that a team of American military and political observers be sent to Yenan to gather intelligence. To this Chiang at last reluctantly consented, despite his conviction that such a gesture would greatly enhance the prestige of the Communists. This is precisely what happened in the month ahead.

It had been easy for Stilwell's political advisers to sell such a man as Wallace a complete anti-Nationalist bill of goods. In a cable from Kunming to President Roosevelt on June 28, Wallace declared that Chiang simply did not possess the necessary "intelligence of political strength to run post-war China." At best, he said the Kuomintang leader was a short-term investment, since the Communist leaders in China would certainly emerge by evolution or revolution. For the purposes of the war against Japan, he cabled, a new "united front" must be achieved as soon as possible. But Wallace, an experienced politician, knew that Chiang meanwhile would have to be placated. In his cable he recommended, therefore, that it might be wise to replace Stilwell with an American general who would prove more compatible to the Chungking leadership. After his return to Washington the Vice President made a further recommendation to the White House: a presidential representative should be sent to China to act as liaison between the Nationalists at Chungking and the Communists at Yenan. On this recommendation, which was actually Chiang's, President Roosevelt acted promptly. On August 18 the White House announced the appointment of the distinguished Republican lawyer and former Secretary of War, Patrick J. Hurley, as special envoy to China.

Like the President, Hurley believed strongly in the effectiveness of personal diplomacy. He had served Roosevelt as an adviser and special representative since early in the war, and now held the rank of major general in the United States Army. Hurley's instructions, written and oral, came down to this: he was to prevent the collapse of the Chinese National government. The President told him to develop some kind of working military relationship between the Nationalists at Chungking and the Communists at Yenan. Roosevelt felt that it must be done now, and that urbane "Pat" Hurley could do it. His chief qualification for the China mission was the fact that he was not doctrinaire. Neither sympathetic nor unsympathetic to either side, he was essentially a broker and a negotiator who approached his ticklish task with objectivity. At Roosevelt's instruction Hurley stopped at Moscow to sound out the current thinking of Soviet leaders on the situation in China. He was told by Foreign Minister Molotov that the Russians had no current connection with the Chinese Communists. Hurley hastened to Chungking, arriving on September 5, and began at once to try to reconcile Stilwell with Chiang. It did not look very promising. Moreover, Roosevelt had already almost decided to bring Stilwell home. But General Marshall kept telling the President that Stilwell was the only high-ranking American officer who could speak Chinese. While he was with Roosevelt at the second Quebec conference, Marshall drafted a blunt message for Stilwell to deliver to Chiang. Generalissimo Chiang was to be asked to place Stilwell in "unrestricted command" of all Chinese forces. If he refused, he must then be "prepared to accept the consequences."

Marshall's ultimatum arrived at Chungking on September 19 with the special instructions to Stilwell to deliver it in person. Stilwell was jubilant; he had waited two and a half years for this moment. "President's message arrived," he wrote in his diary. "Hot as a firecracker." But Hurley, who had just begun his conversations with Chiang, wanted to wait. He advised Stilwell that this was not the proper moment to deliver such a message. "You shouldn't now . . . pile it on him," Hurley said, "at a time he has felt compelled to make every concession that we have asked. He has made them; he is ready to go; he is ready to bring troops down from the North to reinforce you in the Salween front; he is going to appoint you commander-in-chief." Stilwell would not be deterred. He wanted to humiliate Generalissimo Chiang. "I am directed by the President," he told Hurley, "to hand it to him." Hurley then raised the question as to who had the authority to speak for the President, but Stilwell refused to be moved. He meant to have his revenge.

Hurley accompanied Stilwell to the fateful meeting with Chiang. The Marshall ultimatum had been translated into Chinese. When Chiang read it, Hurley thought he looked "like he had been hit in the solar plexus." Silence followed. Then Chiang reached over to his tea cup and put the cover on upside down. Stilwell, in Chinese asked, "That gesture still means, I presume, that the party is over?" Someone in Chiang's staff said, "Yes." Stilwell and Hurley then rose and left the room. This incident is seldom described by the anti-Nationalist school. The reason is that Stilwell looks vindictive in it, and Hurley looks sensible.

To the diplomat it is a matter of routine duty, of course, to record an observed scene fully and frankly, even when the reporting may not be consonant with current policy. The dispatches of Davies and Service can be said, therefore, to be on-the-spot objective reporting of what they actually saw and heard in China. This, precisely, is how their dispatches have been interpreted by the anti-Nationalist school. But their dispatches were not merely reports, they were editorials. They were special pleas so stridently anti-Kuomintang that all objectivity was missing. A remarkable example is a dispatch prepared by Service under date of October 10, 1944. In his "Report No. 40" Service blatantly suggested that Chiang Kai-shek be publicly abandoned in favor of Mao Tse-tung. Certain parts are italicized to highlight the point:

> Our dealings with Chiang Kai-shek apparently continue on the basis of the unrealistic assumption that he is China and that he is necessary to our cause. It is time, for the sake of the war and also for our future interests in China, that we take a more realistic line. . . . In the present circumstances, the Kuomintang is dependent on American support for survival. *But we are in no way dependent of the Kuomintang. We do not need it for military reasons. . . . We need not fear Kuomintang surrender or opposition.* The Party and Chiang will stick to us because our victory is certain and is their only hope for continued power. . . . *We need not fear the collapse of the Kuomintang government. . . .* Actually, by continued and exclusive support of the Kuomintang, we tend to prevent the reforms and democratic reorganization of the government which are essential for the revitalization of China's war effort. . . . We need not support the Kuomintang for international political reasons. . . . *We need not support Chiang in the belief that he represents pro-American or democratic groups.* All the people and all other political groups of importance in China are friendly to the United States and look to it for the salvation of the country, now and after the war. In fact, Chiang has lost the confidence and respect of most of the American-educated democratically-minded liberals and intellectuals. . . .

Finally, we need feel no ties of gratitude to Chiang. . . . Chiang's own dealings with us have been an opportunist combination of extravagant demands and unfilled promises, wheeling and bargaining, bluff and blackmail. Chiang did not resist Japan until forced by his own people. He has sought to have us save him—so that he can continue his conquest of his own country. In the process, he has "worked" us for all we were worth. . . . Our policy toward China should be guided by two facts. First, *we cannot hope to deal successfully with Chiang without being hard-boiled.* Second, *we cannot hope to solve China's problems* (which are now our problems) *without consideration of the opposition forces—Communist, Provincial and liberal.* . . . We should not be swayed by pleas of the danger of China's collapse. This is an old trick of China's. There may be a collapse of the Kuomintang government; but it will not be the collapse of China's resistance. There may be a period of some confusion but the eventual gains of the Kuomintang's collapse will more than make up for this. The crisis itself makes reform more urgent—and at the same time increases the weight of our influence. *The crisis is the time to push —not to relax.* . . . More than ever, we hold all the aces in Chiang's poker game. It is time we started playing them.[3]

Report No. 40, written "from the field" at Yenan, was addressed to General Stilwell at his Chungking headquarters. By the time it arrived, however, Stilwell was about to relinquish the American command in China to Lieutenant-General Albert C. Wedemeyer. When asked in 1951 to comment on its contents by a congressional committee, General Wedemeyer made the following statement:

In my judgment the military capabilities of the Communist forces in Yenan were not great, were invariably overemphasized in this and other reports submitted to me by these political advisers. I think I am qualified to speak knowingly on that subject, because I am a trained military man and those men were not. . . . I state categorically these reports were not consonant with my interpretation of my directive or of American policy. That contravenes American policy as I understand it. . . . If I had followed the advice I would not have been carrying out my orders. . . . When he [Service] talks, when this man writes about other parties, there are no other parties over there worthy of the name. There was no other leadership through which I could work, except Chiang Kai-shek on the one hand, and on the other Mao Tse-tung. . . . They [the Communists] were operating in sporadic efforts to the north of the wartime capital up in the Yenan area and Shensi Province. They never launched a concerted attack in coordination with those attacks that I was putting on down below . . . their military operations did not make the contributions so often one reads in the press or hears about on the radio. The military operations of the Chinese Communists, at least while I was in command of the theater, were not significant. . . . The splinter parties were absolutely impotent. There were not enough people involved. If we threw over the Kuomintang,

[3]*Hurley Papers,* File 312, Document No. 48, *Mss.* Santa Fé.

it meant we were going to assume support and cooperate with the Communists. . . . The Communists, in my judgment—and I have tried to be objective, I have tried to find good in Marxist theories—the Communists will cooperate when the advantage accrues to them. At no time will a Communist cooperate otherwise. . . . Their avowed intention is to destroy capitalism, expressed to me personally.[4]

In early November of 1944 Hurley himself visited Yenan. Here he hammered out a five-point draft agreement with the Communists which embodied the minimum demands for cooperation with the National government. Later that month President Roosevelt named him ambassador to China, succeeding Stilwell's friend the veteran Clarence E. Gauss, and on January 8, 1945 he presented his credentials at Chungking.

By this time, however, Hurley had come to feel that his mission was doomed. Most of the career diplomats on station in China, and especially Davies and Service, bitterly resented his appointment to the ambassadorship as well as his evident willingness to deal with Chiang Kai-shek. The special reports of Davies and Service to their immediate superior in Washington, John Carter Vincent at the "China Desk" of the State Department, were increasingly sharp in condemnation of Chiang, the Kuomintang, and the whole operation at Chungking. On the other hand, when describing conditions in the Communist-controlled northern hills, the careerists were full of buoyant optimism. Their dispatches to the State Department contained the persistent suggestion that all lend-lease military aid be handed over to the Communists at Yenan. They went so far, in fact, as to intimate directly to the Communist leaders that Hurley's efforts to "save" the Chungking administration did not represent the actual American policy.

When Hurley was called to Washington for consultations late in February, 1945, the careerists took full advantage of his absence. The chargé d'affaires of the embassy, George Atcheson, now collaborated with Service in preparing a major position paper that flatly recommended the complete abandonment of the Nationalists. When Hurley realized that he was being seriously undercut by his staffers, he insisted on their recall. So it was that John Paton Davies and John Service, two of the youngest "old China hands" in the U.S. diplomatic corps, finally left the land of their nativity in the spring of 1945. But that was not the end of it. Upon their arrival in Washington they became Ambassador Hurley's superiors, in a sense, insofar as they were now in position to participate in the reshaping of China policy at the front of foreign affairs—the Department of State.

[4]*Institute of Pacific Relations, Hearings,* Vol. 3, pp. 779-783.

The situation is easily summarized. By the time Pat Hurley assumed his duties in China, the views of the Foreign Service officers were so frozen against the Nationalists that Hurley could do little to break the ice. His instruction from the President was to effect a coalition. He opposed giving military aid to the Communists while they were in rebellion against the National government. By withholding it, he hoped to force the Communists to gravitate toward Chungking. But the careerists were solidly of the opinion that the United States should show a sign of friendship first, and then the Communists would gladly cooperate. They believed in the good faith of Mao Tse-tung as much as they distrusted Chiang Kai-shek. Hurley believed, as did President Roosevelt, that Chiang deserved the continuing support of the United States because he had resisted alone for a long time and had rejected their most seductive peace overtures. Hurley and Roosevelt felt that, given time, the Nationalists would make the reforms necessary to stabilize the situation. The careerists believed that only the Communists were capable of reform in China.

Joseph Alsop, in an article in the *Saturday Evening Post* in 1960, neatly assessed the results of the wartime field of the careerists. "Throughout the fateful years in China," he wrote, "the American representatives there actively favored the Chinese Communists. They also contributed to the weakness, both political and military, of the National government. And in the end they came close to offering China up to the Communists, like a trussed bird on a platter, over four years before the eventual Communist triumph."

Hurley continued to serve, however unhappily, as U.S. Ambassador to China until the war in the Pacific was over. In his letter of resignation to President Truman on November 26, 1945, and in a memorable appearance before the Senate Foreign Relations Committee the next month, he explained what had happened. In unequivocal terms he defined the basic disloyalty of his professional staff to the objectives of the mission. The chief obstacle to the accomplishment of President Roosevelt's goals in China, he declared, was a dedicated opposition to those goals on the part of career diplomats in the Chungking embassy and their superiors in the Far Eastern Division of the State Department. The key question was that of lend-lease military aid. In seeking to turn the flow of American military supplies away from Generalissimo Chiang's armies and toward the forces of Mao Tse-tung, the careerists were consciously trying to strengthen an "armed party" which was in rebellion against "the government that I was sent to China to uphold." This, to a patriot like Hurley, was nothing less that a deliberate reversal of that which was the official position of the United States government at the time.

Hurley was too loyal to President Roosevelt to say much about

112

Yalta in 1945, but he well knew what had taken place in February of that year at the fateful Crimean summit. Here the United States was drawn close to a quasi-official endorsement of Communist objectives on the Asian mainland. Here the American president, his health failing fast, bargained with Premier Stalin for the active participation of the Soviet Union in the war against Japan. With the Germans now backed to the wall and ready to capitulate, the Russians were prepared to join the struggle against Japan within two or three months following the Nazi surrender. For this promise by Stalin, Roosevelt agreed to restore to Russia certain prerogatives in the Far East that had been lost to the Japanese in the 1904-05 war. Included were concessions in the southern Sakhalin Islands, the Kurile Islands, the ports of Dairen and Port Arthur, and the Chinese Eastern and South Manchurian railroads. No representative of China attended the Big Three conference in the Crimea, and the terms of this famous executive agreement were committed to secrecy. The Yalta concessions, patently contrary to the whole historic basis of American policy in East Asia as it had stood since Secretary Hay's enunciations almost a half-century before, gave Soviet Russia the toehold Stalin needed to realize the old ambitions of Lenin for the spread of Communism on the Asian mainland.

Soon after the Crimean conference, while in Washington for consultations, Hurley was shown a copy of the secret accord by the President himself. The ambassador immediately complained that it contained clauses which seriously jeopardized the sovereignty and territorial integrity of China. While denying this at first, the President apparently had second thoughts. Two weeks before his death, Roosevelt talked again with Hurley. "I would like for you to go to London," he said, "and see Churchill to ameliorate that agreement. It has got some things in it. I would like you to go to Moscow and see Stalin." Hurley went, but his long conversations with the British prime minister and the Soviet premier came to nothing. Stalin would not repudiate the diplomatic bargain he had obtained from the sick American president. He merely repeated his personal pledge to "respect" the sovereignty of China. Hurley feared that this meant little, and the events of the next few months confirmed such fears.

In conclusion, it is important to note that Stalin's 1941 non-aggression pact with the Japanese was still in effect in July, 1945, when the Big Three met at Potsdam for the last of the wartime conferences. Again, of course, no Chinese spokesman was present, and the Yalta Agreement was still a dark secret. On August 6 the first atomic bomb fell at Hiroshima, and two days later Russia declared war on Japan. Nagasaki was bombed on the 9th, and on the 14th the Japanese government announced its unconditional surrender to the Allies. On that same day the Soviets, with their divisions now pouring into Manchuria, went through the formality of a Treaty of Friendship and Alliance with China by which "moral support" and military supplies were promised to Chiang Kai-shek's Nationalists. But Generalissimo Chiang was hardly deceived by such assurances. He could not expect to see Stalin become the gravedigger of Chinese Communism. Trying to make the best of the situation, Chiang calculated that China could quickly execute its part of the treaty and then he would have his hands free to cope with the Yenan rebels. As it turned out, however, Chiang was never able to deal as freely as he wished with Mao Tse-tung's followers. In 1945 the anti-Nationalist faction in the United States was already manufacturing its disastrous policy of direct political intervention in China's internal affairs. Before the year was out, the very man who had selected Stilwell for the wartime command in China would himself be there—and trying, as Stilwell had, to tell the Chinese what was best for them. In General George C. Marshall's mission to China the anti-Nationalists would find the formula for the great reversal.

4

The First Reversal
[1946-1949]

IN THE FALL of 1945, at the moment of the Japanese surrender, America's leaders had at their disposal the largest military machine the world had ever seen. Also at their exclusive command was the most powerful weapon ever devised, the atomic bomb. Yet, ironically, the masters of the Soviet Union were now able to seize large chunks of territory and extend their despotic control over vast populations in Europe and Asia. The men in the Kremlin took full advantage of the fact that the American people, weary of war, were anxious to bring the boys home. The United States government thus missed the rare opportunity to employ effectively an unparalleled military potential in guaranteeing the frontiers of freedom, a goal for which World War II had been fought in the first place. It is no great exaggeration to say that the United States won the war against one form of totalitarianism and then lost the peace to another form. The loss of the peace, within five years of the winning of the war, may properly be described as the great historic reversal of the twentieth century. Numerically defined, the principal victims of the great reversal were the hundreds of millions of helpless Chinese on the mainland of Asia.

From the outset of its involvement in the Pacific war, it had been the strict policy of the U. S. government to uphold the National goverment of China. As pledged to President Chiang Kai-shek by President Roosevelt at the Cairo conference, American support of the Republic of China had as its ultimate purpose the restoration to that government of legitimate control over all the Chinese territories lost to aggression since World War I. As long as Chiang's armies were in the field against the Japanese, the efforts of the Generalissimo received generally sympathetic consideration in the United States. The American attitude began to shift, however, officially as well as unofficially, as soon as the Japanese had surrendered and Chiang was free to display his Nationalist forces against Mao Tse-tung's insurgent Communists. A hue and cry arose for a united and democratic China, and official suggestions were advanced for curtailing rather than augmenting American support of the Nationalists. Upon accepting Ambassador Hurley's resignation late in 1945, President Truman appointed the distinguished wartime chief of staff, General George C. Marshall, as his personal representative to China. Marshall's mission, as defined in his official instructions, was to seek to bring about a coalition government in China that would include some Communist elements. At this moment, according to the State Department's official *White Paper* of 1949, the Nationalists enjoyed five-to-one superiority in combat troops and rifles, a "practical monopoly" in heavy equipment, and an "unopposed air arm." Marshall's instructions, therefore, were obviously based on somebody's conviction that it was the political leadership in China that was inadequate, and that an infusion into the Chinese governmental set up of Maoist and perhaps other "progressive" factors was not only desirable but imperative. Some key officials in Washington, D. C. apparently believed that the Communists would be happy to cooperate with the Kuomintang in creating on the liberated Asian mainland a nicely unified, democratic, and peace-loving nation of about 600 million people.

This belief was based on somebody's fatal misreading of the practices and objectives, Soviet-inspired and directed, of the 25-year-old Chinese Communist Party. General Marshall arrived at Chungking late in December, 1945, and spent most of the next year in China. A professional soldier whose life had been spent in receiving and handing down orders rather than in negotiating diplomatically, he exhibited little understanding of the nature and aims of Marxist-Leninists. He quickly became, in the words of his old friend Albert C. Wedemeyer, an easy victim of "Crypto-Communists, or Communist-sympathizing sycophants, who played on his vanity to accomplish their own ends." Thus Marshall came to believe, thought General Wedemeyer, that he could "mix oil and water by reconciling the basically antagonistic aims of the Chinese Nationalists and the Moscow-supported Chinese Communists." But the ingredients would not mix, and the slime of Communism soon came to the surface.

General Marshall brought his olive branch to China at a time when Chiang Kai-shek's forces were pushing hard to extend the sovereignty of the National Government into Manchuria. North of Hankow 200,000 government troops had surrounded some 70,000 Communist guerillas and were beginning a methodical job of extermination. The Communists appealed urgently to Marshall to arrange a truce, and he complied. So it was that the fighting ceased while the Communists slipped out of the trap and on to Shantung province, where they organized the large offensive that began about a year later. To the south, on the East River near Canton, some 100,000 Communist troops were likewise trapped by government forces. Again, truce teams effected their escape by allowing them to march unmolested to Bias Bay where they boarded junks and sailed north to Shantung.

But the worst of General Marshall's intercessions came at Kalgan Pass, a gap in the North China mountains that was the historic gateway to Manchuria. At the close of the Japanese war there were no organized Communists in Manchuria, and Chiang Kai-shek considered it strategically essential that the Nationalists gain control of the city of Kalgan. Marshall became convinced, however, that Chiang was pursuing a policy of raw force instead of the desired "negotiation." As a result of pressure from Marshall, Chiang finally agreed to let the Communists occupy Kalgan. As a result the Communists flocked from their bases in northwestern China through Kalgan Pass into Manchuria, where they joined the Russian army of occupation. When Nationalist troops finally entered Manchuria, they found its great industrial centers stripped bare of machinery and the arsenals of Japan's old Kwantung Army already empty.

The tragedy of the Marshall mission is in the fact that U.S. policymakers either deliberately or unconsciously regarded the Chinese Communists as true liberals and "agrarian reformers" interested only in bringing "democracy" to China. General Marshall apparently never grasped the diabolical character of urbane Communist spokesmen like Chou En-lai, who could assume at will whatever intellectual posture the exigencies of the moment demanded. Chou had once defined a truce as "the military equivalent of the political tactic of coalition." Communist strategy on this point has not changed to date. Put simply, when the Communists cannot win, they always ask for a cease-fire. But this is never a move to end the war, only a trick to end a losing phase of it—such as was done in Korea—in order to shift to another operation, such as Vietnam, which they believe will prove more profitable. Father Raymond J. de Jaegher, a Chinese-speaking priest with much experience in the Communist-controlled areas in China, sought to warn General Marshall of such tactics. But his counsel was obstructed by an administrative aide on Marshall's staff who happened to be a Chinese Communist!

117

The Marshall mission to China came at a time when the United States was at the peak of its military potential in the Pacific, and at the time that Chiang Kai-shek's government finally had a chance to assert its sovereignty in North China and Manchuria. Victory was possible for the Nationalists had Marshall been willing to lend the military support that they now desperately needed. The balance of power was with the Nationalists when Marshall arrived, and remained so for at least six months. Chiang's divisions were chasing the Communists northward, with the prospect of victory at its highest, when Marshall arrived with his plan to impose a coalition and began putting pressure on Chiang to force compliance. Marshall applied far more pressure on the Nationalists than on the Communists at the very moment that he should have done exactly the opposite. He could have let it be known to Mao Tse-tung and Chou En-lai that until they were willing to recognize the supremacy of the legitimate government of the Republic of China, its ally the United States would supply the Republic of China with such military aid as President Chiang needed to suppress all insurrections. Instead, says General Wedemeyer, "we were insisting that Chiang both institute democratic reforms and collaborate with the Communists." We were repeating the axiom that we wanted a strong and independent China, but at the same time we were refusing its National government the material and moral support that was to overcome a massive domestic rebellion.

In Greece, when local Communists threatened to seize power in 1947, the United States acted quite differently. President Truman aided the anti-Communist side without restraint. We did not go into Greece and say, "Listen, you ought to arrange a coalition with the Communists. You mustn't have a civil war; you must have a truce." Instead we said, "We will help you only if you resist a coalition with the Communists and fight them instead." And we helped the Greeks to build up their strength for that purpose by sending them our General Van Fleet and authorizing him to "advise and train at all levels." It is interesting to note that the "Truman Doctrine" which saved Greece, was never asserted in China. In Greece we said, "You must win the civil war." In China we said, "You must not win the civil war; you must make a coalition." American policy in Greece was correct, and it succeeded greatly. American policy in China was wrong, and it failed terribly.

The Chinese Communists never had a sincere thought of cooperating with the National government. It was their single purpose to overthrow and replace that government. When it became clear in the summer of 1946 that China was moving neither toward "coalition" nor toward peace, General Marshall finally imposed a strict embargo on all munitions and declared that henceforth the United States

118

would not take sides in what had become a "civil war" rather than a mere rebellion. This was terribly discouraging to the Nationalists, and immensely encouraging to the Communists. The United States government was, in effect, recognizing the legality of Mao's rebellion. At that moment the Communists, after a quarter of a century of insurgent activity, were in effective control of only about one fourth of China's territory; and they had no substantial following outside the ranks of their own armed forces. Moreover, at the very moment that the American government discontinued its material and moral support of the Nationalists, the Russian government began giving substantial material support to the Chinese Communists. Within a year Mao's armies were ready to embark on the major offensive destined to result, in the next two years, in their physical control of all the mainland provinces of China, and the withdrawal of the National government to the island province of Taiwan.

The Marshall mission thus simply provided Mao Tse-tung with the precious time he needed to mount his offensive. It is not hard to understand. When a prizefighter in the ninth round suddenly becomes very affectionate with his opponent, embracing him ardently, we do not misunderstand that maneuver. We do not imagine it is because he has decided to give up; it is because he wants to rest and hang on, if he can, until the end of that round in the hope he can knock out his adversary in the next round. When the Communists suddenly proposed a truce, it was only a skilled boxer's clinch. It meant that they were in trouble and trying to get out of it; their purpose was not to end the war but to win it. But somehow this was misconstrued by General Marshall's truce teams, or by the General himself, or by the Washington administration. The American policies that sprouted from the Marshall mission seriously demoralized the National government of China, on the one hand, and on the other these policies provided substantial encouragement to the Chinese Communists in the final rounds of their long struggle for ultimate domination.

The mistakes of General Marshall's truce teams cannot, of course, be held solely responsible for the tragic outcome of this extended struggle. Basic errors on the part of Chiang Kai-shek's political advisors, such as the hastily conceived currency-reform plan of 1948, resulted in further deterioration of the economy and debilitation of the Nationalist armies. Equally as devastating was the failure of Nationalist spokesmen to counter effectively the ideological offensive of the Communists. And by the beginning of 1949 the Chinese masses were so bewildered and exhausted by seemingly endless war that they were ready to accept peace at any price. Important as such internal factors doubtless were, the adminstration of President Truman must still bear a large part of the blame for the fall of China to Communism. To put it rudely, the United States finally "ditched" its war-time ally Chiang Kai-shek just as some State Department careerists had long been suggesting.

Some years later William D. Pawley, who knew China intimately and knew the State Department from the inside, stated it simply in testimony before a Congressional committee. Those who had advocated as early as 1942 that Chiang be "scuttled" had succeeded, he said. Pawley was annoyed by the failure of the State Department to energetically pursue the same type of anti-Communist program in the Far East as it had carried out in Europe. He went on to describe fully his own experience with the anti-Nationalist group in the Department of State. Late in 1949, six months before the Korean conflict began, Pawley went personally to see President Truman. "If we do not take a strong hand now," he told the President, "and support with tremendous effort the Nationalist movement in China in which Chinese will fight for their own freedom and own independence, China will be lost and you will have a war on your hands in Burma, Indochina, or Korea within one year and you will either commit America or you will lose Asia . . . ." The President did not take a strong hand, or any hand at all. He was committed to his earlier endorsement of General Marshall's estimate of the situation, since Marshall had become Secretary of State upon his return from China. Pawley's prediction came true with the outbreak of war in Korea in June, 1950.

In February of 1951, when Pawley became a special assistant to Secretary Acheson, it did not take him long to learn that there were many in the State Department who despised his views. After the swearing-in ceremony, Undersecretary of State James Webb took him to lunch and said: "Bill, you and I have been friends a long time and I don't want you to feel badly, but at a meeting in the Secretary's office this morning, to which we purposely did not invite you, it has been decided that you are to see no document dealing with the Far East, you are to participate in no conference that is held in the Department of State or anywhere else in Government dealing with this matter, and as a favor to the Secretary just don't discuss Far East matters." When Pawley asked, "Jim am I considered a subversive," Webb replied: "No, let's say reactionary. We have our views on what ought to be done, and they do not coincide with yours and therefore we don't want any trouble." Pawley was dismayed. "Jim," he said, "when we get to a position in the Department of State in which a man with the years of experience in the Far East that I have had where you have had none, the Secretary has had none, and no member of the Cabinet that I know, and they are all my friends, has had and the Secretary rules me out as a devil's advocate, then I think we are in real trouble." By this time the Chinese Communists had crossed the Yalu and enlarged the Korean war. Marshall was Secretary of Defense and MacArthur was soon to be relieved of command in the Far East. We were indeed in real trouble.

Seldom mentioned in books describing China's fall to Communism—or the victory of Communism in China, to put it another way—is the tremendous impact of certain well-endowed foundations on the shaping of public opinion in the United States. The outstanding example was the Institute of Pacific Relations, a "learned" organization of professional propagandists which probably contributed more than any other single factor to the conditioning of the American mind to the abandonment of China to the Communists. The public was "informed" that the Chinese Communists were no kin to the Muscovite Communists: the followers of chairman Mao were simply progressives and "agrarian reformers" fighting uphill against an entrenched bureaucracy rife with the ancient corruptions of Chinese officialdom. Upon the Kuomintang and its leader President Chiang was affixed an image of exploitation, landlordism, reaction, and finally Fascism. The aim of the IPR was to prepare the American people to accept China's fate with indifference. And that aim quickly became a result.

The Institute of Pacific Relations was organized shortly after World War I when a group of Hawaiian businessmen, interested in the social and economic problems of the Pacific area, called a conference of delegates from China, Japan, Korea, Australia, New Zealand, the Philippines, and the United States. Later, of course, there were delegates from the Soviet Union. In its basic structure the IPR was a loose federation of national organizations, each with a separate council but all under an international board. The American branch grew rapidly to include not only businessmen but also scholars, journalists, government officials, and community leaders of various kinds. The bulk of the membership of the IPR, as well as its very trustees, were for the most part inactive and passive, generally without influence over the expanding organization in either its development or its purposes. At its center instead was a small core of hyperactive members who carried the main burden of activities and who, most of the time at any rate, directed its administration and policies.

The IPR board of trustees was studded with names of high respectability and preeminence in business. Their very presence on a letterhead was enough to put at rest any suspicion of socialist intrigue or subversion. Moreover, these names meant money. There was never a financial problem in the IPR bcause funds flowed in from such affluent individuals as Thomas W. Lamont, Henry R. Luce, and Gerald W. Swope as well as from the Rockefeller, Carnegie, and other foundations. Corporations which made regular donations included J. P.

Morgan & Company, International Business Machines, Shell Oil, Matson Steamship, and even *Reader's Digest* magazine.

In its prestigious quarterly *Pacific Affairs* and in the spoken words of its officials, the IPR presented itself as engaged in, and devoted exclusively to, professional research and objective scholarship concerning all phases of life in the Far East. Upon the broad base of this definition of aim, the IPR recommended itself to any and all who were interested in the various problems of the Pacific basin. Specifically, this meant foundations, corporations, and individuals who might contribute funds for its scholarly activities in different fields. But the evidence before the Senate Internal Security Subcommittee clearly disclosed that the IPR was far more than a "research organization." Its chief product was seen to be propaganda, and its chief purpose was to shape American thinking on Far Eastern matters in order to serve Russian and Chinese Communist interests. The Senate committee also discovered that scores of important Communists had been closely associated with the American council of the IPR. Fifty-four persons directly connected to Communism in various ways were identified by witnesses, though IPR officials had always maintained that the organization was strictly objective and that its publications advocated no policy or "line.' But the conclusion of five leading Far Eastern scholars, each of them thoroughly familiar with the history and activities of the organization, was that the IPR functioned for years in the United States as an instrument of Soviet policy.

During the late 1930's and throughout the 40's the IPR maintained a virtual monopoly on public presentation of data concerning the Far East. In educational circles this meant that hundreds of teachers and thousands of students interested in the problems of the Pacific became unwitting supporters of, and propagandists for Soviet aims in East Asia. IPR officials realized that no arena was of greater importance than the school system. Consequently many colleges, and some high schools as well, were heavily and continuously cultivated by the IPR. It was only natural, moreover, and indeed inevitable, that a selfstyled "research" organization should quickly establish close links with the major universities, the home of leading scholars in any society. Thus the voice of the IPR reached far down into American society and was loudly heard at the upper levels.

The Senate committee learned that the IPR inner sanctum established a direct connection with the Communist International in Moscow as early as 1934. In that year an IPR member went directly to the Comintern's Far Eastern chief for instructions on "editing the vocabulary in left and Soviet articles." The active group in the IPR wrote books, articles, and pamphlets not only for publication by the IPR itself but also for release by university presses and other outlets. As a result, Americans cumulatively got the wrong slant on Soviet intentions in the Far East, and it was chiefly because of this slant that the actions of the United States government in the field of Asian affairs were also wrong in the long run.

The IPR thus effectively neutralized the Western nations—particularly the most important one in the post-war world, the United States—in resisting the Communist conquest of China. This was accomplished methodically by way of a massive psychological campaign: The goal of the campaign was simply to mask the design of Soviet strategy and thereby weaken the national will to resist it. Professor David N. Rowe of Yale, in his testimony before a Congressional committee investigating the tax-exempt foundations, offered this elucidating commentary:

> The area of ignorance in the United States about the Far Eastern matters was so great that here was the strategic place in which to strike at the security of the United States by people interested in imperiling our security and fostering the aims of world Communism. They would naturally not pick an area in which we have the greatest intellectual capacities . . . for defense. They would pick the area of greatest public ignorance, with the greatest difficulty of defending against tactics of their attack, and so these people naturally poured into Far Eastern studies and exploited this area as the area in which they would promote the interests of world Communism most successfully in the general ignorance and blindness of the American people.[1]

For the educational system below the university level, the IPR had an ambitious and vigorous program. Pamphlets, slides, films, and such other study materials were distributed in secondary and primary schools by the hundreds of thousands. The American Council's school program met an enthusiastic response from teachers and administrators alike. On two pamphlet series for high school use the gross income from sales of the first five titles amounted to $45,000 in the year 1943 alone. To focus attention of individual teachers on the Pacific area, the IPR cooperated with the *American Observer* magazine in sponsoring a quiz which reached 450,000 children. In conjunction with the American Council on Education and the Foreign Policy Association, the IPR developed an elaborate system of distributing to the schools what were called "resource packets." The 1944-46 official IPR report, *Windows on the Pacific*, boasted that its texts had sold more than a million copies in the three and a half years since Pearl Harbor, and that these publications had been placed in more than 1,300 school systems throughout the United States.

[1]Rene A. Wormser, *Foundations: Their Power and Influence* (Old Greenwich, Conn.: Devin-Adair, 1958), 176.

The publishing operations of the IPR were extensive and varied in kind, range, and type of audience. According to William L. Holland, a ranking official of the organization, some 200 "major volumes" were brought out between 1925 and 1951. A sophisticated journal, *Pacific Affairs*, appeared quarterly under the auspices of the international secretariat of the IPR, and a bi-weekly magazine, *Far Eastern Survey*, was issued as a popular organ by the American council. Both periodicals disseminated their propaganda cannily and persistently.

Another phase of IPR publishing was specially designed to supply materials to U.S. governmental agencies, particularly the armed forces, during World War II. A "Troop Training Orientation Program," designed for military instructors, contained a list of 39 books recommended for young men in basic training. Twenty-two of these were prepared by the IPR, and no less than 230,000 copies were purchased by the Pentagon for distribution at U.S. military installations throughout the world. Raymond Bennett, who for some time was secretary of the American council, told Congressional investigators that the educational and information branches of the Army and the Navy bought "somewhere in the vicinity of several hundred thousand" IPR pamphlets for use in their orientation programs on the Far East. Actually, more than 750,000 such pamphlets were purchased by the government and sent to American troops in the Pacific during the war years. Other IPR services to the U.S. armed forces took the form of lectures and library loan materials. It is logical to conclude that the IPR was, directly or indirectly, the major source of indoctrination in the U.S. armed forces on the subject of Far Eastern affairs. Since most of America's immense military establishment was dispersed throughout civilian life after the war, the IPR obtained a tremendous influence on public opinion in general.

The Department of State, of course, received its full share of influence from the IPR. Publications of the institute were in fact, almost the only materials on the Far East coming into the State Department, and they were always in ample supply in the Department's reference rooms in Washington and overseas libraries. But in estimating the Institute's influence in government, one's view should not be limited to books, periodicals, and pamphlets bearing its own imprint. The IPR was actually a complex of interlocking organizations such as the China Aid Council and the American Russian Institute all neatly tied in. There were looser associations with such outfits as the Foreign Policy Association, certain general-interest magazines, and the trade departments of key publishers. The functional lines of IPR influence stretched very far indeed. Wherever there was, (or could be roused) a call for a book review or an article or memorandum on the Far East, the IPR was almost certain to be heard. "There was a tendency on the part of the staff," Raymond Dennett admitted, "to pick people as authors and to submit their manuscript to other writers for critical comment who, by and large, tended to agree with the point of view of the staff prior to the selection of either the authors or the readers of the manuscript." This, he added, "tended over the whole period to give less than a complete objective picture." Indeed, the IPR operated what might be called a boosters-and-knockers club. Members would boost each other's writings and knock anyone, even another IPR member, who was outside—or had stepped partly or temporarily outside their ideological circle. It was obligatory on all inside members to give loud public praise to each other's work and in that way to build each other up, little by little, in public esteem.

The wartime influence of the IPR penetrated even the White House. This was possible because Dr. Lauchlin B. Currie, a real insider, was one of the President's executive aides and his special adviser on Far Eastern affairs. From his vantage point on Pennsylvania Avenue the ubiquitous Dr. Currie kept in close contact with the IPR by meeting frequently with its secretary-general, Edward C. Carter. Currie was responsible for setting up a conference on October 12, 1942, between Undersecretary of State Sumner Welles and two officials of the American Communist Party, Earl Browder and Robert Miner. Professor George Taylor, of the University of Washington, told a Congressional committee that Currie was "very friendly" and invited him to his office every Wednesday—until Taylor wrote a memorandum suggesting that arms be provided to Chiang Kai-shek for the specific purpose of fighting the Communists. After this, Taylor was never asked again to lunch, and he never again saw Currie.

One of Dr. Currie's most curious involvements concerned the Washington visit of Vladmir Rogoff, a former *Tass* correspondent and one of the principal Soviet intelligence agents in the Far East. Through the good offices of the IPR, Rogoff was closeted with American policymakers for long periods in 1944, a year of many important decisions. Also involved in the Rogoff episode was Alger Hiss. As head of the postwar plans staff at the State Department, Hiss enjoyed limitless access to the closest secrets of the United States government. His association with the IPR was such that when he left the government early in 1947, Carter wrote: "You have done so much for the IPR, in cooperation and wise advise, that I am hoping this fine relationship can continue in your new post." Then as an IPR trustee, Hiss was about to become president of the Carnegie Endowment for International Peace where he would be in a key position to recommend people for overseas appointments. The IPR submitted various lists to the Carnegie Endowment, and to other foundations, with names of expert personnel who might then be recommended for appointment to the

U.S. occupation forces in Germany and Japan. These lists contained the names of many members of the American Communist Party. Professor Kenneth Colegrove of Northwestern University, then the executive secretary of the American Political Science Association, was "shocked" when he saw such a list of civilian personnel prepared for appointment to General MacArthur's staff in Japan. "I wanted to find out where the list came from," he recalled in Congressional testimony, "and I was told it had come from the Institute of Pacific Relations."

From the early 1930's onward the IPR gave friendly publicity to the Chinese Communists. After the Japanese invasion of Manchuria in 1931, and again after the strike against China proper six years later, the IPR called for activity of such a sort that the Soviet position in Siberia, and the Communist strongholds in China, would not be endangered. From 1937 to 1943, in keeping with Moscow policy, the prevailing line of the IPR called for a Chinese "united front" of Communists and Nationalists. But as soon as American military power in the Pacific had hurt the Japanese to a point where they were no longer a threat on the Asian mainland, the IPR cranked up a potent propaganda campaign to discredit the Nationalists and glorify the Communists. Chiang Kai-shek and the Kuomintang were decried as "corrupt reactionaries" while Mao Tse-tung and his disciples were christened "native agrarian reformers" quite independent of Moscow. In the July 14, 1943, issue of *Far Eastern Survey*, the prolific T. A. Bisson published an article which foreshadowed the change in the official line. There were really two Chinas, Bisson wrote, and they were very different. One, Kuomintang China, might better be called "feudal" China; the other, Communist China, might be called "democratic" China.

Other IPR writers quickly took up this theme. Their consistent assertion was that the Chinese Communists were not really Communists in the Bolshevik sense. Instead they were "patriots" or "native radicals" or "liberals" or "populists." Maoism, it was said, "springs out of the Chinese soil and Chinese history." Mao's followers were the honest, efficient "liberators" of the peasants; the only true and genuine revolution in China was the movement led by Mao. It was democratic, progressive, and "good." All anti-Communist movements, on the other hand, were stranglers of the revolution, reactionary, fascist-oriented, and "bad." Chiang Kai-shek and his "clique" are grafters, agents of foreign powers. The Communists were riding the wave of the future. Since Mao was inevitably going to win, Chiang was through as a national leader. This was the IPR line after 1943. These were perennial points in the books, articles, reviews, lectures and panel discussions of IPR activists.

The IPR was more valuable to the Chinese Communists than ten field divisions. It is doubtful that they would have been victorious without the exertions of the IPR. The IPR immobilized the only force—American public opinion—that could have blocked their advance. For this achievement, which has no real parallel in the history of propaganda, the Communist manipulation of the IPR must be acknowledged a political masterpiece. And, even though the organization was exposed and discredited, its influence has persisted in American thinking and governmental policy. For several years following its citation on the Attorney General's list as a subversive organization, the IPR continued to enjoy tax-exempt privilege. This was finally removed, only to be restored in 1960.

Manchuria was the key to control of the continent. Most of the postwar problems in China can be traced to the concessions made at the Yalta conference of 1949 inviting Soviet armies into Manchuria. In spite of the Sino-Soviet Treaty of that year, Stalin was able to obstruct the efforts of the Nationalist government to restore its authority in Manchuria. Stalin's agents accomplished this by timing the withdrawal of Russian troops from Manchuria so as to allow Mao's guerillas to seize large stockpiles of surrendered Japanese military equipment. The Soviets also diverted many thousands of tons of United States Lend-Lease supplies, originally earmarked for use against the Japanese, by directing hundreds of ships crossing the Pacific to their main port at Vladivostok. Much of the material later paraded by the Chinese Communists under the guise of having been obtained in battle from Chiang Kai-shek's armies was actually Lend-Lease equipment that the United States had sent to the Russians.

In 1947, as the struggle for control of the strategic areas of Manchuria seemed to be going against the Nationalists, demands arose in Washington for a reevaluation of American policy. At this juncture President Truman decided to send Lieutenant-General Albert C. Wedemeyer on a fact-finding mission. Instructed to make a full appraisal of the political, economic, and psychological climate as well as the military situation, General Wedemeyer arrived in Nanking with a full staff of experts. They spent a month gathering diverse information. Touring the major cities and talking with many official and unofficial persons, Wedemeyer quickly sized up China's immediate needs. He was hard-headed and objective. At one point he sharply criticized the Kuomintang for permitting corrupt practices and countenancing inefficiency. "The Central Government cannot defeat the Chinese Communists by the employment of force," he said, "but can only win the loyal, enthusiastic, and realistic support of the masses of people by improving the political and economic situation immediately." Kuomintang officials were naturally taken aback by such words. They acknowledged that certain weaknesses did exist, but they insisted that such deficiencies should be weighed alongside the Kuomintang's accomplishments while engaged in years of struggle against the Japanese, the greedy entrenched landlords, and the rebellious armed party of Mao Tse-tung.

Returning to Washington, General Wedemeyer submitted an elaborate "China Report" to President Truman. It remained in a secret drawer at the White House for the next two years—and never would have been brought to light if certain Senators had not demanded that its contents be made public. General Marshall, then posing as Secretary of State, was directly responsible for supressing the report. His own views differed sharply from those in Wedemyer's assessment of Communist strategy and tactics. Wedemeyer's prediction of how America's security would ultimately be threatened by Communist expansion in Asia was not in accord with Marshall's estimate of the global situation. Wedemeyer viewed the situation as critical enough to require "prompt action" to block Communist extension in the Far East. China's industrial resources were simply not yet capable, he thought, of supporting adequately its military forces in the field. Urgently needed, then, was American ammunition and technical assistance to contravene Soviet aid to Mao's armies in North China.

Any reasonable prospect of success for the Nationalists, Wedemeyer reasoned, would require a hard decision for more American aid. It should begin with the desperately needed spare parts which the United States government had already promised for the 16,000 motor vehicles the Nationalists had on hand. They should then be permitted to purchase on credit the heavy equipment necessary to complete Chiang Kai-shek's master plan for a coordinated regular army, which had been stymied for two years because of Lend-Lease shortages. The United States government was "morally obligated to complete this program," Wedemeyer declared, and further credits should also be made available to enable the Nanking officials to make some sensible projections. These were the recommendations of a master military strategist who knew China well and who enjoyed great respect for the part he had played in the planning of the D-Day operation in Europe. But the Wedemeyer report was shelved, its suggestions ignored, and its very existence kept secret.

Why was General Wedemeyer's report so completely suppressed for the two critical years between 1947 and 1949? Was it for security reasons, or was it to cover up the administration's past errors in China? In the State Department's *China White Paper*, released in 1949, the reader is told that the report contained a recommendation that Manchuria be placed under the guardianship of five powers, including the Soviet Union, and that, if this had been made public at the time, it would have been highly offensive to the Chinese as an infringement of their sovereignty. But this explanation does not hold much water. There was little concern about Chinese interests at Yalta when President Roosevelt bargained away China's sovereignty in Manchuria for Stalin's promise to enter the war against Japan. The Wedemeyer report contained proposals that would have greatly strengthened Chiang's hand against the Communists had they been even partially implemented. Might it be that this report was suppressed because some American officials, perhaps Secretary of State Marshall, feared at the time that a five-power protectorate in Manchuria would cause Mao's "agrarian reformers" to lose out there?

Certainly the sensitivity of General Marshall on the China question was a major factor. General Wedemeyer later summed it up in these words:

> I knew that the delay in implementing my recommendations for immediate moral and material support to the Chinese Nationalist Government was serving the purpose of the Communists. The State Department knew as well as I that the situation was deteriorating rapidly, yet the hands-off attitude prevailed. I asked myself with increasing anxiety why I had been sent to China. Had General Marshall simply wanted me to reinforce his own views by submitting a report completely confirming his existing do-nothing policy? Had he wanted me to join the host of sycophants whom he had despised in the earlier years when he told me that he valued those who frankly expressed their honest convictions? . . . .
> *I feel positive today that the publication of my report would not have caused embarrassment to my Government or to the Chinese or the Koreans.* If I am wrong, then it would appear that the subsequent publication of my report in the White Paper in 1949 was a serious mistake in diplomacy.[2]

When appearing before the Senate Committee on Appropriations in December, 1947, General Wedemeyer was asked if he had brought a copy of his report. He replied that General Marshall had "admonished" him and furthermore had instructed every member of his mission not to reveal its contents. When Marshall later testified before the Senate Armed Services Committee, he was asked why he had "joined in" the suppression of the Wedemeyer Report. To this he answered bluntly: "I did not join in the suppression of the report. *I personally suppressed it.*" But he gave no convincing reason why he had done so.

As Mao's military successes began to mount, pressure for aid to Chiang's armies became more intensive in the halls of Congress. The

---

[2]Senate Armed Forces Committee, *Hearings on the Nomination of George C. Marshall to be Secretary of Defense*, 82nd Cong., 2nd Sess. (1950), 22.

Republicans charged the Democrats with purposely letting China "fall" into the hands of the Communists. They complained that it was futile to challenge the Soviets in Europe while simultaneously leaving the door to Communism wide open in Asia. President Truman's first Secretary of Defense, the far-sighted, James E. Forrestal, now took up the plea for aid, but Labor Secretary Lewis B. Schwallenbach and some other Cabinet members argued that there was no valid reason for the United States to continue to "interfere" in the internal affairs of China.

At the same time repeated warnings came from the American ambassador, John Leighton Stuart, a former missionary with many years of experience on the Asian mainland. Dire consequences would result if the foot-dragging in Washington continued, he wrote, but "the tide may turn quickly in our favor" if adequate American material began to flow immediately to the Nationalist forces. "The Chinese people do not want to become Communists," Stuart said, "yet they see the tide of Communism running irresistibly onward. In the midst of this chaos and inaction, the Generalissimo stands out as the only moral force capable of action."

Another sharp warning came from William C. Bullitt, onetime ambassador to the Soviet Union, in his memorable "Report on China" published in *Life* magazine on October 13, 1947. Bullitt strongly recommended that United States military advisers be sent to help Chiang, and called for the immediate release of stockpiled munitions to the ill-equipped Nationalist forces in Manchuria. The probable cost of such a program of military aid, he estimated, would be $200 million annually for three years. This price, Bullitt thought, was small enough if China could be saved.

The critical military situation in China required prompt action on the part of U.S. officials if the Asian mainland was to be saved from a Communist takeover. When Chiang Kai-shek asked Truman for a high-ranking military officer to assist in planning operations against the Communists, the President would not send one. He would make no commitments beyond the amount of aid already voted by the Congress. Madame Chiang Kai-shek then came to Washington to make a personal appeal to Secretary of State Marshall, and the Chinese government made another urgent request directly to the Congress. The failure of these frantic efforts was very discouraging and demoralizing to Nationalists at all levels, and the tide began to shift to the Communists. What little material actually reached China arrived too late to be effective against the Soviet-supported military offensive of the Maoists. As William C. Bullitt told the House Committee on Foreign Affairs, the Truman administration had not delivered to the Chinese "a single combat plane or a single bomber since General

Marshall, in August 1946, by unilateral action, broke the promise of the American Government to the Chinese Government and suspended all deliveries of planes and dishonored the pledge of the United States."

Senator Pat McCarran, the Nevada Democrat, tried to reassure the China Nationalists by introducing a bill calling for a $1.5 billion loan for economic and military aid. But the new Secretary of State, Dean Acheson, was strongly opposed to extending further assistance. Aid to China since VJ-Day, he argued, had reached a point "aggregating over $2 billion." According to Acheson, Chiang Kai-shek's government did not have "the military capability of maintaining a foothold in South China against a determined Communist advance"; and there was "no evidence that furnishing of additional military material would alter the pattern of current developments in China." The Secretary's statement that aid to China since September of 1945 had reached more than $2 billion was sharply contested by Senator McCarran as "inaccurate and misleading." In a statement to the press, McCarran reported that his own analysis showed that effective military aid since VJ-Day came to only $110,000,000—or about one-twentieth of the total added up by Acheson.

What is important about this episode is that Acheson's figure of $2 billion was so immediately impressive, as the official estimate of the State Department, that Americans began to take seriously the line that what was really wrong in China was the corruption and outright inefficiency of Chiang Kai-shek's party, the Kuomintang. Yet when broken down by items, the State Department figures are highly suspect. A case in point is the $333,817,910 charged to the Chinese for the disarming and repatriating of Japanese troops. On the item of "grants," the State Department runs up an astronomical total of $1,596,000,000 by the device of including non-military ECA and UNRRA aid. Not only were the UNRRA payments of $474,000,000 altogether non-military, but also they were doled out impartially in both Nationalist and Communist areas.

A substantial percentage of the surplus military material which went to the Nationalist forces, moreover, was unusable for actual combat. Because much of the material abandoned after VJ-Day was left in tropical areas, most of it was in a state of deterioration. In the papers of transmittal a truck was defined as "a vehicle with less than 20 percent of its parts missing." Approximately one-third of the total of the Pacific surplus comprised such "vehicles" of all kinds. President Truman himself admitted, in a report to Congress, that the so-called "surplus sales" to China, as included in the State Department's two-billion dollar estimate, did not include "weapons which could be used in fighting a civil war." Indeed, when compared with the totals of

131

postwar "reconstruction" aid to America's former enemies (Japan, $1.7 billion; Italy, $2 billion; and Germany, $3 billion), the U.S. dollars invested in the Republic of China seems inconsequential indeed.

General Edward Stratemeyer has related a stirring story about shortages of equipment. He ferried 90,000 Chinese troops by air north from Canton into the Tientsin-Peiping area where, according to our promise, we would supply them; but the troops were left there, stranded, at the mercy of the Communists. "They had no ammunition, they had no spare parts, they couldn't fight. They had to live, so the Communists took them over, and those they didn't kill, I think they forced into their services." Admiral Oscar C. Badger has described another lamentable situation in North China which he personally witnessed. Some unequipped Chinese divisions, going up to take the place of others in the front, actually lined up to receive from the outgoing divisions their rifles and small arms. Chiang's troops, the Admiral reports, were often asked to go to the front with fifteen or less rounds of ammunition per man.

There is yet another point to be considered. The Truman administration's wait-and-see, let-the-dust-settle policy in China ultimately caused such confusion and demoralization that the Chinese masses finally lost their will to resist the Communists. President Roosevelt's original policy of firm support to the Republic of China should have been the continuing policy of the United States. The sudden disappearance of such support, both moral and material, had a tragic disheartening effect on the Chinese people. In 1947, when Dean Acheson appeared before the House Foreign Affairs committee, Congressman Walter Judd asked a pertinent question: "Mr. Secretary, a great many Americans obviously are confused by what seems to be a contradiction in our foreign policy with respect to the government which becomes Communist-dominated. If it is a wise policy for us to urge, for example, the Government of China to unite with organized Communist minorities there, why is it a wise policy to assist the Greek Government to fight against the same sort of armed Communist minorities in Greece?" Acheson replied that the Greek government and economy had collapsed. "The Chinese government is not approaching collapse. *It is not threatened by defeat by the Communists.* The war with the Communists is going on much as it has for the past twenty years."

Actually, of course, there were many obvious similarities between the civil war in China and the one in Greece. The chief difference was in the American response in material aid and moral support. Greece was given much more. Aid to China was less than half the amount given to Greece during the same period. When the civil war involving Communists started in Greece, American officials adopted an attitude entirely different from theirs on the conflict in China. The President enunciated the so-called Truman Doctrine and promptly sent a special mission under General Van Fleet to supervise the training of Greek national troops to resist the Communists. While American soldiers did not actually fire on the Communists in Greece; they were clearly recognized by the Communists as the enemy. American officers were instructed to go down to battalion level in their advice to the Greeks. There was no pull-out and Van Fleet did not try to avert a civil war. His instructions were simply to help the Greek government, our ally, to *win* the civil war. This is not what General Marshall tried to do in China. His subordinates were prohibited from going down to levels where they might risk coming into contact with the Communists. The U.S. military advisory group in China was under strict orders not to permit any officer to enter combat areas or even "disputed" areas to which both sides, Communists and Nationalists, laid claim. Even with the material shortages, General Wedemeyer has observed, the Chinese Nationalists would probably have been able to "operate against the Communists effectively provided American advisers were present."

In the China White Paper released in 1949 under the title of *United States Relations with China,* it is stated that "a large proportion of military supplies has fallen into the hands of the Chinese Communists through the military ineptitude of the Nationalist leaders, their defections and surrenders, and the absence among their force of the will to fight." No serious students of the situation can deny that Chiang Kaishek's commanders were faltering by 1947 and 1948. Yet it is important not to forget what they had been through in the debilitating years between 1937 and 1945. When asked by Senator Brian McMahon of Connecticut whether he thought Chiang's government was corrupt and inefficient, General Wedemeyer answered, "Yes . . . but I think it is dangerous to overemphasize . . . because we find corruption in our own government and it was inevitable with a government that was down and out economically."

The actual value of the material which did reach the Chinese foot-soldier was often nothing more or less than scrap iron. "A lot of it," said General Wedemeyer, "was equipment that they were not capable of using. . . ." Some equipment has been described as broken, rusting, and lacking parts. One shipment of automatic weapons actually arrived without magazines, making the guns about as useful as broomsticks. Colonel L. B. Moody, who served under Donald Nelson on the War Production Board chairman's visit to China, stated that the defeat of the Nationalists was made inevitable by the appalling deficiency of infantry supplies. What Chiang's troops really needed, he said, were small arms and ammunition, but these were exactly what the United States denied. What we sent instead were "billions of moldy cigarettes" and "blown-up guns and junk bombs and disabled vehicles from the Pacific islands, which have been totaled up with other real or alleged aid . . . to create the impression that we have furnished the Nationalist government with hundreds of millions or even billions of dollars worth of useful fighting equipment."

As Mao Tse-tung's armies swept southward and eastward in China, fifty-one Republican members of the House of Representatives addressed an urgent letter to President Truman which asked bluntly: "What is our policy toward China?" Secretary Acheson told the Congressmen in a private session that it was the President's intention to wait "until the dust settles" before defining a policy. But the dust was already settling over China, and it was a Red dust. The Chinese people may still have had the will to combat the Communists in 1947 and 1948, but what America offered in the form of material aid and moral support was the difference between effective resistance and hopeless capitulation. What we did give them in the way of material aid was both too little and too late to be of any real use, and as a result Chiang Kai-shek's commanders were forced to surrender one strategic position after another. Each loss of area was followed by a new faltering of morale.

Strangely enough, it is sometimes asserted that the U.S. government actually supported the Chinese Nationalists after 1945. The critics of the Chinese National government have always talked a great deal about how much in dollars was the value of our alleged aid to China. But they never explain how much of what was delivered, to whom, when, where, and in what condition. And they never mention such intangibles as moral support and effective training. The American public was told then, and is being told again, that the U.S. government gave enormous amounts of aid to China, that it was all wasted, that we did everything we could, that Nationalist officials never took our advice, that Chiang Kai-shek's soldiers had no will to fight—in short, that the Republic of China was so hopelessly inefficient and corrupt that there was nothing we could have done that would have saved it. Aid that arrives too late, no matter how much its dollar value, is not real aid. Lend-Lease supplies that were dumped into the Bay of Bengal was not aid to China, no matter how many hundreds of millions of dollars it totals. The equipping of Chiang's best divisions with American 30-caliber rifles, and then placing an embargo on 30-caliber ammunition—as General Marshall did from the summer of 1946 until at least the late spring of 1947—is not aid, no matter how much the value in dollars of the rifles. Marshall's actions, in fact, had the net result of effectively *disarming* Chiang's ablest troops instead of arming them. When 30-caliber ammunition finally was released for shipment to China, it was charged against the funds provided by

Congress at the rate of the replacement cost of $85 per thousand rounds, instead of its actual cost to us on original manufacture of $46 per thousand rounds. Yet ammunition from the same dumps was sent to the Greeks at a surplus price of $4.60 per thousand rounds. And General Marshall's refusal to allow Chiang to obtain, either by purchase or by grant, the aviation gasoline for the air force built up by General Chennault was not effective aid, no matter how many dollars show up in the tables as the cost of the planes.

Most serious of all defects in the American program was the refusal to let our military mission give real advice and training to Chiang's forces at all levels in the field. It was virtually impossible to train any army in the field with a thousand advisers sitting in Nanking working on tables of organization. And, still worse, was the refusal to give one word of encouragement to the Nationalist Chinese during those dreary months and years of civil war. There is no other case in American annals where a supposed ally spent several years in active vilification of a friend it was posing before the world as trying to help. In short, what the Chinese government needed was *proper* aid rather than *more* aid. Proper aid was what the U.S. government systematically, and with obvious forethought, refused to give. If we had treated the Greeks, the Italians, the French, or even the British the way we treated the Nationalist Chinese, they probably would have gone down too. It is the sorriest chapter in the whole history of U.S. relations with foreign governments.

Deprived of moral and material support from the United States and weakened by the Communist infiltration of their ranks, the Nationalists were forced to give up the ancient capital of Peking in January, 1949. Successive military victories by Mao Tse-tung encouraged some American journalists, scholars, and political leaders to advance the fond hope that he would become a second Tito and break away from the influence of Moscow. This assumption was altogether unrealistic, however, since Mao's military potential at this time was hopelessly tied to the Soviet Union by the umbilical cord of supply. Few American opinion-makers noted that Mao Tse-tung showed his close affinity to the Soviet Union on July 1, 1949 in a manifesto commemorating the twenty-eighth anniversary of the birth of the Chinese Communist Party. Mao's text failed to reveal any sign of Titoism, and its appeal to Communists everywhere was blatant:

> Unity in the common struggle with the countries of the world which regard us as an equal nation, and with the peoples of all countries. This means alliance with the U.S.S.R. . . . . Internationally, we belong to the anti-imperialist front headed by the Soviet Union, and for genuine friendly aid we must look to this front and not the imperialist front.[3]

[3]*Congressional Record*, July 13, 1949, 9396-7.

While Mao grew more confident of victory, the Nationalist cause in China was weakening under constant Communist military pressure. Shortly after Shanghai fell it became necessary for Chiang Kai-shek to withdraw the last of his forces to Taiwan. By the end of July, 1949, the Communists were converging on Changsha, from which there was a direct rail line to Canton. These military developments caused little apprehension along the corridors of the State Department, however, because few Asian specialists in the department were really very much disturbed by the prospect of Chiang's collapse.

At the State Department the book-length report known as the China White Paper was being prepared under the editorship of Professor Philip H. Jessup. It was ready for issue several months before the Communists proclaimed their victory. The timing of its release was extremely damaging. It shattered the morale of the Chinese Nationalists. The White Paper was released despite warnings that its publication would have precisely this effect. Jessup rejected a strong plea from General Chennault, for example, who was certain that the document would undermine the National government at a critical hour in the struggle. Another vigorous protest came from William C. Bullitt, veteran diplomat and onetime ambassador to Russia, who argued that the State Department's official version of how China fell to Communism was proof of the length to which the Washington administration would go to protect a vested interest in its mistakes. To publish this inquest on an old and faithful ally, fighting in despair to preserve its national integrity, was incompatible with any standard of decent conduct, Bullitt said. And in his opinion the State Department had done so not to serve a national American interest but to serve domestic political expediency. Ambassador John Leighton Stuart, who had spent a lifetime in China, was just as critical.

> The White Book served to inform the world that the Nationalists, in the opinion of the United States Government, had lost the "civil war." Without admitting any mistakes in United States policy, it tried to place all the blame upon the Nationalist Government of China. United States policy, it claimed, had been in no way responsible for the "ominous result." By implication it announced that the United States support of the National Government and the efforts of the United States toward survival of that government were at an end.[4]

Even the Secretary of Defense, Louis Johnson, raised the question of its accuracy. He suspected that the files of the Defense Department contained data that would be found to conflict with proposed things in the then draft.

[4]"How the Communists Got China," *U.S. News and World Report*, October 1, 1954, 124.

Many hard questions need to be asked on the whole complex subject of post-war U.S. aid to China. For example, why was it that, following the Japanese surrender, shipments of lend-lease supplies to China from India were stopped? Why were large quantities of munitions and equipment intended for China either destroyed or dumped into the Indian Ocean? Why were two officials of the Department of Commerce, Michael Lee and William Remington, permitted to hold up gasoline permits to the Republic of China? Why did American officials place an embargo on all supplies to the Chinese National government when at the same time they had irrefutable evidence that Soviet officials were aiding Mao's rebels? These are some of the perplexing questions that caused such confusion in America's postwar China policy.

Fleet Admiral William D. Leahy, a brilliant man who served long and expertly as a senior aide to President Roosevelt, simply could not comprehend what was happening in China. "Our postwar attitude toward the Government of China," he said, "is completely beyond understanding." But the Communists were not confused. Shortly after V-J Day an explicit instruction from the Kremlin was sent William Z. Foster, head of the American Communist Party. "On the international scale," it read, "the key task is to stop American intervention in China." Chiang Kai-shek, who was hailed as a gallant ally by the Kremlin as long as he was fighting the Japanese, was now to be vilified by Moscow as corrupt, inefficient, a born Fascist, and a typical warlord. The switch of official attitude on Chiang Kai-shek in 1945 is one of the most remarkable and significant shifts in the long history of Kremlin duplicity.

At a White House Conference early in 1944 Secretary Acheson and his Ambassador-at-Large, Philip S. Jessup, proposed to the President that supplies then being loaded into ships at San Francisco and Honolulu for transport to Chiang Kai-shek's government be dramatically stopped as a move toward world peace. Attending this meeting was Senator Arthur H. Vandenberg, chairman of the Foreign Relations Committee, who observed in his diary:

> If, at the very moment when Chiang's Nationalists are desperately trying to negotiate some kind of peace with the Communists, we suspend all military supplies to the Nationalists, we certainly shall make any hope of negotiated peace impossible. We shall thus virtually notify the Communists that they can consider the war ended and themselves as victors. We virtually withdrew our recognition of the Nationalist Government. We sealed China's doom. . . . Regardless of the justification of previous charges that our American policy has been largely responsible for China's fate, if we take this step at this fatefully inept moment, we shall never be

able to shake the charge that "we are the ones who gave poor China the final push into disaster. . . ."[5]

While President Truman did not accept the suggestion of a dramatic move, he did gradually cut off aid to the Nationalists after the capture of Peking. He thus acted shrewdly in a manner that was intended to avoid the shock of any sudden cessation of support of America's old ally.

In appraising the causes of the fall of the Nationalist Chinese Government, there is no single or simple interpretation. Secretary Acheson tried to put most of the blame on Chiang Kai-shek and the Kuomintang and admitted no mistake in American policy. Nothing that this country did or could have done, within the reasonable limits of its capabilities, he wrote, could have changed that result; nothing that was left undone by this country has contributed to it. It was the product of internal Chinese forces, forces which this country tried to influence but could not. From this, one might derive that China could never—and perhaps should not—have been saved from Communism. Secretary Acheson insisted that nothing that was left *undone* by the United States government had the effect of contributing to the fall of the Nationalists. He did note, however, what was *done* by American officials that helped Mao's forces to gain the advantage in the struggle.

There is a catalogue of such things that the United States *did* which contributed decisively to the loss of China. Consider, for instance, the Yalta decision giving the Soviets effective control of Manchuria, thereby negating what the Nationalists had fought for eight years against the Japanese to regain, and which was promised to Chiang Kai-shek at the Cairo meeting. Or consider the four cease-fires which General Marshall imposed upon the Nationalists at times when they had the upper hand, thus undercutting the morale of their fighting forces. Or consider the American embargo on .30-caliber ammunition and the deactivation of some 180 of Chiang's 300 divisions, which demoralized the officers and noncoms of these units and left the rank-and-file little alternative except to go over to the Communists. The Acheson statement simply does not provide an adequate explanation of the loss of the Asian mainland to Chinese Communism.

While the Washington government waited on the sidelines, Mao Tse-tung consolidated his newly won military victories. On October 1, 1949, the rebel leaders proclaimed the establishment of the "Central People's Government of China," declaring his to be the "sole legal government representing all the people." He served notice that his government was ready to establish diplomatic relations with "any

[5]Arthur H. Vandenberg, Jr., ed., *The Private Papers of Senator Vandenberg* (Boston: Houghton Mifflin, 1952) 531.

foreign government willing to observe the principles of equality, mutual benefit, and mutual respect of territory and sovereignty." The next day the Soviet Union extended full diplomatic recognition to Mao's regime and severed all relations with the "provincial government" of the Nationalists. Other Communist-controlled countries quickly followed suit.

From the outset Great Britain, the Netherlands, and some other nations with major Far Eastern investments and interests leaned toward recognition of the new regime on the Asian mainland. Apparently the Department of State harbored a desire to do the same, but clumsy Communist mishandling of American nationals caused second thoughts on the matter. The American vice consul in Shanghai, William M. Olive, was arrested and subjected to harsh treatment. Communist soldiers invaded the bedroom of Ambassador Stuart in the American embassy at Nanking, and the U.S. consular offices at Peking were seized. The most flagrant violation, however, was in the case of Angus Ward, the American consul-general at Mukden, who was rudely detained under house arrest. In addition to these humiliations, Mao Tse-tung's vitriolic anti-American propaganda became more conspicuous day by day as his allegiance to the Soviet Union became increasingly evident. When Admiral Charles M. Cooke sent a ship with supplies for the American naval personnel on station at Dairen, the Russian commander at that port gave the U.S. ship an ultimatum to leave the harbor within two hours. No State Department action was taken against the Russians, but such a wave of popular resentment was produced in the United States that any official action "affirmatively favorable" to the Chinese Communists was precluded.

Late in 1949 the question of Formosa was discussed extensively with senior U.S. military officers, of course, and the State Department view was strongly urged on them. When Admiral C. Turner Joy met Dr. Philip Jessup in Tokyo, he got the unwelcome impression that this professor was trying to convince him that the large island, which the Navy regarded as an unsinkable aircraft carrier, was of no real strategic importance to the U.S. military position in the Pacific. Similarly, Jessup attempted "over and over" to persuade General Stratemeyer that Formosa was unnecessary as a link in the perimeter of Pacific defense. The military experts, on the other hand, repeatedly warned that it would prove seriously detrimental to American interests to let the island fall into "enemy hands." General Wedemeyer was emphatic on this point when asked to comment on Secretary Acheson's December 23 directive. "All the military men," he said, "recognize that Formosa does have strategic significance." All, that is, except Wedemeyer's old boss, General Marshall, whom President Truman was about to recall from retirement to become Secretary of Defense!

On December 22, 1949 the Joint Chiefs of Staff sent a memorandum to the National Security Council urging that an American military mission be sent to Formosa to assess defensive and operational needs. This recommendation was ignored by President Truman. Instead, on January 5, 1950, the White House issued this statement: "The United States Government will not pursue a course which will lead to involvement in the civil conflict in China. . . . Similarly, the United States Government will not provide military aid or advice to Chinese forces on Formosa." Acheson's personal influence on the President's decision was direct and visible, and no one tried very hard to hide it. After a visit to Formosa to see for himself, Senator Knowland of California was sharply critical of the decision. "Munich should have taught us," he said, "that appeasement, then as now, is but surrender on the installment plan." Knowland subsequently was caricatured by liberal journalists, and by the Communist press, as "the senator from Formosa."

Secretary Acheson paid another installment on appeasement when, in a well-remembered speech at the Washington Press Club on January 22, 1950, he conspicuously omitted not only Formosa but also Korea from our strategic line of Pacific defense. It is little wonder that the American people, were utterly confused as to the intention of the Truman administration. Acheson's failure to include Formosa and Korea as areas vital to American security in the Western Pacific became a fiery controversial point when the Korean war broke out. Acheson's critics insisted that his Press Club speech had, in effect, invited the Communists to invade South Korea. Some members of Congress were soon calling for his resignation and the appointment of a Secretary of State better able to understand strategic considerations. But it was not Acheson alone who was responsible. By now President Truman had allowed himself to be sold completely on the Asian viewpoint of Acheson's predecessor in the State Department, General Marshall, the new Secretary of Defense.

It is difficult to believe that the key officials in Washington, having access to every kind of intelligence, could fail to realize that the Chinese Communist movement constituted an aggressive threat to the Pacific world. But consider the fact that no representative of any of the intelligence agencies of the U.S. government was permitted to set foot in Formosa in 1949 or 1950, and all reports made by naval and military attaches had to filter through the screening of the State Department. While Secretary Acheson and other Washington officials waited for "the dust to settle," south of the Yangtze Mao's forces added one victory to another. With the fall of Chungking in December, 1949, all effective resistance ceased and the Nationalist government was forced to the island of Formosa. Not until the outbreak of the Korean War a few months later was the State Department forced into a policy of aid to the Chinese Nationalists—too late to save the mainland, of course, but in time to save Formosa. "What the policy of the State Department is," said Senator Vandenburg in a floor speech, "I am unable to testify." Ambassador John Leighton Stuart, the last American envoy on the mainland, was more pointed. "I found the attitude of the Department of State on the whole subject of China," he said, "essentially one of frustrated unsympathetic defeatism."

At the beginning of 1950, Great Britain recognized Mao's mainland regime. Norway, Finland, Sweden, Switzerland and the Netherlands soon followed suit. The United States government would also have done so early in 1950 had it not been for the continuing humiliations suffered by our diplomatic personnel at the hands of the Chinese Communists. In January, 1950, American consular property in Peking was seized in violation of both treaty rights and the most elementary standards of international conduct. The State Department then announced the recall of all U.S. personnel on station in China, as it had notified the Chinese Communists that it would do if humiliations did not cease. Secretary Acheson later explained: in a speech to the Commonwealth Club in San Francisco:

> . . . as old friends of the Chinese people, we say to them that the representatives of our country are leaving them not by any wish of ours. They are leaving because the normal and accepted standards of international conduct have not been observed by the Chinese Communist authorities in their treatment of our representatives and because they have, in effect, even been summarily ejected from their offices in Peiping. Under such conditions our representatives could not fulfill their normal functions. We regret this leaving of our people, but our Chinese friends will understand again where the responsibility lies.[6]

Segments of the public and members of Congress now began to demand that no step be taken which might weaken Chiang Kai-shek's position on Formosa. The question of U.S. recognition and U.S. admission of Mao's regime was hotly debated in the press, on public platforms, and in Congress. On May 10, 1950, thirty-five senators asked President Truman for clear assurances that the United States would not intend to recognize the Peking regime nor support any movement for admission in the United Nations. Former President Herbert Hoover, when asked for his personal views on the critical China situation by Senator Knowland, strongly asserted that America should not only continue to recognize the Nationalist government in Taipei but should support it with air and naval protection if necessary.

[6]*Department of State Bulletin*, March 27, 1950, 469.

With the outbreak of hostilities in Korea, the Administration's plans for recognition of Mao's regime were hastily set aside. On June 27, 1950, President Truman castigated the Chinese Communists for their aggressive actions and made it clear that any attack upon the island of Formosa would be taken as a direct challenge to the security of the United States. Truman's change of attitude is very significant in view of his earlier statement abandoning the island. Formosa now became strategically important, and American aid began to flow to Chiang Kai-shek's forces. In the House and Senate unanimous resolutions were passed against the admission of the Chinese Communist regime to the United Nations and the State Department evinced a willingness to use the veto, if necessary, in the Security Council to keep the Chinese Communists out. In December, British Prime Minister Clement R. Attlee hurried to Washington to discuss with the President the widening Korean conflict and offered a compromise: A Korean cease-fire in exchange for a UN seat for Mao Tse-tung. President Truman turned it down flat.

To many Americans, what happened in China two decades before the Korean conflict is still sadly misunderstood. Congressman Walter Judd of Minnesota, once a medical missionary in China and a long-time student of Far Eastern affairs reminds us of Chiang Kai-shek's leadership in China:

> We Americans ought never to forget this one fact, which outweighs every other contention—namely that when our fleet lay at the bottom of the sea and Japan had carried out in six months (1942) the single greatest conquest in the history of warfare, only one thing prevented her from completing and organizing her new empire, and turning all her efforts against us. It was this . . . old, so-called backward, corrupt, undemocratic, inefficient China that refused to yield. Chiang could have had peace (with Japan) on very generous terms and saved his people most of the suffering and the economic dislocations and the Communists and the war. Instead he chose to buy for us the precious months and years in which we would rebuild our fleet and capture the islands, one by one, and build the atomic bomb and ultimately bring our superior air power and the bombs to bear upon Japan and give her the final blow. That is a fact that takes precedence over every other in the picture.[7]

"Squeeze," or graft, was an old and accepted practice in China as in most Asian countries, but it was not until runaway inflation had made salaries almost meaningless that such irregularities reached menacing proportions. At a press conference in Shanghai in 1947, General Wedemeyer remarked that he might not be incorruptible if he had to live on the salary of a Chinese general. The revenues of the National

[7]*Congressional Record,* June 19, 1948, A4560.

government actually shrank instead of increasing after V-J Day. "More and more appropriations," Wedemeyer said, "had to be made for the repair of railways, mines and industries, and military expenditures were swollen to ever greater proportions. Hence the demoralizing inflation, corruption and a general decline of morale greater than during the long years of holding out against Japan." The reforms that American officials kept urging upon the Nationalists, he said, would have been "hard enough to carry out in peacetime even with United States aid" and were "totally impossible in the midst of the civil war, which was in fact a Sino-Russian war." To label Chiang Kai-shek a "Fascist dictator" was a ridiculous perversion of the truth. "The powers of the Chinese National Government," he said, "far from being totalitarian, were much too limited. It interfered with the individual too little, not too much. Its sins of omission were the cause of its eventual downfall."

It cannot be denied that there existed, between 1945 and 1949, some valid grounds on which to criticize the Nationalist government of China. Indeed valid grounds can be found on which to criticize any government that ever existed, be it in China or in the United States. But the real motive behind most of the attacks on Chiang Kai-shek's government was not reform of the Kuomintang. It was, instead, removal of the Kuomintang from China, and replacement of it by Mao Tse-tung's party. The actual motive of many of Chiang's critics is obvious in the sheer venom of their attacks. To tear down the National government it was necessary to destroy the Kuomintang, and to destroy the party it was necessary first to demean and discredit Chiang himself.

Up to the middle of 1944 the official policy of the United States was one of unequivocal support of the government headed by Chiang Kai-shek. As the Japanese military machine then began to show definite signs of wearing down, the importance of Chiang Kai-shek as an ally began to diminish. Chiang had done his part by holding down the best of the Japanese armies, but the long years of war had ruined China economically and financially. Her giant population was exhausted and demoralized, and she needed the moral and material support of her American ally now more than ever. It was not forthcoming. The reason that aid was cut may be discovered in the wrong-headed sympathies of certain U.S. Foreign Service officers, the Yalta Agreement, and the Marshall Mission. As William D. Pawley put it: "It is my judgment, and I was in the Department of State at the time, that this whole fiasco, the loss of China and the subsequent difficulties with which the United States has been faced, was the result of mistaken policy of Dean Acheson, Phil Jessup, Lattimore, John Carter Vincent, John Service, John Davies, [O. E.] Clubb, and others. In answer to Senator McClellan's question as to whether he thought the mistaken policy a result of "sincere mistakes of judgment," Pawley replied: "No, I don't, Senator."

Whatever their motives, the key American officials of that day cannot forever be absolved of their wrong-headedness on the fateful China question. Blindly or deliberately, they failed to shape a positive policy. The fact that the Soviet Union had a pervasive and dominating influence in the Communist party in China had long been well-known to Washington officialdom. Army intelligence continued to submit documented reports describing the extent of this influence, but Secretary Acheson and his associates just did not accept these as authoritative. It is hard to understand how American officials of the postwar period could have overlooked the fact that since 1922 successive Communist International party congresses at Moscow had announced to the world their determination to overturn all non-Communist governments. Apparently, such old echoes were not heard in Washington after 1945, and new warnings from first-hand observers in the Far East were similarly unheard.

It can no longer be doubted that there were some important people in Washington in those times—either actually in the government or close by as consultants—who sincerely believed that the corpus of Marxist-Leninist ideology contained the best answers for the problems of most of the world. Others, many more in number, were motivated by fuzzy but seemingly practical visions of "one world" to be achieved by "cooperation" at all levels with all existing regimes, regardless of the totalitarian nature of Communist regimes. Taken together, there were simply too many such misguided people in positions of power and decision at one of the truly critical junctures in American national history.

5

Our Friend, Free China
[1950-1968]

IN THE CLOSING year of the last century the eminent American diplomat John Hay uttered one of the truly prophetic statements of modern history. "The storm center of the world," he said in 1899, "has gradually shifted to China." No phenomenon of the twentieth century has been more striking than the fulfillment of this remarkable prediction. World War I may have been strictly European in origin, but certainly one of the most significant results of that "crusade for democracy" centered on the inclusive question of the fate of China and the future of Asia. World War II was at least one-half Asian in origin, and the fate of China was the question which finally brought the United States into that crusade as freedom's champion. What befell that hard-won freedom in the years immediately following V-J Day was nowhere more pointedly illustrated, and nowhere more tragic in its implications for so many millions, than on the Asian mainland. The smashing of freedom in China, at the very moment when the fulfillment of freedom in that most populous country on earth seemed at last possible, provides the classic example of Communist ascendency in the Cold War.

With the seizure of the Asian mainland by the Chinese Communists, the island of Taiwan now became a paramount issue in American diplomatic deliberations. On December 22, 1949 the Joint Chiefs of Staff, under the chairmanship of General Omar Bradley, decided that it was in the best interest of the United States to help the Chinese Nationalists defend the island against a possible Communist invasion. They therefore advised the establishment of a military mission there.

The day following this decision Secretary Acheson sent a directive, which later leaked out from Tokyo, to American diplomatic and consular representatives throughout the Far East telling them of the abandonment of Taiwan by the United States. The message read in part:

> Formosa (Taiwan) has no military significance . . . we should occasionally make clear that seeking United States bases in Formosa, sending troops, supplying arms, dispatching naval units, or taking similar action would (a) accomplish no material good for China or its Nationalist regime; (b) involve the United States in a long-term venture, producing at best a new era of bristling stalemate and at worst possible involvement in open warfare.[1]

At a meeting of the National Security Council a week later President Truman, after hearing the opposite views of Secretary Acheson, overruled the Joint Chiefs and upheld the hands-off idea. The President maintained this negative posture in a policy statement of January 5, 1950:

> At the present time the United States has no intention of seeking rights from Taiwan, establishing military bases there, or interfering militarily. . . . The United States Government will not adopt any measures to become involved in the Chinese civil war, and similarly will not offer military aid or suggestions to the Nationalist forces in Taiwan.[2]

Yet there was another element in the Chinese equation which the President failed to mention. That element was the fiefdom of Korea. It will be recalled that the Cairo Declaration of 1943, to which Russia later subscribed, supported the idea of Korean independence "in due course." Before steps could be taken to implement this declaration, however, Japan surrendered and Korea was divided into two zones at the thirty-eighth parallel for the purpose of effecting the Japanese capitulation. It was agreed that the Russians would occupy the northern zone, the Americans the southern. This temporary military line, the thirty-eighth parallel, promptly became a semi-permanent political line, an eventuality which should have been foreseen, if indeed it was not, by all the statesmen and generals concerned.

In his well remembered speech at the Washington Press Club on January 12, 1950, Secretary Acheson declared that henceforth neither Taiwan nor South Korea would be considered as within the American "defensive perimeter." On February 24 he said that the policy of the United States was to "wait until the dust settles." Acheson made this

---

[1]*Military Situation in the Far East,* Part 5, 167 ff.

[2]*American Foreign Policy 1950-1955, Basic Documents* (Washington, D.C.: Government Printing Office, 1957) 2458-59.

statement in an informal interview with fifty-one Republican members of Congress, thirty of whom had signed a letter to President Truman asking for a reappraisal of the China situation. Until the dust had settled, he said, he could not clearly predict the outcome of the Chinese struggle. In his memoirs Acheson complains that this statement was deliberately distorted by opponents of his policy. What he meant to say, he insists, is that it is always impossible, after a big tree falls in the forest, to "perceive the degree of damage until the dust settles." He was not describing any government, he insists, but merely stating that the future on the Asian mainland was uncertain.

Whatever its meaning today, Acheson's remark certainly invited the aggression of the North Korean Communists. In the early morning hours of Sunday, June 25, 1950, North Korean forces, supported by Russian-made tanks, crossed the thirty-eighth parallel in a surprise attack that shattered the uneasy peace of the cold war. South Korean troops, lightly armed, broke under the impact of armor and fled in disorganized retreat. The North Koreans claimed that the South Koreans had attacked first and that they were merely counterattacking, but a United Nations investigating commission concluded that the northern Communists had initiated the "well-planned, concerted, and full-scaled invasion" of the south.

With the outbreak of the Korean crisis, the United States government once more altered its official attitude on the China question. Any effort to repel the aggression in Korea would be in jeopardy if a Communist attack on the island of Taiwan should occur concurrently. In his dramatic statement of June 27 President Truman, after announcing that he had ordered U.S. air and sea forces to give the South Koreans "cover and support," went on to say:

> The attack upon Korea makes it plain beyond all doubt that Communism has passed beyond the use of subversion. . . . In these circumstances the occupation of Formosa by Communist forces would be a direct threat to the security of the Pacific area and to United States forces performing their lawful and necessary functions in that area. Accordingly, I have ordered the Seventh Fleet to prevent an attack on Formosa. As a corollary of this action I am calling upon the Chinese Government on Formosa to cease all air and sea operations against the mainland.[3]

With this pronouncement, the American government in effect reentered the Chinese civil conflict. Secretary Acheson's decision to abandon Chiang Kai-shek's Nationalists had been reversed. The Peking press immediately denounced President Truman's action, of course, and in a newspaper article Chou En-lai admitted that Chairman

[3]*American Foreign Policy, 1950-1955*, Vol. II, 2468.

Mao Tse-tung's plan to "liberate" Formosa had suffered a major set-back.

Some friends of the Free Chinese, however, could scarcely interpret President Truman's order as anything other than the deliberate "leashing" of Chiang Kai-shek. Truman's decision to deter any Nationalist move against the mainland was, to be sure, a distinct advantage to the Communists. Relieved of the necessity of guarding against a possible sea attack from across the Formosa Strait, Mao's generals were able to shift large numbers of troops from Fukien province to the Korean frontier in preparation for their momentous autumn crossing of the Yalu. Yet the President had committed the United States to the primary objective of keeping Taiwan out of Communist hands, and Republican leaders on Capitol Hill did not hesitate to express themselves strongly on this issue. Senator Alexander Smith insisted that under no circumstances should the Chinese Communists be allowed to seize the island. Senator Knowland urged that a team of U.S. military observers be sent, and Senator Taft called for direct naval assistance to the Nationalists.

In the opening weeks of the war, the North Koreans quickly overran most of the south. The United States rushed in with air, naval, and ground forces under General MacArthur, and various other members of the United Nations sent manpower or equipment and supplies. During the summer MacArthur's hard counterattack drove the invaders northward across the thirty-eighth parallel and, in full flight, almost to the border of China proper at the Yalu River. There was talk of "the boys" being "home for Christmas." The war, MacArthur told newsmen, "very definitely is coming to an end shortly." Then came the incredible swarm of Mao Tse-tung's "volunteers" across the Yalu to the rescue of the North Koreans. With flares lighting the sky and bugle blasts piercing the cold air, hordes of Chinese Communists slammed into the center of the United Nations lines. As the outnumbered U.N. forces fell back in bloody retreat over frozen ground, General MacArthur announced dramatically that "an entirely new war" had begun. His command, he told his superiors a few days later, was now faced with "the entire Chinese nation in an undeclared war."

According to General MacArthur, victory would not be possible unless he was permitted to bomb strategic targets in China, use Chinese Nationalist troops on the ground in Korea, and blockade and execute diversionary attacks on the China coast. But the State Department under Secretary Acheson and the Department of Defense under General Marshall flatly opposed the course MacArthur suggested. It would certainly lead to a third world war, they warned, and President Truman agreed. "If we began to attack Communist China," Truman wrote in his memoirs, "we had to anticipate Russian intervention." He reasoned that Red Russia and Red China were ideological allies, after all, and the Soviets had not yet established their remarkable record of bluffing in international affairs. Moreover, the feisty little man in the White House appears by this time to have cultivated an immense personal dislike for, and distrust of, his famous and highly esteemed commander in the Far East. According to Merle Miller's so-called "oral biography," *Plain Speaking,* published twenty-three years later, Truman by 1951 regarded General MacArthur as an overdressed poseur and a "dumb son of a bitch." In his mind he linked MacArthur with the Republican supporters of Nationalist China in the United States, those whom he believed to be the "China Lobby" people so hated by Marshall, Acheson, and the whole liberal wing of the Democratic party. The fact that MacArthur had once been Army Chief of Staff under President Hoover and Secretary of War Patrick J. Hurley doubtless helped the aggressively partisan Truman to hate him all the more. The upshot, of course, was the dismissal of MacArthur in April, 1951, and the ensuing stalemate in Korea which persists to this day.

A major factor in hardening the official attitude toward Mao's regime was the continuing struggle between the French and the Ho Chih Minh's Communists in Indo-China. The newly elected president, General Eisenhower, correctly felt in 1953 that a Communist victory in Indo-China would mean that all Southeast Asia would finally be threatened. American officials participated, along with delegates of the Peking regime, in the Geneva Conference that "declared" peace in Vietnam in the summer of 1954. But Washington did not like the result, and Secretary of State Dulles' fear of "falling dominoes" led the Americans to promote the formation of the South-East Asia Treaty Organization (SEATO) in the aftermath of the final French defeat at Dienbienphu.

The SEATO treaty was signed on September 8, 1954. Five days earlier the Chinese Communists had laid down a heavy artillery barrage against the tiny offshore island of Quemoy, which was strongly occupied by the Nationalists though less than two miles from the mainland port of Amoy. Tension had been rising in the Formosa Strait for some months. The Eisenhower administration was now faced with the problem of defining an official attitude toward all the Nationalist-held offshore islands—the Quemoy group, the Matsu twelve miles off the port of Foochow, and the Tachens farther north. The Seventh U.S. Fleet, which since 1950 had cruised in the Formosa Strait for the purpose of protecting Taiwan, had no orders to defend the offshore islands.

The shelling of the little islands of Quemoy and Matsu was a typical Communist maneuver. The initial stake seemed indeed small in comparison with the risks that the United States would have to take to prevent their seizure. Many Americans naturally felt that these islands

149

were mere "pieces of real estate" for which the endangering of a single American life would never be justified. This, however, was not the official view in Washington. Unwillingness to protect these islands, however insignificant they might seem as real estate, would indicate on America's part an unwillingness to stand firm in the Far East. Fear would spread, and this would give the Communists a confident expectation of further gains which, in all likelihood, would lead to early hostile action of a more daring character. The United States decided, therefore, that the challenge must be met.

Although the Eisenhower administration clearly desired to maintain good relations with the Chinese Nationalists, the question was how far to go. Would the United States support a Nationalist counterattack against the mainland? The Washington government had no intention of attempting to overthrow the Chinese Communist regime by force. Rather it hoped that the application of U.S. military pressure would serve to deepen the internal crises in China and encourage the mainland population to revolt against Mao's policemen. This idea of the maintenance of pressure was what Secretary Dulles meant by "peaceful liberation."

The conscious effort in Washington to build up the image of Taiwan demonstrated unmistakably that the United States had again recognized the status of the Republic of China. As such it seemed to herald a bright new era in Sino-American relations. Secretary Dulles contended that the Republic of China would prove a trustworthy and valuable ally and that its elevation to international status matched the interests of the United States. American connections with the Nationalist government grew stronger day by day. Late in 1954 a sweeping "mutual defense" treaty was signed in Washington. It gave the United States the right to deploy such land, air, and sea forces in and about Formosa and the Pescadores Islands "as may be required for their defense as determined by mutual agreement." Since the treaty was to remain in force indefinitely, Secretary Dulles felt that it would "put to rest once and for all" the recurring rumor that the United States was about to abandon what the cynical pro-Communist "China expert" Owen Lattimore had called "that driftwood government of the beaches of Formosa." Dulles was warmly congratulated by President Chiang for forging a necessary link in the protective chain of freedom in Asia. Newspapers in both countries lauded the treaty, including the *New York Times* which conceded in an editorial that the pact expressed "a position that most Americans strongly support."

The treaty committed the United States only to defend Taiwan and the Pescadores; it left open to question the defense of "other territories" such as the offshore islands. A clarifying exchange of notes, kept secret for a month, extracted an agreement from the Nationalists not to attack the mainland unilaterally. Chiang was "leashed" again, but Secretary Dulles pointedly declared that Taiwan was now an integral part of America's "defense perimeter" on the western rim of the Pacific. Moreover, he insisted, the United States had proven its total disinterest in "trading" Taiwan as part of some future settlement or accommodation with Peking. Dulles thus injected into American policy an unmistakeable obligation to defend the Republic of China against any and all, and there was no doubt as to which enemy he meant.

On the positive side for both the Republic of China and the United States, the 1954 treaty strengthened all the vital ties between the two nations and made possible a reasonable arrangement of military cooperation. On the negative side from the viewpoint of the Chinese Nationalists, the treaty was strictly defensive in nature and thereby a means by which the United States might possibly frustrate a timely counterattack against the mainland. According to Article 5, all measures taken by the Nationalists to counter an armed attack by the Communists "shall immediately be reported to the United Nations Security Council, and these measures shall be halted when the Security Council adopts the necessary measures to restore and maintain international peace and security." In other words, any and all military action taken by the Republic of China, (*i.e.*, a counterattack against the mainland) was subject to interference by the United Nations which, conceivably, could declare Chiang's government guilty of aggression. The United States, moreover, had no obligation to help the Republic of China in case a Nationalist action against the Chinese Communists precipitated an attack by the latter. By the exchange of notes on December 10, 1954, between Secretary Dulles and Foreign Minister George K. C. Yeh, it was agreed that no military unit "created through the joint efforts and contributions of the two contracting nations" could leave the area circumscribed by the treaty "if such departure will reduce the defense capabilities of the said territories."

The State Department viewed this exchange of notes as a positive guarantee by the Nationalists that they would never attack the mainland without "prior consent." From the viewpoint of the Republic of China, however, the 1954 treaty contained no absolute prohibition on a Nationalist counterattack against the mainland. On the day it was signed Foreign Minister Yeh asserted that the mutual defense in no way signified that "Free China did not have the right to recover the mainland." Simultaneously the Vice Minister of Political Affairs, Shen Chang-huan, told a press conference:

A counterattack against the mainland is an affair which lies within the scope of our sovereignty. The national policy of mainland recovery was mapped out long ago and will continue to be carried out in the future,

151

without interference from any quarter. The text of the treaty carries no stipulations prohibiting a counterattack against the mainland.[4]

The exchange of notes between Foreign Minister Yeh and Secretary Dulles on December 10 arose from Article 4 of the treaty, which stipulated that the signatories might consult with each other at any time concerning implementation of the treaty. This exchange, therefore, did not constitute a secret agreement outside of the treaty, and neither was it an appendix to the treaty. But even though the official text of the treaty contained no stipulation prohibiting a counterattack against the mainland, the ability of the Republic of China to carry out such an action was in fact restricted in some degree because the United States did not endorse the idea. While the 1954 treaty did give real impetus to further mutual cooperation, its side effect was to reinforce the concept of "Two Chinas" which had long been popular among some Asian experts of the U.S. government.

Important persons in Washington had long nurtured the notion of "Two Chinas." The idea originated with the British, who feared for their vast investment in Hong Kong. Then, with the outbreak of the Korean War, the United States effectively froze the political status of both Taiwan and the mainland. The popularity of the "Two Chinas" idea in the United States was grounded in selfish economic considerations only, for such a hypothesis was politically unacceptable to both Taipei and Peking. The first official American mention came at a press conference on January 19, 1955, when President Eisenhower remarked that formal recognition of "two Chinas" was one of the "possible approaches" being considered by his administration. This suggestion, of course, was sternly condemned by officials of the Republic of China.

The obvious American objectives in the Mutual Defense Treaty were twofold: to warn the Chinese Communists that the United States would not tolerate an armed attack on Taiwan or the Pescadores, and to declare to the world that Taiwan and the Pescadores would never be traded away in any American negotiation with the Chinese Communists. Yet, by subtler interpretation, the treaty can be said to have contained three "understandings" or "reservations": (1) the legal status of Taiwan and the Pescadores was unaffected, *i.e.*, the United States still regarded the status of Taiwan "unsettled," as it had been since 1950; (2) the United States had no actual obligation to garrison troops in Taiwan except to take such action when the Republic of China was forced to fight in self-defense; and (3) since the United States made no commitment to protect Quemoy or the other offshore

[4]Kuang Chung, *A Review of the U.S. China Policy* (Taipei, 1971), 13.

islands, the defense of any additional areas must be approved by the U.S. Senate.

Since the Mutual Defense Treaty did not cover the several offshore islands, Mao Tse-tung saw a fine chance to put American policy to a test. He chose the tiny Tachen Islands, about 250 miles northwest of Taiwan, where no outside aid could easily be brought in and a heavy Communist bombardment could quickly make the Nationalist position there untenable. President Chiang was stubbornly determined to defend the Tachens until he was persuaded, and wisely so, by his American military advisers to evacuate with the help of the U.S. Seventh Fleet.

At the same time, however, Foreign Minister Yeh received assurances from Secretary Dulles that the United States would defend the remaining offshore islands. President Eisenhower, angered by Mao's naked action against the Tachens, vowed that the Pescadores would not be allowed to fall to "aggressive Communist forces" and asked Congress for a resolution authorizing him to prevent any such attack. Responding to this urgent request, Congress spoke almost unanimously. The affirmative vote in the House was 409-3; three days later the Senate concurred by a vote of 85-3. The "Formosa Resolution" of 1955 thus authorized the President to "employ the armed forces of the United States as he deems necessary" to protect Taiwan, the Pescadores, and related territories. As the resolution did not mention by name the offshore islands of Quemoy and Matsu, the question arose of what to do if the Communists attacked these atolls. Secretary Dulles clarified the matter somewhat at a press conference by declaring that the President would certainly use American air and sea forces if he deemed an attack on these two islands to be part of a "larger assault" on Taiwan.

On February 19, 1955, President Eisenhower put some interesting words into a letter to Winston Churchill. All of the non-Communist nations of the Western Pacific, he said, were "watching nervously to see what we do next." If the United States appeared "strong and coercive only toward our friends" and compelled the Chinese Nationalists to "make further retreats," other Asians would feel that they "had better plan to make the best terms they can with the Communists." On March 10 Secretary Dulles, returning from a tour in the Far East, told the President: "The situation out there in the Formosa Strait is far more serious than I thought before my trip. The Chinese Communists are determined to capture Formosa. Surrendering Quemoy and Matsu won't end that determination."

The tension momentarily was taken out of the Formosa Strait crisis by none other than Chou En-lai. On April 23, 1955, during the course of the Afro-Asian conference at Bandung, Indonesia, the Red Chinese premier issued a statement expressing the willingness of his government to negotiate with the United States. The Chinese people, he said, were always "willing to settle international disputes by peaceful means." But when the United States took up Chou's suggestion and indirectly sought reciprocal renunciations of force, his ambassador at Warsaw finally had to admit that the Chinese Communists did intend to use armed force to "take Taiwan" unless they could "get it in some other way." A negative response from the State Department was cautiously worded by Dulles.

On July 25 it was agreed to raise the consular-level talks, initiated the previous year at the Geneva conference on Indo-China and Korea, to ambassadorial level. These talks opened a week later in Geneva. The only specific item on the agenda concerned the mutual return of civilians—several thousand Chinese students in the United States and forty Americans in China. Agreement on this subject was reached in six weeks. Sixteen years later, as President Nixon's visit to Peking was being arranged, this was still the only subject on which the two sides had ever reached agreement in the ongoing ambassadorial talks. And even this one agreement was quickly swamped by charges and counter-charges of reneging.

The question of admitting the Peking regime to the United Nations now came up again. It had been a perennial issue since 1949, but Mao Tse-tung's crude invasion of Korea necessitated a shift of attitude in the State Department and forfeited the hopes of certain "experts" for an early American endorsement. The British had applied some pressure for the quick seating of a Chinese Communist delegation, but President Truman declared the Red Chinese to be merely "Russian satellites." The Senate felt called upon, therefore, to adopt the first of eight unanimous resolutions against the admission of the Chinese Communists into what its critics already were calling the East River Debating Society.

On January 23, 1951, acting on a resolution introduced by John L. McClellan of Arkansas, the Senate voted 91-0 that "the Communist Chinese government should not be admitted to membership in the United Nations as the representative of China." By the following September, the various pressures for UN admission and, as well, formal U.S. diplomatic recognition again so alarmed the Senate that a majority of 56 members of both parties addressed a letter to President Truman opposing "the recognition of Communist China by the Government of the United States, or its admission into the United Nations." Among the senatorial signers were the liberal Paul Douglas of Illinois, the conservative Robert A. Taft of Ohio, and Richard M. Nixon. Again in 1953 both houses, now Republican-controlled, adopted unopposed expressions against admission. The Senate, acting on an amendment to an appropriations bill offered by Senator Styles Bridges of New

Hampshire, resolved 76-0 that "the Communist Chinese Government should not be admitted to the United Nations as the representative of China." The House, on a motion by Congressman Robert B. Cheperfield of Illinois, concurred by a vote of 379-0.

Robert J. Donovan, Eisenhower's biographer, has suggested that the general was basically unconvinced that "the vital interest of the United States" was actually best served by "prolonged non-recognition." But on many occasions President Eisenhower and Secretary Dulles made it very clear that they did strongly oppose both UN admission and U.S. recognition of the Peking regime. The President expressed himself with considerable emphasis as follows:

> I am completely and unalterably opposed, under the present situation, to the admission of Red China to the U.N. I personally think that 95 per cent of the population of the United States would take the same stand. There is a moral question first of all. . . . The U.N. was not established primarily as a super-government, clothed with all the authority of a super-government. . . . On top of that, Red China is today at war with the U.N. They were declared an aggressor by the U.N. . . . That situation has never been changed.[5]

To move against admission, Secretary Dulles relied heavily on the inhibition in the United Nations charter against admitting any state answering to Red China's description. At the San Francisco founding conference, Dulles recalled, the proposition that the United Nations should be "unselective" and universal was "strongly argued," but the "proponents of selectivity" won out. Furthermore, said the Secretary, the objection to Red China as less than "peace-loving" was strengthened by the charter provision that "any nation against which enforcement action was taken," as with Red China in the Korean War, "should be liable to suspension from membership in the U.N."

Among the influential private citizens in those days who argued the unacceptability of Red China, Adolf A. Berle, Jr., the brilliant former Assistant Secretary of State, was conspicuous. A profound student of international affairs, Berle made his point convincingly:

> The United Nations charter names the Republic of China as a permanent member of the Security Council. It is absurd to suggest bringing into the peace-keeping machinery of the United Nations a country which has made war against Korea and signed an armistice there but which has refused to make peace. . . . It is one thing to admit a member to an organization, being convinced that the member will join in and forward its work. It is another to admit a tough, or a gangster, who hammers at the door with a gun butt.[6]

[5]U.S. News and World Report, November 26, 1954.
[6]"The Soviet-Chinese Complex." Annals of the American Academy July, 1954.

Organized expressions of public concern underscored such personal anxieties. The American Federation of Labor, the United States Chamber of Commerce, the American Federation of Women's Clubs, and other national organizations stood solidly opposed to UN admission for Mao's regime. A poll conducted in 1954 by the Council on Foreign Relations among 800 selected "leaders of American thought and action"—including businessmen, lawyers, educators, and newspaper editors—showed that eighty per cent were opposed to admission and seventy-six per cent were generally satisfied with the administration's posture in Far Eastern affairs. In a speech late in 1954 President Eisenhower was explicit. Reviewing Mao's spasmodic aggressions from 1950 in Korea to the current bombardments of the offshore islands, the President adverted to the disastrous attempts by the Atlantic Powers to appease the Japanese warlords in Manchuria, Mussolini in Ethiopia, and Hitler in the Rhineland, Austria, and Czechoslovakia. He said:

> Let us suppose that the Chinese Communists conquer Quemoy. Would that be the end of the story? We know that it would not be the end of the story. History teaches that, when powerful despots can gain something through aggression, they try, by the same methods, to gain more and more.... The shooting which the Chinese Communists started on August 23 ... is part of ... an ambitious plan of armed conquest ... (which) would liquidate all the free world positions in the Western Pacific area and bring them under captive governments ... hostile to the United States. ... Thus the Chinese and Russian Communists would come to dominate at least the western half of the now friendly Pacific Ocean.[7]

In 1956, Congress again spoke with a united voice (391-0 in the House, 86-0 in the Senate) to reemphasize previous interventions against the seating of Red China. Congress expressed the conviction that such admission would "gravely injure the United Nations and impair its effective functioning in accordance with the provisions of the United Nations charter." Visiting Taipei in July of that year, Vice President Nixon delivered a personal message from President Eisenhower to President Chiang Kai-shek which, besides paying lavish tribute to Chiang's leadership, asserted: "Let there be no misapprehension about our own steadfastness in continuing to support the Republic of China." The next month, at the Democratic and Republican national conventions in Chicago and San Francisco, both parties inserted planks in their platforms pledging continued opposition to the seating of the Peking regime in the United Nations. On that occasion President Eisenhower spoke with deadly seriousness:

[7]Forrest Davis and Robert A. Hunter, *The Red China Lobby* (New York: Fleet Publishing Co., 1963), 103.

I must say to you very frankly and soberly [that] the United States cannot accept the result that the Communists seek. Neither can we show . . . a weakness of purpose, a timidity, which would surely lead them to move more aggressively against us and our friends in the Western Pacific. . . . A Western Pacific Munich would not buy us peace or security.

Congress has made clear its recognition that the security of the Western Pacific is vital to the security of the United States and that we should be firm. The Senate has ratified, by overwhelming vote, security treaties with the Republic of China covering Formosa and the Pescadores, and also the Republic of China. We have a mutual security treaty with the Republic of the Philippines, which could be next in line for conquest if Formosa fell into hostile hands. . . . In addition, there is a joint resolution which the Congress passed in January, 1955, dealing specifically with Formosa and the offshore islands of Free China in the Formosa Straits.

If the present bombardment and harassment of Quemoy should be converted into a major assault, with which the local defenders could not cope, we would be compelled to face precisely the situation that Congress visualized in 1955.[8]

What were the arguments on the other side? Secretary of State Dulles specified them in his speech to the Lions International in San Francisco on June 28, 1957. Some people were saying that the United States should accord diplomatic recognition to the Chinese Communist regime because it had existed so long that it had earned the right to recognition. This, said Dulles, was not sound international law. Diplomatic recognition was always a privilege, never a right. But diplomatic recognition gave the recognized government both rights and privileges, and recognition by the United States would give Mao's regime new prestige and influence at home and abroad. But Mao's was a bandit regime, and the United States would continue to act in accordance with principles which contribute to a world society of order under law.

Secretary Dulles clearly understood that the programs of guerrilla warfare directed and supported by the Chinese Communists against other Asian countries were real and increasing by the month. Linked with the threat of these subversive programs was the problem of large Chinese minorities that for centuries had lived on the fringes of the mainland. The problem was that these "overseas Chinese" had often demonstrated an inability and unwillingness to assimilate with the native population. Dulles warned that recognition of Mao's regime would provide stepped-up Communist activities among these populations. (This position was supported by a former Air Force Secretary, Thomas K. Finletter, in his book *Foreign Policy: the Next Phase*. "A

[8]*Ibid.*, 104.

recognition of Peking by the United States," he wrote, ". . . would undoubtedly help the mainland Communists in their efforts to manipulate the Overseas Chinese and to swing them to the Communist cause.")

A test often applied, Dulles noted, was the actual ability of a regime to govern. Nations often maintain diplomatic relations with governments-in-exile, and they frequently deny recognition to those in actual power. Other tests were whether, as Thomas Jefferson put it, the recognized government reflects "the will of the nation, substantially declared;" or whether the government conforms to the code of civilized nations, lives peacefully, and honors its international obligations. Recognition, Dulles insisted, was an instrument of national policy to serve enlightened self-interest. There was nothing automatic about it, and it was never compelled by the mere passing of time.

Another argument beginning to be heard, Dulles said, was that since diplomatic recognition was "inevitable," why not now? But when had the United States ever succumbed to the argument of "inevitability"? We had never accepted the mastery of totalitarian forces. Communist-type despotisms were not so immutable as they might sometimes appear. There was often an optical illusion in the fact that police states give an external appearance of hard permanency while the democracies, often speaking through different and discordant voices, seem the unstable members of the world society. But the reality was that a system which tolerates diversity has a long life expectancy, whereas a system seeking to impose conformity was always in danger. Of all the arguments advanced for recognition of the Chinese Communist regime, the "least cogent" to Dulles was the argument of "inevitability."

There was always the possibility, Dulles admitted, of influencing the Chinese Communist regime to better ways by means of diplomatic relations with it. But the experience of those who had recognized and dealt with Mao's regime convinced him that the probable result, internally, would be the opposite of what was hoped for. If the United States recognized the mainland regime, many of the millions of Overseas Chinese in free Asian countries would reluctantly turn to the guiding direction of the Maoists. This would be a tragedy for them, Dulles said, and would imperil friendly governments already menaced by Chinese Communist subversion. The Republic of China, of course, would feel betrayed by its American friends. The Nationalist government was our firm ally in World War II and earlier had borne alone the burden of the Far Eastern fight against totalitarianism. It had many tempting opportunities to compromise with the Japanese on terms which would have been gravely detrimental to the United States, but it never did so. The United States was honor-bound, therefore, to give its old ally, to whom we were now pledged by a mutual defense treaty, a full measure of loyalty. If we were to do less than this, the free Asian governments of the Pacific and Southeast Asia would be gravely perplexed. The unifying and fortifying influence was, above all, the spirit and resolution of the United States. If we appeared to waver or to compromise with Communism in China, that would in turn weaken Asian resistance to Mao's regime and assist international Communism to score a signal success in its design to "encircle" the United States.

The Chinese Communist regime, Dulles concluded, simply did not conform to the practices of civilized nations. It did not live up to international obligations, had not been peaceful in the past, and gave no evidence of being peaceful in the future. Its foreign policies were hostile to ours. But were our policies merely negative? Did not we see any prospect of resuming the many friendly ties which, for many generations, the American people have had with the Chinese people? Did we not see any chance that the Chinese, with their ancient culture and rich wisdom, would again be able to play a constructive part in the councils of the nations? Dulles answered these questions in the affirmative. American confidence, he said, was based on a belief in the future of human freedom and on the conviction that Communism was repugnant to the individualistic people of China. He ended his speech by quoting the brave words recently uttered in Red China by a university lecturer: "To overthrow you cannot be called unpatriotic, because you Communists no longer serve the people."

On August 12, 1958, the State Department circulated a memorandum to its overseas missions on the question of recognition. It reflected the thinking of Secretary Dulles:

Chinese Communist leaders . . . are not primarily interested in promoting the welfare of their people while living at peace with their neighbors. Their primary purpose is to extend the Communist revolution beyond their borders to the rest of Asia and thence to the rest of the world . . . Mao Tse-tung himself has said that his regime's policy is to give active support to the national independence and liberation movements in countries in Asia, Africa, and Latin America. . . .[9]

Ten days later the Chinese Communists launched their fierce bombardment of Quemoy as a prelude to the second crisis in the Taiwan Strait. They clearly planned to seize Quemoy and Matsu before the United States had time to interfere or to force the United States, through threat of war, to negotiate with them and thus pave the way for admission into the United Nations. Mao's spokesmen strictly avoided using the phrase "liberation of Taiwan" in their propaganda. By carefully separating the "Quemoy problem" from the "Taiwan

[9]*American Foreign Policy, 1958*, 1136-43.

problem," they hoped to force the United States into making concessions on the former.

The question was now simply this: would the United States come to the defense of Quemoy and Matsu? The offshore islands were not within the scope of the Mutual Defense Treaty of 1954, and in approving the treaty the Senate had specifically noted the proviso that no military action would be taken in areas other than Taiwan and the Pescadores except through "special revision" of the pact. But while the Eisenhower administration was bound by no public or official guarantee of the defense of Quemoy and Matsu, the American position was clear enough. In his press conference on May 4, 1954 President Eisenhower had called attention to the fact that the Chinese Communists never mentioned that their objective was merely to occupy Quemoy and Matsu; indeed, they always said that they meant to occupy Taiwan itself. The same clear indication appeared in a letter from President Eisenhower to Prime Minister Churchill about the same time—and now again, four years later, in a letter to Premier Khrushchev during the second Taiwan Strait crisis.

On the offshore island problem, the President was especially concerned about the morale of the citizens of the Republic of China. His disregard of the clamor of appeasers at home and abroad, and his willingness to recognize the ideological importance of two tiny islands off the China coast, were indeed admirable. During the 1958 crisis the United States not only strengthened its conventional forces in the Far East as a warning to the Chinese Communists, but went so far as to install rockets and nuclear launchers on the offshore islands as a guard against the possibility of mass invasion from the mainland.

Frustrated in their designs, the Chinese Communists could now only back down and insist that they had no intention of challenging the United States. As might be expected, they proposed continuing the ambassadorial-level negotiations at Warsaw. But now Mao's representatives reversed their previous position by separating the two "problems" of Taiwan and the offshore islands. They no longer talked of Taiwan and Quemoy in the same breath. This strategy finally worked. As a result of some rather soft statements coming out of Peking on the remoteness of any resolution to the "Taiwan problem," the United States began to effect a fundamental change in policy to avoid repetition of the explosive Strait situation. Washington now asserted that the offshore islands were not worth risking a nuclear war, and that the problem could only be resolved through negotiations with the Chinese Communists. In summary, the American government gave proof of its staunch determination to protect not only Taiwan, but also Quemoy and Matsu, during the 1958 crisis; yet at the same time Washington officialdom began to reflect a different view of the Chinese Communists. There now emerged a faint hope for some permanent improvement of relations with Mao's regime—in place of the older view of the regime as a temporary aberration in Chinese history.

Yet Secretary Dulles himself remained staunch. After meeting with President Chiang Kai-shek at Taipei in October, 1958, the Secretary issued this unequivocal statement: "The United States recognizes that the Republic of China is the authentic spokesman for Free China and of the hopes and aspirations entertained by the great mass of the Chinese people. . . ." On their part the Chinese Nationalists agreed that the use of military force to recover the mainland should be avoided "if possible," stressing instead that their major means would be an implementation of Dr. Sun Yat-sen's Three Principles of the People. As long as he was on the job, Secretary Dulles held firmly against any softening of the official American attitude toward the Peking regime. In the lower echelons of government, however, there remained a persistent interest in the notion that some basic revision was desirable. When ill health forced the retirement of Dulles, the rumbles from below became more audible. Senator John F. Kennedy, for instance, was beginning to express strong opposition to the Formosa Resolution of 1955. He, and his foreign policy advisers were obviously thinking in terms of some "Two-China" solution as a Democratic plan in the upcoming Presidential campaign.

In the memorable contest of 1960 the China question was hotly debated. Particularly sharp was the issue of the offshore islands as aired in the famous televised confrontations of the candidates. The position of Vice-President Nixon was predetermined. He was obliged to uphold the actions and attitudes of the past eight years. Senator Kennedy, on the other hand, was under no such wraps. With nothing to lose, the senator gave dramatic expression to his view that the defense of the offshore islands was "not worth American blood." The larger question of the defense of Taiwan, if that became necessary, was left hanging.

Kennedy's hairbreath victory brought to Washington a new group of officials and advisers whose collective commitment to Free China was, to put it mildly, somewhat less than enthusiastic. But the American people were clearly unready for any drastic shift of policy. The brutal record of Mao's regime, as evidenced most graphically by the recent atrocities in Tibet, was still too fresh in the public consciousness. Moreover, the new President was perhaps still aware of what he had once said on the subject of the loss of mainland China to Communism. Early in 1949, as a young Congressman, he had spoken boldly and plainly on what had gone wrong in the Pacific at the end of World War II:

A sick Roosevelt . . . gave the Kurile Islands, as well as the control of various strategic ports . . . to the Soviet Union. . . . The responsibility for the failure of our foreign policy in the Far East rests squarely with the White House and Department of State. . . . What our young men had saved, our diplomats and our President have frittered away.[10]

Ten years of intense partisanship, however, had changed JFK's views on some related issues. After his inauguration in 1961, therefore, the policy of the past decade was certain to be subjected to reappraisal.

What the young President's advisers on foreign policy finally advanced was the naïve "Two China" solution. Under the chairmanship of J. William Fulbright, the Senate Foreign Relations Committee quietly commissioned a study, prepared by the private research firm of Conlon Associates, Ltd., of San Francisco, recommending a gradual shift in policy. The suggested shift would lead, on the one hand, to formal U.S. recognition of Communist China and support for the seating of Mao's delegate in the UN Security Council; and, on the other hand, to U.S. recognition of Taiwan as an "independent republic" and its seating in the UN General Assembly. But the current behavior of the Chinese Communists was so bad that no hints of such a shift in the official American position could be advertised. Yet the "new" China policy proclaimed by President Nixon in 1971 was clearly in the making during the first year of the Kennedy administration, for the United States government had begun to accept the "fact" of Chinese Communist "existence."

President Kennedy hoped to improve relations with the Chinese Communists through the use of friendly gestures, but he was a cautious man. According to a close adviser, he was dissatisfied with his failure to "break new ground" in China. He "began and remained . . . disturbed and baffled" by Peking's "instant and constant antagonism," and was appalled that the Chinese had "spewed unremitting vituperation" on him personally since his inauguration. The unkindest cut of all seems to have been Chairman Mao's remark that he was worse than Eisenhower. In mid-1962 the President told newsmen that he would certainly take "the action necessary" to assure the defense of Taiwan and the Pescadores, as provided for in the 1955 Formosa Resolution, if the Chinese Communists were to attempt any "aggressive action" against Quemoy or Matsu. "Any threat to the offshore islands," he now said, "must be judged in relation to its wider meaning for the safety of Formosa and the peace of the area."

President Kennedy was particularly aggravated by Chinese Communist efforts to associate themselves with the progress of American blacks in the field of civil rights. Chairman Mao had said: "I call upon

[10]*Congressional Record,* January 30, 1949.

162

the workers, peasants, revolutionary intellectuals, enlightened elements of the bourgeoisie and other enlightened personages of all colours in the world, white, black, yellow, brown, etc., to unite to oppose the racial discrimination." The President rightly concluded that any friendly initiative on his part would be regarded by the Chinese Communists as a reward for their aggressiveness. He was also concerned about how Congress and the people at large would react to any such move. He decided, therefore, to postpone a policy shift until his second term. Accordingly he sent the veteran globe-trotter W. Averill Harriman to New Delhi upon the outbreak of the Sino-Indian border war in November, 1962. Harriman's mission was to arrange military assistance to India.

One point on which the Kennedy administration was forced to make a change was the matter of the UN seat. Since 1951 the United States had been able to secure majorities in the General Assembly to block discussion of the perennial Soviet proposal to seat Mao's delegation. But the majority on this resolution had been dwindling over the years and was about to disappear in 1961. The President changed the American tactic, therefore, and abstained on the resolution to postpone discussion. The resolution finally failed, but the United States instead secured a favorable vote on its proposal to make Chinese representation an "important question" that would require a two-thirds vote of the General Assembly. The "important question" device was to be successful in excluding Mao's regime from the UN for another decade.

The assassination of the President in November, 1963, caused some amount of rejoicing in mainland China. A periodical carried a cartoon of a man sprawled on the ground with the caption "Kennedy Bites the Dust." But some State Department officials evidently thought the moment was ripe for a basic change of policy. A few weeks after the assassination the Assistant Secretary of State for Far Eastern Affairs, Roger Hilsman, delivered a remarkable speech at the Commonwealth Club in San Francisco. After commenting at length on how "unaware" Mao and his cohorts were of the "vital ideas which have moved civilization" and how they "comfortably clothe their own dictatorship in a cloak of doctrinal righteousness," Hilsman came finally to the point. American policy, he said, could no longer be predicated on the assumption that the Communist domination of the mainland was about to pass. Instead the United States must be prepared to coexist with Mao's mainland China while retaining, of course, its commitments to Chiang's "China on Taiwan." While this variation on the old theme of Two Chinas was acceptable to neither Peking nor Taipei, for naïve Americans the solution seemed ideal. According to Hilsman, the reality of the existence of the People's Republic could be recognized without sacrificing the Republic of China. Thus in late 1963 the State

Department took its first unmistakable step, however cautious, toward rapprochement with the Chinese Communists. It is no exaggeration to say that Hilsman's ambiguous speech was a milestone in the transformation of American policy toward China.

But the change would be very gradual. The succession of Lyndon B. Johnson to the presidency resulted in no immediate alteration of official policy. Deepening troubles in Indochina—together with Mao's flat rejection of President Johnson's suggestion that American scientists and other selected persons be permitted to visit the mainland—prevented much progress in the easing of tensions with the Communist regime. While Senator Goldwater's candidacy in 1964 raised many basic questions regarding future American military involvement in Asia, the challenger and the incumbent did not disagree publicly on the matter of the American commitment to the Republic of China. Yet in April of that year Secretary Rusk's visit to Taiwan produced a rather weak statement. Rusk neatly avoided any mention of the Republic of China as the only government legally representing the Chinese people. Instead he merely referred to U.S. treaty obligations and declared America's continuing opposition to handing over the UN seat of the Republic of China to the Chinese Communists. What he was saying between the lines was that the United States would not object to Chinese Communist admission into the United Nations as long as the Republic of China was not expelled. This attitude was unacceptable to the Republic of China, of course, and no joint communique was issued even though Rusk held three meetings with high-level Nationalist officials.

After his mandate at the polls in 1964, President Johnson began to drop some hints of a policy change. But the deepening American involvement in Vietnam effectively prevented the Chinese from making any direct response, especially after Soviet insinuations that Peking talked belligerently about Vietnam but was quite ready to negotiate with Washington. By 1966 the Chinese Communists were in the convulsion of their so-called Great Proletarian Cultural Revolution, and for the next year and more they had little time for international negotiation. All of Mao's ambassadors abroad, except Huang Hua in Cairo, were recalled for "re-education." Foreign Minister Chen Yi came under strong criticism from the Red Guards and eventually ceased to exercise his office. The most conspicuous aspect of Chinese foreign relations at this time was a succession of clashes, of varying degrees of severity, between the Red Guards and foreign diplomats in Peking. The worst incident was the sack of the British mission and the beating of its personnel in the summer of 1967.

Such incidents tended to postpone rapprochement. Early in 1966 William B. Bundy, Assistant Secretary of State for Far Eastern Affairs, delivered a telling speech at Pomona College:

These are samples of what we are up against. We are Peking's great enemy because our power is a crucial element in the total balance of power and in the resistance by Asian states to Chinese Communist expansionist designs in Asia. That is the really controlling fact, not sentiment, not whatever wrongs may have been done in the past, but that very simple fact and the very fundamental conflict between their aims and objectives and the kinds of aims that we have—above all, our support for the right of the nations of Asia to be free and independent and govern themselves according to their own wishes.[11]

But the war in Vietnam was not going well. An air of appeasement began to spread domestically and internationally, and gradually the Johnson administration began to look for practicable measures to improve relations with the Chinese Communists. As the "schism" between Red China and Soviet Russia became more apparent, the illusion again arose in the United States that Mao would imitate Tito of Yugoslavia in resisting the Russians.

Early in 1966, spurred on by such arguments, both the Senate and the House of Representatives conducted hearings on the China question. The Senate Foreign Relations Committee, under the chairmanship of J. William Fulbright of Arkansas, invited three well-known "experts" to testify. All three echoed the view that the proper American policy toward mainland China should require military *containment*, to be sure, but not diplomatic, cultural, or commercial *isolation*. Since those hearings the cry of "containment without isolation" has been a favorite slogan of the advocates of a "new" China policy.

Professor A. Doak Barnett of Columbia, the first witness before the Foreign Relations Committee, came on in quite subtle style. He advocated continued American military defense of Formosa while at the same time suggesting "self-determination" for the "13,000,000 inhabitants of Taiwan." The "myth" that the Kuomintang "regime" was the legitimate government of mainland China, he said, must be abandoned. It should be recognized as the legal government of only those areas over which it held effective control, *i.e.*, Taiwan and the Pescadores. Barnett was downright classic in his assertion of the Wilsonian principle of self-determination for the people of Taiwan, but he failed to extend its coverage to the people of the mainland.

Professor John K. Fairbank of Harvard advanced a second idea with perhaps even greater aplomb. After we stop isolating Peking, he said, "we may expect the Chinese revolution to mellow." Professor Fairbank's long and intimate acquaintance with Chinese thought permitted him to surmise that "it would not be illogical" for Mao's Communists to "adopt a somewhat milder policy."

The third "expert," Professor Hans Morgenthau of the University of

[11]For an assessment of this important speech, see Robert A. Hunter and Forrest Davis, *The New Red China Lobby* (Whittier, Calif.: Constructive Action, Inc., 1966), 6.

Chicago, went even further. We should terminate our policy of military containment, he said, as well as our policy of isolation. Advocating immediate and total withdrawal from Vietnam, he recommended that the U.S. policy of military containment of Communism in Asia ought to be gradually phased out. This policy, he said, was "not only irrelevant" to the interests of Americans but "actually runs counter to them."

Shortly after the hearings ended, one of the most prestigious names in the U.S. Senate—albeit one of the least experienced senators—was added to the list of those urging changes in China policy. In May of 1966 Senator Edward M. Kennedy of Massachusetts surfaced with a proposal for the creation of a special presidential commission to review the whole matter. His speech suggested that a softening of policy would be a "new direction." The inference was that this was desirable simply because it was "new." The time had come, he declared portentously, "for the American government and the American people to make a major reassessment of our policy toward China." Following Kennedy was his equally inexperienced friend from South Dakota, George McGovern, with a speech truly remarkable in its naïveté. Senator McGovern declared flatly that since the 1940's Mao Tse-tung's party had been dedicated to "throwing off outside control" so as to secure "a better life for the people." Further on in his speech McGovern argued that the Chinese Communists had a perfect right to resist "U.S. military power in Asia" and to establish "a Monroe Doctrine" that would provide them "the kind of role in Asia which we proclaimed for ourselves in the Western Hemisphere." Either he conveniently forgot that the Japanese had once asked for just such a right, or else the analogy meant nothing to him.

About this time—right in the midst of the "Cultural Revolution"— Secretary Rusk appeared before the Asian and Pacific subcommittee of the House Foreign Affairs Committee and made some odd observations. His statement comprised ten points. The first four mildly restated the old U.S. position while the remaining six demonstrated a perceptible softening of spirit toward the Chinese Communists. Emphasizing that the United States had no intention of trying to overthrow Mao's regime by military means, he declared that the Chinese Communists had achieved a "stable" political condition on the Asian mainland. They should therefore now disavow their old dictum that force was the best means of resolving disputes, and they should also renounce their strategic goal of violent world revolution. If Mao's regime would just do these things, he said, the American government would welcome the advent of friendly relations.

Secretary Rusk's expressed views at this time differed importantly from those of certain Democratic leaders in Congress, like Senators Kennedy and McGovern, who felt that the deep hostility and isolation of the Chinese Communists was largely a result of their frustration over American "acts of aggression." Rusk, on the other hand, seemed to be saying that the Chinese Communists themselves were responsible for their isolation. Improvement in Sino-American relations would not be difficult, Rusk thought, if Mao's people would only change their ways a little. Some of Rusk's critics in Congress condemned his attitude as a Dulles-like obstinacy which would prevent detente with Peking. To assuage a rift in party ranks, both Secretary of Defense McNamara and Vice President Humphrey now started to advocate "bridge-building" with the Chinese Communists in their speeches.

In June, 1966, the majority leader of the Senate, Mike Mansfield, boldly proposed the opening of ministerial-level talks with the Chinese Communists. On July 12 President Johnson indicated clearly what his future policy would be. It would be "firm but flexible." Acknowledging that his administration was anxious to reach a rapprochement, the President observed that cooperation rather than antagonism was the true course of action, but in the end he had to admit that every American overture to improve relations had been rejected by Peking.

A few months earlier the American ambassador to the United Nations, Arthur Goldberg, had said that if the Chinese Communists would accept "certain conditions" the United States would no longer oppose their admission. The "Two China" idea was spreading, and State Department spokesman Robert J. McClosky made no secret of the fact that the administration was working on a plan along these lines. At a Washington press conference on April 19, 1966, Goldberg set these four conditions: (1) that the Chinese Communists drop their demand that the Republic of China be expelled before they enter the United Nations; (2) that the Chinese Communists retract their demand that the United Nations formally apologize for aiding South Korea during the recent war; (3) that the Chinese Communists retract their demand for revision of the UN Charter; and (4) that the Chinese Communists abide by the UN Charter, especially in regard to renouncing the use of force over peaceful methods to resolve disputes. Then, in a speech before the General Assembly on September 22, Goldberg made the following points in answer to a question on the subject of the China seat:

> The American policy does not aim at isolating the Chinese Communists from the rest of the world. . . . the United States is staunchly opposed to efforts at expelling Republic of China delegates to the United Nations. . . . The United States has historical bonds of friendship with the great Chinese people, and hopes that they will become a part of rather than a threat to the world body, practicing forbearance under the spirit of the UN Charter and coexisting peacefully with their neighbors.[12]

[12]Kuan Chung, *A Review of U.S.– China Policy;* (1949– 1971), pp. 63–64.

These statements met with resentment from all quarters in the Republic of China. A flurry of telegrams to Washington lodged strong protests and sternly repudiated such overtures on the part of American officials. On May 18 thirty-four members of the Legislative Yuan in Taipei sent a letter of protest to the U.S. Congress, and two weeks later sixty-four members of the Control Yuan took the same action. No less than sixty-five civic organizations, including colleges and universities, joined in a letter to President Johnson declaring that appeasement would lead to disaster. Most representative, however, was an "Open Letter to the American People" signed by more than 1,500 Chinese scholars and professional men. Published as an advertisement in various American newspapers, it refuted one by one the recent conciliatory statements of American officials. The scholars declared that Mao Tse-tung's "Thought" was in no sense "a manifestation of China nationalism," and that the Peking regime did not hold effective control over the mainland population. The idea of "encirclement but not isolation" was a contradiction, they insisted, for isolation must always result from encirclement. What guarantees existed, they asked, for "peaceful evolution" on the mainland in the next generation?

Secretary of State Dean Rusk made two hurried visits to Taiwan during the second half of 1966 to explain the American position to the Taipei government. Ironically, the so-called Cultural Revolution was then raging on the mainland, and many leaders in Taiwan felt that an excellent, and unprecedented, opportunity was at hand. The restrictions in the Mutual Defense Treaty had cost the Republic of China two earlier opportunities to counterattack the mainland—the first during Mao's abortive "Hundred Flower" movement in 1957-58, the second during the "May exodus" of refugees in 1962. But this third opportunity was perhaps the best. An editorial in the Hong Kong *Commercial Daily News* on June 28, 1966, declared: "It's time to revise the Mutual Defense Treaty." But Secretary Rusk, who visited Taiwan the next week, evidently did not think so.

When in January of 1967 the Chinese ambassador to the United States, Chow Shu-kai, said in a press conference that this might be "a decisive year for the Republic of China to recover the mainland," his statement was sharply refuted by the State Department. Spokesman McClosky quickly pointed out that the Mutual Defense Treaty prohibited the Republic of China from taking any offensive action against the mainland without first receiving the approval of the United States. Declaring that the State Department was not aware of any counterattack plan of the Republic of China, McClosky took pains to mention the 1954 "exchange of notes" between Secretary Dulles and Ambassador Yeh. Ambassador Chow answered in a television interview on January 13, 1967, that the present situation on the mainland was "totally different" from that which existed when the Mutual Defense Treaty was signed a dozen years earlier. Chow hinted broadly that the United States, as an old ally of the Republic of China, should not now be quoting the treaty in this negative and discouraging way.

In a subsequent letter to the *New York Times* in answer to an unfriendly editorial, Ambassador Chow insisted that the issue of mainland recovery was an "internal" Chinese affair that could not possibly be surrendered to the interference of "foreign opposition." News of the success of the Chinese Communist atomic tests in October of 1964, as well as the first tie vote in the United Nations on Chinese Communist admission, was providing new fuel for the idea of "normalization" of relations with Red China and acceptance of Mao's regime as "a member of international society." Officials of the Republic of China, Chow wrote, had good reason to be extremely displeased with the negative attitude of the American government. They were not requesting the United States to become directly involved militarily in a civil war in China; all they wanted was for the United States to remember its pledge to support their government "spiritually and morally" as the legal representative of the Chinese people. Was the United States now really considering the vital interests of its ally? Were Washington officials considering the position and viewpoint of Taipei? Mainland recovery was, after all, the fundamental national policy of the Republic of China, and the very basis upon which the Taiwan government existed. That policy was well known throughout the world. Now, however, Washington was suggesting that a "Two China" solution was in its own interests, and adding that the Republic of China could not "interfere" in those interests. How then, Chow asked, could the United States justly quote the language of the Mutual Defense Treaty in a blatantly selfish gesture of contempt for a faithful ally? It was more than the Confucian Chinese were able to grasp.

Ambassador Chow explained the thinking of President Chiang Kaishek by way of a graphic analogy. If Communism should suddenly sweep over the American mainland and the Washington government were forced to establish its headquarters in Hawaii, what attitude would its officials entertain? Would they not actively plan for the day that the invaders would be driven out of power on the mainland? Would not the Americans long for their old homes, their friends, and their enslaved compatriots on the mainland—or would they be content with a status quo in which Hawaii was the only free piece of American soil? What would they do? Without a doubt, said Chow, they would assert their sacred right to return to their home shores and wrest back their legal property. "This," he concluded, "is exactly how the Chinese people feel at the present time."

The ambassador made a telling point. The Communist victory in

China was not a victory of, by, or for Maoist ideology. It was achieved instead by the skillful use of well-equipped armies and by the marvelous propaganda of big lies and bigger promises. In 1945 the Communists were the "outs" capitalizing on conditions which, after the Japanese, they themselves had helped create. Over the next four years Mao's cadres worked ceaselessly to convince the Chinese masses that such adverse conditions were all the fault of the Nationalists. They promised to replace the "corrupt" and "incompetent" government of the Kuomintang with a system of, by, and for the peasants and coolies. Millions of Chinese—impoverished and frustrated by two decades of warfare, yearning for peace, discouraged and demoralized by the discontinuance of American moral and material support to the National government, and noting the success of the Soviet-supported Communist armies, were taken in by that seductive line.

As the American humorist Will Rogers, used to say, "Communism is like Prohibition; it's a nice idea, but it won't work." Two decades ago, as his cadres extended their control over the cities and villages of mainland China, Chairman Mao was masquerading before the Chinese people as a kind of magical master chef. He was supposed to have in his hat, or somewhere in his apron, the best recipes for the intellectual, political, and economic diet of the whole country. If the proof of the pudding is in the eating, as the English say, then Chairman Mao has proven himself a poor chef indeed. After more than twenty years in control of a barren kitchen, he still cannot cook for the people of China. Thousands flee from his sorry table every year, and countless others try unsuccessfully to get away. The reason that he has failed as China's chef is that the Chinese people are proudly individualistic, and Mao's cupboard of spices contains no dash of freedom.

Mao's siren song to the intellectuals is more seductive than ever as it echoes around the radicalized world today, and the outpouring of party-line propaganda from Peking is as steady and abundant as ever. But inside China, where Mao has been free to experiment with his recipes for more than a generation, his promises to the people are still nothing more than pie-in-the-sky. As long ago as 1957 some of his own cadres were beginning to complain about the thin diet, and Mao responded to that early disillusionment with the deceptive and devastating "Hundred Flowers" campaign. Then in rapid succession came his backyard furnaces, his people's communes, his so-called "Great Leap Forward," his destruction of the family unit, his distribution of the land to the peasants, and then the repossession of that land by the regime.

As each program failed in turn, the disillusionment spread and deepened, and the Chinese people reacted with the only protest possible under Mao's system of political enslavement. This was the silent protest of peasants refusing to work, and it brought on three years which caused great suffering among the voiceless masses but also shook the regime to its bottom.

In desperation, Chairman Mao went again to his cupboard of political stratagems, and came up this time with a new recipe grandiosely labelled the "Great Proletarian Cultural Revolution." Launched in 1966 under Mao's personal guidance, it was entrusted to the one group left in China still naïve enough and immature enough to swallow Mao's paper recipes, that new generation of student radicals calling themselves the "Red Guards." Born and bred under Maoism, these deluded boys and girls knew nothing better and in fact nothing else, for they had been schooled to follow the leader with a blind faith reminiscent of the Hitler Youth of Germany in the 1930s.

The ostensible purpose of the Red Guard movement was to declare unremitting ideological war on Western imperialism in all its forms, on Soviet "revisionism" of the original teachings of Marx and Lenin, and on the four so-called "olds" of Chinese life—Old Thought, Old Culture, Old Customs, and Old Habits. The actual purpose, of course, was chiefly diversionary, *i.e.*, to turn the attention of China's urban and rural masses away from their daily misery and away from the insurmountable practical problems of economic survival under Mao's oppressive, unproductive system.

That, put simply, is the record to date of what the Chinese Communists have done, or tried to do, since their usurpation of the mainland in 1949. It has been all recipe and no repast, all kitchen blundering and no banquet. By their deeds, not their words, we now know them. "Communist China," writes the famous globetrotting novelist James Michener, "is the most frozen-faced society I have ever seen. I met no one who greeted me voluntarily with a smile and only a few who would smile back if I tried to break the ice."

The best tool of the Chinese Communists has always been their high mastery of the art of disguise. By carefully concealing their aggressive tendencies on their way up to power, they succeeded in deluding not only many leading Chinese intellectuals but some important foreigners as well. Once in power, however, they soon dropped the facade and consolidated their gains by the mere expedient of establishing a police state. But the Chinese masses were not long deceived. Traditionally conservative and wise in the teachings of Confucius, they could not reconcile Mao's atheistic materialism with their own ancient cultural concepts of filial piety, parental love, and individual morality and dignity. They have endured the Communist regime for more than two decades only because they have had no means of confronting the Red Army, which upholds the regime with its millions of rifles.

One of Mao Tse-tung's most quoted sayings is that political power grows out of gun barrels. It is important to remember, and to repeat, that he got most of his guns in the first place from the Japanese. These were the Japanese weapons obtained through Russian generosity in 1945 when the U.S. government made the incredible mistake of permitting the Soviet Union to accept the surrender of Hirohito's armies in Manchuria. Without those guns to back up their rhetoric today, the Chinese Communist leaders would soon be talking to themselves in the fraudulently named "Great Hall of the People" at Peking. Fear fills the Communist halls today, as it has for a long time, but no form of intimidation can force the Chinese people finally to forsake Confucius and open their ears willingly to the godless arrogance of Mao's cadres. If history has any meaning at all, the cultural heritage of Confucianism will never be destroyed in China. On the contrary, that which confronts Confucianism head on—as Chinese Communism must do if it is to remain consistent with Mao's teachings—will eventually destroy itself.

The fact that the so-called "People's Republic" of Chairman.Mao was somehow very un-Chinese, as well as anti-Christian and anti-Western, was seen quite clearly by many informed Americans in 1949. While few Americans at that time were as yet deeply suspicious of the Chinese Communists as possible aggressors on an international scale, most of the thinking citizens of the United States had a feeling that the old Confucianism was dovetailing pretty well with Western and Christian concepts in the emerging Republic of China founded by Sun Yat-sen and led since his death by Chiang Kai-shek. For almost a quarter of a century it had been Chiang Kai-shek who represented China to the world. The retreat of President Chiang's Nationalists to the province of Taiwan was viewed generally with dismay, therefore, by Americans to whom the name of Mao Tse-tung then meant nothing at all. Moreover, when the Nationalists left the mainland for Taiwan, an extraordinary collection of art objects came with the retreating forces. Paintings, porcelain, bronzes, enamelware, carved jade—all the unique styles and media of a great civilization's esthetic flowering—are represented in such profusion at Taipei that the National Palace Museum, which houses the collections, must continually rotate exhibits to reveal its dimensions. How substantial a part of the total Chinese artistic heritage these masterpieces of the National Palace Museum represent remains, of course, uncertain. But it is safe to surmise that more of China's heritage of art is to be seen today in Taipei than in Peking.

Some American diplomats predicted in 1949 that Taiwan would be lost to the Communists within six months at the most. Now, a quarter of a century later and despite the recent diplomatic setbacks, the government on Taiwan is still on a solid footing, still undaunted, still looking to an ever brighter future. "Valience, resiliency, determination and conviction shown by the Republic of China . . . is without parallel," said Walter P. McConaughy, the American ambassador at Taipei, before a dinner meeting of the Sino-American Cultural Society in Washington in September, 1972. The American envoy spoke highly of President Chiang who, at the age of 85, "retains his moral fortitude, vigor and sensitivity." The ambassador expressed unreserved admiration for the "dignity and grace" with which President Chiang has borne the weight of the years.

The foreign trade of the Republic of China passed the $5 billion mark in 1972. According to some predictions, the Taiwan trade may move out ahead of the Chinese Communists' total volume of commerce by 1975. An island of less than 14,000 square miles and 15.5 million people will be out-trading a subcontinent of 3,700,000 square miles and some 725 million people. No less an authority than Ambassador McConaughy has predicted that Taiwan's trade advantage over the mainland will reach $1 billion within the next two years. Moreover, Taiwan is no longer receiving American economic aid. All economic assistance to the Republic of China was phased out in 1965. Moreover, the Republic of China now finances ninety-six percent of its annual military expenditure.

The miracle of Taiwan has not been wrought in a day. It has been in the making since those dark days of 1949 when the Communists usurped the mainland and the Free Chinese began transforming their island province into a bastion for its recovery. What Taiwan has over the mainland, of course, is the element of private enterprise. The Ford Motor Company late in 1972 announced its decision to invest $40 million in a production plant in Taiwan. The island is not rich in natural resources. It has, for example, scarcely any discovered and exploited petroleum, while the mainland now claims self-sufficiency in crude oil. Taiwan's coal seams are running out and the potential for additions to hydroelectric power is small. What Taiwan has in plenty, however, is entrepreneurship encouraged by a responsive government. Entrepreneurs are motivated by the expectation of a fair and legitimate profit. Workers are motivated by a rising standard of living and, in many cases, by the attainable hope of themselves becoming entrepreneurs.

In the twelve years between 1958 and 1970, according to data reported by the Chinese Communists themselves, the national income on the mainland grew at an annual rate of just 1.12 percent. Taiwan's annual growth rate of 9.32 percent has been eight times larger. According to research by experts, the per capita income on the mainland during this period could have been only a little more than $90 at the highest, which was less then a third that of Taiwan, and it may have been as low as $60, which is not even comparable with the Taiwan level. When a contrast is made between the living standard on the mainland today against that of Taiwan in terms of food, clothing, housing, travel, education and entertainment, the figures become ludicrous. For example, according to the experts, the average daily calorie intake for Taiwan is 2,680 and protein consumption 69.2 grams while respective figures for the mainland are 1,780 and 30 grams. Taiwan's annual per capita consumption of cotton fabrics is about 7.8 pounds, synthetic fibres 10 pounds, and woolen fabrics 1.2 pounds, on the mainland the figure for cotton is only 1.7 pounds. Annual per capita electricity consumption in Taiwan is 216 KWH, that on the mainland is a mere 13 KWH. For every thousand persons Taiwan has 139 bicycles, 49 motorcycles and 9 automobiles. For every thousand on the mainland there are 20 bicycles, 0.3 motorcycles and 0.8 autos. In Taiwan 98.5 percent of school-aged children are receiving a primary education, and of these about 80 percent are continuing into high school and 70 percent are going on to universities and colleges. On the mainland corresponding percentages are 78, 50, and 20. In terms of medical care and facilities, Taiwan has a hospital or clinic for every 13,000 persons compared with one for every 110,000 on the mainland. In Taiwan there are 210 radio and 53 television sets for every thousand persons. On the mainland the figure for radios is only 0.5 sets, and there is no TV at all except at designated public locations.

From the above statistics one can readily judge the wide gap between living conditions in the Taiwan cities and countryside and those on the mainland. This is a record of which all Americans, once they understand it adequately, may be tremendously proud, for the United States alone has had the wisdom and courage to distinguish consistently between freedom and slavery in the Far East. The Chinese mainland is virtually a closed economy. Open economies cannot sell goods in such a closed market except upon the humiliating terms of Mao Tse-tung's go-between. There can be no hope of reasonable profits, therefore, as long as the puppet masters of Peking are able to rig every transaction to their own narrow advantage and gain. American businessmen who are now expecting early, easy profits from the anticipated "thaw" in Washington-Peking relations should heed the words of C.W. Robinson, president of the Marcona Corporation, who has had long experience in Far Eastern ventures. "In new trade with the Peiping regime," he says, "we may have to learn to crawl before we can walk—and we may have to do a lot of crawling." The primary need of the Chinese Communists is for machine tools, and electronic equipment, and in general, what will help them to produce tanks, trucks, planes, ammunition, and other military items. The *Wall Street Journal* has predicted that the mainland will prove to be "more a mirage than a market," and the *London Observer* recently stressed that "the masses of the people on the mainland have neither the means nor the freedom to buy imported goods."

The contrast between the Republic of China on Taiwan and the People's Republic on the mainland is stark, arresting, and vivid. Regardless of how the prism is turned, the contrast is there. It was sharp two decades ago, and it has become sharper with each passing year. When President Johnson left office in January of 1969, the contrast between Taiwan and the mainland was perhaps more dramatic in every aspect than at any previous time. The reasons for this marked difference between the two Chinese societies can be reduced to the single issue of individual human dignity. On Taiwan, the Chinese individual possesses all the dignity of his ancestors. On the mainland he is under constant and massive pressure to surrender it to the State. For more than two decades the United States government gave official recognition to this difference, and the American people generally understood it. The difference remains, but the American response is presently inconstant and the future uncertain.

6

The Second Reversal
[1969-1971]

FOR ALL PRACTICAL purposes, the China policy of the United States remained officially unchanged while Lyndon Johnson was in the White House. The highly visible role of the Chinese Communists in the Vietnam War was the compelling reason, of course, why it could not then be changed. It was too glaringly evident that Peking was deeply involved in the war by proxy, supplying not only material but military advisers and engineers to bolster Hanoi against the increasing numbers of American troops sent to Indochina by the Johnson administration. Because of Mao Tse-tung's sustained support of North Vietnam, any policy alteration on the China question had to be held in abeyance until after the 1968 election.

Surprisingly little was said about China in the campaign that brought Richard M. Nixon to the Presidency. With the coming of a veteran anti-Communist to the White House, the prospect of a change in Sino-American policy seemed more remote than ever. Yet just a few weeks after he assumed office, President Nixon requested his special adviser on national security, Dr. Henry Kissinger, to prepare a policy paper on the China question. It was at the very outset of the Nixon administration, therefore, that the machinery was set into motion for perhaps the most momentous shift of policy in the diplomatic history of the United States.

Dr. Kissinger quickly proved unique as a Presidential adviser. A man of unusual and conspicuous intellect, he enjoyed tremendous sway in the White House from the start. According to *U.S. News & World Report,* he spent more time in the President's office than any other member of the official family. The same magazine quoted a White House staffer: "Kissinger briefs the President every morning, and they generally talk things over at the end of the day. On a typical working day, they may also confer half a dozen other times. Kissinger . . . [has] instant access to the President at any hour of the day or night." So it was. Every piece of information from the State and Defense departments and the Central Intelligence Agency was scrutinized by Dr. Kissinger before it went to the President. In the December 1969 issue of *Atlantic* this clue is found as to how Kissinger looked at his job:

> One of his oldest and most intimate friends at Harvard says there has never been a shadow of doubt that Kissinger went to the White House in the hope of playing a Bismarck to Kaiser Nixon. He would certainly be a disappointed man if he failed to leave his own imprint. He is the insepa-rable adviser, confidant, counselor, apologist, and spokesman for the President. The two men are constantly in each other's company: Kissinger is at his side for all important meetings and on all foreign journeys. He rents (partly at his own cost) the nearest villa to the Western White House at San Clemente, and at moments of major decision (how to retaliate when the North Koreans shot down an American spy plane, when and whether to announce the next withdrawl from Vietnam), the two men are often closeted alone together for hours on end. . . . And Kissinger is not the man to waste time as the servant of a constitutional monarch.[1]

Kissinger, a refugee from Nazi persecution in Germany, clearly relished a role he never dreamed of as a soccer-playing youngster in his native Bavaria. Brought to New York at the age of fifteen by his Jewish parents when they fled from Europe in 1938, he finished high school and enrolled in the City College of New York with the intention of becoming an accountant. After non-commissioned service in the Army during World War II, he headed for Harvard in 1946 and earned his three degrees in the next eight years. A brilliant student, he was able to stay on at Harvard to teach as a specialist in foreign affairs.

It was directly on the advice of Governor Nelson Rockefeller, who described Kissinger as "the smartest guy available," that President Nixon attached him to the White House staff as special adviser on national security affairs. Kissinger's appointment, the first one the President made to a major policy-making position, won wide praise from the halls of academe. An ultraliberal Harvard colleague, Professor Adam Yarmolinsky, who himself spent six years at the Pentagon under Presidents Kennedy and Johnson, is reputed to have said: "We'll all sleep a little better each night knowing that Henry is down there." One liberal scholar who viewed Nixon's choice with outright mis-giving, however, was Ralph Lapp. The famous nuclear scientist, who

[1]*Atlantic,* December, 1969, 78.

has often been at odds with the nation's scientific establishment for overinvolvement with the military, declared Kissinger to be an unreconstructed hard-liner. Lapp's statement was a smokescreen, for Kissinger's written words do not indicate this. The President doubtless was familiar with *Nuclear Weapons and Foreign Policy,* a small book published in 1957 which established Kissinger as a sort of international authority on the application of military power in the modern world. In it he argued against the Dulles doctrine of "massive retaliation" and in favor of what he called "flexible response."

In his perceptive volume, *Kissinger: The Uses of Power,* David Landau described Dr. Kissinger's spoken words as "deep, authoritative, deliberate, whimsical yet profound." His personal style was further revealed in an interview in the *Washington Star* on November 19, 1972. The article explains that he likes to make his own decisions and do things alone, and that the power of his conviction is an essential ingredient of his success. "I am always convinced that I must do what I am doing," he was quoted as saying. "And people believe it. They feel it. It is important to me that people believe me. . . . I do not look for popularity. I do not ask for popularity. If I would let myself be bothered by people's reaction . . . I would not be able to do anything." Kissinger acknowledged that "when one holds power in one's hand, and when one holds it formally for quite a long time, you get used to considering it as something you are entitled to have." But, he added, "Power as a self-conceited medium does not have the slightest attraction to me. I don't wake up every morning with the thought of, by the way, isn't it fantastic to have at my disposal a plane, a car with a driver waiting for me at the door? What I am interested in is what you can do with power. You can make marvelous things with it, believe me. . . ."

Dr. Kissinger was not well known to President Nixon at the time of his appointment. They are said to have met in passing at a cocktail party in 1968 while Kissinger was acting as foreign-policy adviser to Governor Rockefeller of New York, who was then contesting Mr. Nixon for the Republican presidential nomination. "If you should go through my past political life," Kissinger told an interviewer with characteristic absence of modesty, "you wouldn't imagine that President Nixon could fit in with my plans." He admitted having opposed Nixon in three political campaigns, but added that the President showed "a great vigor, a great ability" in choosing him. According to Charles Ashman in a recent book, "Kissinger was hired out to Nelson Rockefeller in 1968 to gun down Nixon for the presidential nomination." Mr. Ashman adds:

It is ironic that, when Rockefeller announced his candidacy for the Republican nomination, he gave a speech knocking Nixon's 'lack of understanding of the public's criticism of the Vietnam war.' Buried in the press reports of Rockefeller's announcement of May 3, 1968, when he talked about the Vietnam war and domestic problems, was a suggestion that the president of the United States should visit Red China. This idea had come from one of his new foreign affairs advisers . . . none other than Henry Kissinger.[2]

Kissinger was also an unabashed admirer of the late Senator Robert F. Kennedy. His friends say that he would have been happy to serve Bobby Kennedy if the New York Senator had gone on to become President.

Favoring a new balance-of-power instead of containment, Dr. Kissinger took occasion to assail Secretary Rusk's "domino" theory during the last days of the Johnson administration. His views were clearly expressed in a revealing article he published in December of 1968. The incoming administration, he wrote, must realize that the United States can no longer carry out the old policy of containment on a worldwide scale. It can only encourage other nations, including the Communist states, to join together in establishing a system of global security. Containment made necessary the direct involvement of the United States, as in Vietnam; with the new balance-of-power, the United States could remain on the sidelines but still have a voice in the signal-calling.

The concepts advocated by Dr. Kissinger, and pursued since 1969 by President Nixon, are intriguing to observe in action. These concepts are yet more interesting in light of the fact that all earlier ideas have been either openly disavowed or quietly reversed. During the Truman years the prevailing idea of the makers of American foreign policy was to obtain collective security against Communism by reconstructing the devastated areas of Europe along democratic lines and by bolstering America's allies in Asia. In the Eisenhower administration, and directly as a result of the Korean experience, Secretary Dulles stressed instead the concept of containment—the idea of keeping Communism confined within its current boundaries—even though an ideological schism was then developing in the Communist camp. During the Kennedy and Johnson administrations the policy of containment was continued and ultimately tested in Vietnam. For fully a quarter of a century, therefore, the foreign policy of the United States was rooted in the reality of a "cold war" between what Americans called the Free World on the one hand and the Communist Bloc on the other. The Kissinger-Nixon departure is rooted in the notion that the "cold war" has ceased to exist.

Dr. Kissinger's overall view of the new American destiny was neatly outlined in a major speech at Princeton University early in 1969. Here

[2]Charles Ashman, *Kissinger: The Adventures of Super Kraut* (New York: Dell Publishing Co., 1972), 90.

179

he stressed that the guiding principle of American policy in the years ahead should be preventive, *i.e.,* to avert the outbreak of a sudden crisis, not merely to take appropriate action after a crisis has occurred. The United States, he said, could no longer chart the entire course for a rapidly changing world. It could only encourage other nations to follow a good example. While in a material sense the United States was a superpower, yet its foreign policy would be meaningful only when other nations could be brought to cooperate willingly in reducing tensions. The new administration, he added, must realize that as long as the American people lacked a clear understanding of the changing modern world, a stable world was unattainable.

On the other hand, Dr. Kissinger pointed out, the Chinese Communists might now wish to utilize the United States to protect their own security. To counter the threat of the forty Russian divisions deployed along their borders, they might turn in desperation to the West. Their industry had suffered a great setback during the chaos of the Cultural Revolution, and in his opinion they now were hoping for American technology and material aid to improve the situation. Conversely, the United States might anticipate large wheat sales to mainland China and hope for Peking's help in ending the Vietnam war.

Most important, according to Dr. Kissinger, was an understanding that a nation's foreign policy was itself the real goal while technique was only secondary. For the United States to continue to take upon itself all the responsibilities of the free world would be eventually to exhaust all America's psychological resources, and these he considered the major weapons in present-day foreign relations. It was safer, he thought, to "analyze" the sabre-rattling and boasting of certain governments than to view such bombast automatically as a threat to U.S. security. No third nation would be able to catch up militarily with the United States and Russia for at least ten years, and moreover it should be realized that the strong military posture of a nation does not automatically endow it with political influence. The embarrassing position in which the United States now found itself, he said, was basically due to the absence of a masterplan for solving its own domestic problems. A global revolution, he thought, was taking place in the value of all things and in all structural organizations of man. The future would be built upon a balance of ideas rather than upon a physical balance of power alone. The military strength of the United States and the Soviet Union might be enormous, but such power would be difficult to transform into political influence should these nations continue to confront each other in the international arena. America's old allies were vacillating, he said, and the newly emergent nations were proceeding along independent and nationalistic lines leading directly to more global instability. The challenge to

American foreign policy during the next decade, therefore, would be more philosophical than military in nature, and this required Americans to develop a new concept of world order.

Dr. Kissinger did not think that diplomacy should be restricted in any way by so-called international obligations or laws. He simply did not believe in "philanthropy" in foreign affairs. Like Prince Metternich, on whom he wrote his doctoral dissertation, he tended to regard all nations except his own as enemies. His goal was simply a new balance of power involving both the Russians and the Chinese Communists. Whereas Japan and Southeast Asia could balance the Chinese aspirations in the East, West Germany and Western Europe could balance Russian designs in the West. Since border negotiations between the Chinese and the Russians had made no substantial progress, there was bound to be continued armed confrontation between the two Communist powers, and the United States should take advantage of this, using the Russian military superiority along the Sino-Soviet frontier to tip the scales for its own benefit. Implicit in Dr. Kissinger's plan was the maintenance of some degree of power balance in Asia as the United States gradually withdrew its commitments under the Nixon Doctrine. To offset the possibility that the Russians might fill the vacuum, Japan might want to become a nuclear power overnight. To avoid this, it was necessary to ease the tension between mainland China and Japan.

The above are Dr. Kissinger's basic ideas as he outlined them early in 1969. What may be said of his grand strategy for global peace? It is commonplace to think of the United States, Russia, and mainland China as forming a power triangle in the world today. It is not quite proper to think of the three sides of the triangle as perfectly equal. It can be argued, of course, that a lasting balance of power is possible with the United States at the apex of the triangle and thereby playing the role of a flexible referee. But the advocates of the "three-legged stool" seemingly overestimate the military power and internal stability of the Chinese Communists. Many things may happen on the mainland with the passing of Chairman Mao. Secretary of State Rogers said in 1970 that the United States had no intention of stirring up trouble between the Russians and the mainland Chinese. He did not say that the United States had no intention of utilizing the present confrontation between Moscow and Peking. To make proper use of this confrontation is apparently the primary objective of Dr. Kissinger's overtures toward a *detente* with Mao's regime.

It has often been suggested that Dr. Kissinger, as a keen student of 19th-century European politics, regards himself quite seriously as a modern Prince Metternich in search of an equalitarian structured world. Metternich's concept of power balances was a guiding principle among 19th-century diplomats. But the political systems of the last century and the present one are obviously quite different. Regardless of whether enmity existed between France and the German states, or between France and Tsarist Russia, the real difference then was between the two political systems of democracy and monarchy. Today the difference is between totalitarian Communism and non-totalitarian regimes, with Communism itself apparently split by divisions between Russian and Chinese centers of power. In Metternich's world there were no permanent friends or enemies; all parts were interchangeable. If Dr. Kissinger's balance of power is indeed a modern imitation of Metternich's theory, then the United States should forsake all its security alliances and start treating erstwhile foes as friends and vice versa. But if Prince Metternich's ideas seem somehow inapplicable in the modern world, it is precisely because Communism as an international movement did not exist in his world.

In January, 1970, the *Washington Post* editorialized on the relative positions of the Soviet Union and mainland China. "A balance of power such as that existing between Russia and the Chinese Communists," the newspaper declared, "is rarely seen in history. Soviet Russia is of course a more technologically advanced country, and it is impossible to imagine that the Chinese Communists could come marching up to the gates of Moscow. On the contrary, the huge population controlled by the Chinese Communists and the vast numbers which they could mobilize, along with a widespread distribution of human and material resources, would cause Russia to become bogged down if it ever tried to occupy the Chinese mainland." Accepting such an argument, advocates of Dr. Kissinger's new balance of power are wont to predict that the tense Sino-Russian border situation will continue indefinitely in stalemate, thereby encouraging the rise of peaceful co-existence between Communism and capitalism.

Many Americans had trusted or hoped that President Nixon would finally reverse what they considered a suicidal trend toward appeasement of Communism. But by welcoming the Red Chinese into the United Nations—which his four predecessors had steadfastly refused to do—Richard M. Nixon set a new record for political inconsistency. In 1950, while running for the Senate, he asserted that "our own security" required a firm support of Taiwan "to stop the Communists from moving further in the Far East." Later that year he said: "All that we have to do is take a look at the map and we can see that if Taiwan falls the next frontier is the coast of California." In 1951 he described as "the greatest error" the inclination of Washington policymakers to accept advice from those "experts" who had reached "the false conclusion that Chinese Communists were somehow different from other Communists, that Chinese Communists were 'agrarian reformers and liberals'." Secretary Acheson, he said, was the head of a "cowardly college of Communist containment." Then, as the Republican candidate for the Vice Presidency in 1952, he assured his audiences that the Republicans would carry out "a thoroughgoing house cleaning of Communists and fellow travelers in the administrative branch of the government."

In his own campaign in 1960 Mr. Nixon's attitude on Communist China was still uncompromising. "I have been asked sometimes," he said at Fordham University in October, "wouldn't it be a small price to pay for peace to give Mao Tse-tung his way on Formosa? And my answer to this is . . . anybody who even suggests that this kind of argument would lead to peace doesn't read history. . . . When you deal with a dictator and make concessions that he doesn't deserve, whenever you appease him, you don't serve the cause of peace. You serve the cause of surrender." Later, speaking at the Fair Grounds in Tulsa, he hit it again: "And I can tell you today that I know, that when you're dealing with a man like Mr. Mao Tse-tung, the dictator of Communist China, or any one of the Communist leaders in the world, they have only one objective . . . and that is to conquer the world. . . . They will use any means. . . . If America is to retain its freedom—but, more than that, if we're going to keep peace—we must recognize these men for what they are and develop our policies accordingly, and these are the things we must do, and these are the things we will do."

Both General Eisenhower and Mr. Nixon took pains to notify John F. Kennedy, following his hairbreath victory, that while they would try to support him on foreign policy questions they would be obliged to speak out in opposition should he make any move toward diplomatic recognition or UN membership for Peking. Indeed, reporting on this in his book, *Six Crises*, Nixon takes pride in his part in preventing the new President's left-wing advisers from moving him toward accommodation of the Chinese Communists:

> I then brought up an issue on which I told him I had particularly strong views—the recognition of Red China and its admission to the UN. . . .
>
> In expressing my strong opposition to this policy, I pointed out that . . . what was really at stake was that admitting Red China to the United Nations would be a mockery of the provision of the Charter which limits its membership to "peace-loving" nations and what was disturbing was that it would give respectability to the Communist regime which would immensely increase its power and prestige in Asia, and probably irreparably weaken the non-Communist governments in that area.[3]

In a television debate with Kennedy on October 13, 1960, Mr. Nixon had defined the ambitions of the Chinese Communists as

[3]Richard M. Nixon, *Six Crises* (New York: Doubleday, 1962) 408-409.

global. "They don't just want Quemoy and Matsu," he said, "they don't just want Formosa. They want the world." Later statements by Mr. Nixon were these: "Appeasement is not safety, but suicide. . . . Our actions must always be based on what is right for the United States and the cause of freedom, not on the anticipated reaction of world opinion."[4] "We must understand that the Communist threat is world-wide, and if Communism takes over in one country the tremors are felt clear around the world. . . . And the eventual target is the United States."[5]

His stand, unequivocally expressed during a visit to Thailand in 1965, was that the only correct American attitude toward Peking was the hard-line. "I for one," he said, "would strongly oppose any change in that position in the future." Were he president, he would use the U.S. veto if necessary to keep Red China out of the United Nations.

From such remarks it can be seen that there was no evident weakening of Mr. Nixon's stance on the China question prior to 1966. But by the end of the next year he was exhibiting some new perspectives. In an article in *Foreign Affairs* in October, 1967, he wrote: "Taking the long view, we simply cannot afford to leave China forever outside the family of nations, there to nurture its fantasies, cherish its hates, and threaten its neighbors. There is no place on this small planet for a billion of its potentially most able people to live in angry isolation." This change of attitude had not come overnight. The deepening American military involvement in Southeast Asia doubtless was a factor, as was Mr. Nixon's realization that he might have a good chance for a political comeback in the presidential sweepstakes of 1968. His changing view developed slowly as he went along, possibly in some ways he had not himself expected. He was still thinking largely in terms of the continuing containment of Chinese Communism by the application of American military and economic powers. Whoever was elected president in 1968, he felt, ought to study how to "develop the power around the perimeter of China which will convince the Communist Chinese leaders that they will not gain—as a matter of fact that they will run very great risks—in the event that they attempt to expand through the area of the Pacific." Then, in a major foreign policy speech in 1968, Nixon the Republican candidate declared:

Any American policy toward Asia must come urgently to grips with the reality of China. This does not mean, as many would simplistically have it, rushing to grant recognition to Peiping, to admit it to the United Nations and to ply it with offers of trade—all of which would confirm its

[4]*Los Angeles Times,* April 6, 1962.
[5]*Reader's Digest,* November, 1964.

184

rulers in their present course. . . . Instead this means a policy of firm restraint, of a creative counter-pressure, designed to persuade Peiping that its interests can be served only by accepting the basic rules of international civility.[6]

It may be mere coincidence, therefore, that President Nixon's new China policy was remarkably akin to recommendations contained in a paper prepared just after the election by a team of Ivy League "China hands." This paper most likely came to the attention of the president-elect via Dr. Kissinger. In any case, Mr. Nixon's inaugural address indicated that he was ready to experiment. He intimated that a dialogue with the China mainland was no longer out of the question because, as he said, an era of negotiation was now succeeding the age of confrontation.

In his first press conference, the new President carefully avoided any reference to a policy change. The masters of China, he felt, had to change first: "We will be interested to see," he said, ". . . whether any changes of attitude on their part on major substantive cases may have occurred."

Yet a change was clearly coming. During his visit in 1969 to Rumania, a nation friendly to Mao's regime, President Nixon stated that henceforth the United States government would deal with Communist states on the basis of their foreign policy rather than their internal policies. This was correctly interpreted as an overture to the Chinese Communists. When asked at a press conference in March of that year about the prospects of some understanding with Peking, the President had said: "Looking further down the road, we could think in terms of a better understanding with Red China's breaking off the limited Warsaw talks that were planned, I do not think that we should hold out any great optimism for any breakthrough in that direction at this time."

A year later, in his second annual foreign policy report on February 25, 1970, he reiterated the American commitment to the Chinese Nationalists but added that the United States was now prepared to "see the People's Republic of China play a constructive role in the family of nations." Significantly, this was the first time that Mr. Nixon had ever referred in public to Communist China by its formal name. Previously he had always called it Communist or Red or Mainland China. The President's personal wish to visit the Chinese mainland was noted in *U.S. News and World Report* with this quote:

And I would finally suggest that I hope and, as a matter of fact, I expect to visit mainland China sometime in some capacity. I don't know what

[6]Article by William L. Ryan in *Dallas Times Herald*, Feb. 20, 1972.

capacity. . . . And I hope to contribute to a policy in which we can have a new relationship with mainland China.

He continued:

I'm not referring to any invitation. I'm referring only to a hope and an expectation that at some time in my life and in some capacity—which, of course, does not put any deadline on when I would do it—that I would hope to go to mainland China.[7]

The shift in Mr. Nixon's attitude had been gradual, but it was dazzling. During the Korean War he had urged the bombing of China, and the Peking press had long assailed him as "a cunning and crafty swindler and a murderer." He may have seen, in his image as a hardliner, a chance to do what virtually no other American public figure could do with the same immunity. In a briefing of newspaper editors in Kansas City he predicted that mainland China would one day be "an enormous economic power." Its continued isolation from international dialogue, he said, must therefore be ended before Mao's government became a practical threat to world peace. Since the Soviet Union would do nothing to break China's isolation because of "differences that at the present time seem to be irreconcilable," the United States was the only power that could "take steps" toward such a dialogue. Mr. Nixon was looking into the future. He went on: "Mainland China outside the world community, completely isolated, with its leaders not in communication with world leaders, would be a danger to the whole world that would be unacceptable to us and unacceptable to others as well."

More personally, the President often talked to his White House staff about how the Chinese-Americans in his native California had proven peace-loving, law-abiding, and industrious for several generations. He spoke glowingly of the Chinese as the most "creative" people in Asia and foresaw the day when the mainland would furnish a "reservoir of talent" for a world at peace. That the mainland leaders were Communists no longer seemed an overriding or irredeemable fault. Ideologies new seemed less important than the need of the world's billions to live at peace in an age when so many could die so swiftly.

President Nixon's scenario for Asia, as fashioned by Dr. Kissinger, envisaged a new balance of power, and the increasing tension on the Sino-Soviet border in 1969 presented some interesting possibilities. Administration officials were coming to believe that Peking's fear of Moscow might not be entirely unfounded. The Central Intelligence Agency, for example, became convinced in 1969 that the Russians were not beyond planning a pre-emptive "first strike" to destroy the

[7]*U.S. News and World Report,* May 10, 1971.

Chinese nuclear arm before it became operational. Recognizing the validity of Chinese apprehensions, President Nixon and Dr. Kissinger speculated that this would be enough to cause Peking to welcome some opening vis-a-vis the United States as soon as this might be politically feasible. The key was seen to be in the fact that the Soviet Union was keeping no less than forty divisions and a thousand warplanes along the 7,000 miles of frontier shared with China.

News of simultaneous developments at Peking gave further encouragement. In April, 1969, the ninth congress of the Chinese Communist Party formally brought Mao's "Great Proletarian Cultural Revolution" to a close. Official interest in foreign relations suddenly resumed, and Premier Chou En-lai ordered Chinese ambassadors to return to their posts. In the major address of the congress, General Lin Piao, who had been named Mao's successor in the new Party constitution, used far more words denouncing the Soviet Union than the United States. His chastisement of the Russians was not surprising since the previous month there had been a grave border clash on the Ussuri River. There was subsequent trouble on the Sinkiang frontier in August, and rumors emanating from East European sources suggested that the Russians had been sounding out their allies on the possibility of a pre-emptive strike against China. In light of the justification of the Soviet invasion of Czechoslovakia of 1968 by the "Brezhnev Doctrine"—which apparently was meant to provide a rationale for the overthrow of governments in other Communist states—the Chinese may well have felt it timely to seek an avenue of communication with the United States.

Fundamental changes were also underway in the American public attitude toward the mainland regime. As a result of the widespread disillusionment throughout the United States over the Vietnam War, there was a growing tendency to listen to the analyses of Far Eastern "experts" long identified as sympathetic to the Chinese Communists. The American people may indeed have been psychologically prepared for a "new" China policy by 1969. In any case, by the time Mr. Nixon came into office many of his countrymen were prepared to regard Mao's regime as a permanent government which was no puppet of the Soviet Union and was indeed hostile to Russian influence. China was now being viewed by many not as an expansionist aggressor but rather as a defensive victim of Soviet aggression. The memories of the Korean conflict had faded by this time, and Vietnam was hardly being viewed as a new crusade. Many war-weary Americans were prepared to buy the argument that the United States should help to bring the isolated Chinese into the world community. President Nixon took office at the precise time when a drastic change in overall Asian policy seemed somehow long overdue, and at a time when the domestic political situation made it particularly easy for him to act. There was a bit of suspicion in the conservative wing of the Republican Party as to what the President might do, but because it could not be charged that Mr. Nixon had ever been "soft on Communism" he found himself far more at liberty to act than any Democratic incumbent could have been.

Another step in the direction of the Chinese Communists was now taken in the mid-Pacific. At Guam in July, 1969, the President enunciated what became known as the "Nixon Doctrine." It seemed to foreshadow a lessening American commitment in Asia. This meant that in any future Vietnam-type situation the United States would expect the nation directly threatened to assume the "primary responsibility" of providing the manpower for its own defense. The President's statement must have been received hopefully in Peking, though Mao Tse-tung's satisfaction doubtless was diminished by the hint that Japan might be expected to fill gaps left by the departing Americans.

The Nixon Doctrine was indeed ambiguous. It asserted that the United States would continue to meet its commitments and therefore still needed to maintain a substantial military capability in East Asia. America's allies, it was hoped, would be persuaded that the United States was more likely to remain involved if they could make a greater contribution to their own security. In essence, the Nixon Doctrine attempted to strike a balance between what America would do for her allies and what they ought to do for themselves. It pledged that the United States would keep its treaty commitments and would provide a nuclear shield, but it did not guarantee that Americans would again be sent to fight for freedom in Asia.

As a result of its "winless" policy the United States was bogged down in the Asian war, suffering from loss of face internationally, and wracked by unprecedented domestic turmoil. President Johnson had been forced to abandon all hope for another term, and Mr. Nixon was elected on a platform whose most conspicuous plank pledged a prompt end to the war. The obvious purpose of the Nixon Doctrine was to reinforce this promise. But, because the greatest obstacle to peace in Asia was the implacable hostility of the Chinese Communists, it now seemed sensible to seek a detente with the mainland regime. To do this, it would be necessary for the President to make some real concessions to Peking, on the one hand, while paying lip service to Taipei on the other. The "Two-China" policy of the Nixon administration was rooted in this dual purpose.

President Nixon's gestures were being carefully watched in Taipei. In April of 1970 Premier Chiang Ching-kuo visited Washington to convey his government's alarm at the prospect of a "Two-China" approach on the part of the United States. To the President and Secretary Rogers he outlined the attitude of the Republic of China in these terms: (1) under no circumstances would his government abandon its mission of mainland recovery, for only through restoration of the mainland could the "Source of Scourges" in Asia be eliminated and true stability be restored to the world; (2) his government would strive to build up Taiwan to even greater power and prosperity as a bastion and a base for mainland recovery; and (3) the Republic of China, while requesting the continued spiritual, moral, and material support of the United States, had no intention of asking that a single American soldier fight its battles. The Premier went on to describe the Maoists as "a renegade clique . . . which oppresses seven hundred million Chinese people." The Republic of China, he said, naturally objected to any contact between its allies and this ruthless regime, for such contact merely gave encouragement to its aggressive intentions. The formal reply of Secretary Rogers included guarantees to the effect that the United States would observe all its treaty obligations and commitments, would continue to support the objectives of the Republic of China in the United Nations, and would uphold the fundamental rights of the Chinese Nationalists in international affairs.

To the great satisfaction of some Washington officials, the Warsaw talks with the Communist Chinese were being reopened after a two-year suspension. In addition, trade concessions were announced by the Nixon Administration. In his 1970 foreign policy message the President noted that the Soviet Union and Communist China, once bound by an alliance of friendship, were now "bitter enemies"—and Mao's government now possessed thermonuclear weapons. A new Asian policy, he said, would thus have to consider the possibility that the Chinese might deploy intercontinental missiles in the future. With such weapons at Mao's disposal, it was time to think of approaching Peking for a possible detente. "We will deal with the Communist countries," he declared, "on the basis of a precise understanding of what they are about in the world, and thus of what we can reasonably expect of them and ourselves. Let us make no mistake about it—leaders of the Communist nations are serious and determined. Because we do take them seriously, we will not underestimate the depth of ideological disagreement or the disparity between their interests and ours. Nor will we pretend that agreement is imminent by fostering the illusion that they have already given up their beliefs or are just about to do so in the process of negotiating with us." This applies to China and the Soviet Union alike. The President did not expect American policy to have much impact on China's behavior. "But," he concluded, "it is certainly in our interest and in the interest of peace and stability in Asia and the world that we take what steps we can toward improved practical relations with Peking."

The time seemed indeed ripe for a basic change in American policy. Those wishing to curry favor with the Chinese Communists now surfaced in all sectors of American society. At a hearing of the Asian and Pacific Affairs subcommittee of the House Foreign Affairs Committee on October 6, 1970, Assistant Secretary of State Marshall Green clearly indicated that the administration was preparing to take a long step toward "recognizing the reality" of the China question. On the one hand, he said, the United States would strive to safeguard the international status of the Republic of China. On the other hand the administration was prepared to set aside the "Taiwan problem" in order actively to seek detente with the Chinese Communists. Shortly thereafter, at a state dinner for President Ceaysescu of Rumania, Mr. Nixon again referred to mainland China by its formal name, the People's Republic, and at a meeting of NATO foreign ministers at the end of 1970 Secretary Rogers went so far as to predict that the Chinese Communists would soon be admitted to the United Nations.

Some members of Congress were by now anxious to have a hand in fashioning the new China policy. In his "State of the World" address to Congress on February 21, 1971, President Nixon not only clearly voiced his "Two-China" view but also unequivocally designated the mainland regime as the People's Republic of China. It was remarkable for President Nixon to make a point of the "national designation" of a regime which was unrecognized by the United States and which was regarded as a rebel regime by one of America's allies. Such lack of consideration for the Republic of China met with heated indignation in Taiwan and elsewhere among overseas Chinese.

The section on the China question in President Nixon's February 25 message proved to be a concrete description of things to come. "We are prepared," the President said, "to establish a dialogue with Peking. We cannot accept its ideological precepts or the notion that Communist China must exercise hegemony over Asia. But neither do we wish to impose on China an international position that denies its legitimate national interests." His "Two-China" approach seemed to pledge that the United States would continue to protect the UN seat of the Republic of China, but on the other hand it seemed to welcome Chinese Communist participation in the UN on the condition that the Nationalists were not expelled. President Nixon was saying, in effect, that he would treat Red China and Free China as two separate nations. His rejection of the interests of the Republic of China had now formally come into the open.

Meanwhile the official wooing of Mao Tse-tung grew more ardent. In announcing that American citizens would no longer need special passport stamps to visit the Chinese mainland, State Department spokesman Charles Bray noted that this decision was consistent with

President Nixon's "publicly stated desire to improve communications" with China. Reviewing the unilateral steps taken by the Nixon administration to ease tensions between Washington and Peking, Bray listed the following:

JULY 1969: Relaxation of travel restrictions to allow persons with a "legitimate purpose" to travel to mainland China on an American passport.

DECEMBER 1969: Permission for American tourists to make unlimited purchases of Chinese goods and for collectors, museums, and universities to import Chinese items.

DECEMBER 1969: Permission for American-controlled subsidiaries abroad to conduct trade in non-strategic foreign goods exported to mainland China.

AUGUST 1970: Lifting of restrictions on American oil companies abroad and refueling free world ships bearing non-strategic cargoes to Chinese mainland ports.[8]

Asked by correspondents if Peking had ever responded to these initiatives, Bray admitted that there had been no visible reaction. But, he added, "we would hope that lifting these restrictions on travel would result in greater travel to the mainland." The administration was now also scrupulously avoiding any gesture which could be interpreted by the Maoists as hostile. In fast order Washington ordered a large-scale reduction in military aid to Taiwan, reduced and finally halted altogether the patrol activities of the Seventh U.S. Fleet in the Taiwan Strait, and discontinued all manned and unmanned reconnaissance flights over the Chinese mainland.

Then, in April of 1971, came an unexpected and highly dramatic move. The Chinese Communists, responding to the President's obvious overtures, invited the U.S. Table Tennis Team and a group of American newsmen to visit Peking after finishing a tournament in Japan. Had it been any other sport like baseball or basketball in which American players were known to excel, it is unlikely that any invitation from Chou En-lai would have come at this time. But the Communist Chinese, because of their exclusive and almost fanatic concentration on this game, had what were probably the best table tennis players in the world, and a victory by them over the Americans would have great propaganda value in Asia. The match was held, and the Chinese won easily. NBC's John Rich, one of the newsmen accompanying the team, commented on how "sportsmanlike" the Chinese players were in not beating the U.S. team too badly. That the Americans were beaten should not have been so surprising, however, since their star

[8]*U.S. Information Service*, London, Press Release, March 16, 1971.

191

player, D. J. Lee of Cleveland, did not make the trip at all. Lee, a native of South Korea, had lost most of his family when the Chinese Communists overran his homeland, and he refused to participate in any match with the Maoists as a matter of principle.

Mao Tse-tung's "ping pong diplomacy" proved a great psychological coup for his regime. It caused one American writer to quip: "If Hitler had invited the United States to a game of badminton, we probably would have called off the Normandy invasion." Chou En-lai's invitation to the American ping pong team is already being regarded by scholars as the great turning point in Washington-Peking relations. This assessment will probably stand. In any case, some prominent official voices were quick to predict that Chou's new "smiling" diplomacy would result in a United Nations seat. This viewpoint was happily echoed by Professor Edwin O. Reischauer of Harvard, the former ambassador to Japan, and by other academics across the country.

The American team had come into China by way of Canton. The party comprised only fifteen people: seven players, a coach, five officials, and two wives. Among the newsmen invited to cover the matches were John Roderick of the Associated Press, who had been briefly in China after World War II, and John Rich of NBC. In welcoming the American athletes, Premier Chou spoke some warm words: Contacts between "the peoples of China and the United States," he said, had been "frequent" in the past but then they were abruptly broken off. This visit would reopen the door to friendly contacts between the "peoples" of the two countries. "We believe," Chou concluded, "that such friendly contacts will be favored and supported by the majority of the two peoples."

It is perhaps odd and ironic that the Chinese media gave scant attention to the visit of the American athletes. But the reason is not far to seek. Visiting in Peking at exactly the same time as the U. S. Table Tennis delegation were three Black Panther leaders: Huey Newton, Elaine Brown and Robert Bay. Along with sixteen other young American radicals, this delegation from the American "New Left" had been invited to China by a "friendship association." Newton at the time was out on $50,000 bail and awaiting trial on a voluntary manslaughter charge in the 1968 death of an Oakland policeman. The Peking press took advantage of his presence, of course, to editorialize on the plight of American Negroes and their need to rise in revolt against all imperialist oppressors in the United States. At the same time only a passing mention of the presence of the American ping pong players was made over Peking Radio, and provincial newspapers and radio stations seem to have ignored the Americans entirely. Though a set of matches in Shanghai were televised, it is unlikely that the audience was large since there were not many individually owned sets in the city.

The Americans did manage to find time for shopping in Shanghai, but only after declining some spending money offered by their hosts. Glenn Cowan, a nineteen-year-old with hippie-style hair and attire, became a center of attention among the curious Chinese. Upon his return to Los Angeles, young Cowan cutely remarked that he could easily mediate all differences between Chou En-lai and President Nixon. Mainland China was "primitive," reported eighteen-year-old Olga Soltesz, who noted that even a large city like Peking wasn't anything like her hometown of Orlando, Florida. "I thought Peking would be a miniature Chicago," she said, "but there were no cars, only a few buses and everybody rode bicycles. I never saw a man and a woman together. When people were together it was either all men or all women. They are trying to discourage the people from having children. All the women wear baggy pants. I never saw a dress."

Conservative reaction to the new "smiling" diplomacy of Mao and Chou was cautious. The visit of the American players, said Senator Peter Dominick of Colorado, marked the first time that ordinary Americans had made a "goodwill tour" to China since the Communists came to power, and it would be well to remember that "the same men who smile at our ping pong players are those who subjected Tibet to the most dangerous type of colonialism the world has ever seen." They were the same slavemasters "who operate such a cruel and hated dictatorship that more Chinese attempted to escape in one recent month than all the East Germans who attempted to scale or penetrate the Berlin wall in ten years," the same ideologues "who continue to declare their resolute adherence not to peaceful means of settling disputes but to the use of revolutionary force."

When Vice-President Agnew's opinion was finally sought by the President in a meeting of the National Security Council on the subject of diplomatic ping pong with the Chinese Communists, he flatly declared himself against it. He considered it a cheap propaganda victory for Peking and said so. The Maoists were still a menace, he declared, and he was not about to change his opinion because of a couple of ping pong games and a few tentative smiles. Marshall Green, the assistant secretary of state for East Asian and Pacific Affairs, seconded the vice president. Despite Peking's new "flexibility," he said, the Mao regime still sought dominance over free Asian countries.

The invitation to the American athletes to visit the mainland did not come, as some have imagined, from the hearts of the Chinese peasants. It came from the tiny ruling clique in Peking. The fact is that Mao

Tse-tung and his cohorts decided to allow a few young, impressionable Americans to get a fleeting glimpse of China only because to them it seemed a timely move. The ballyhoo that was expected in the United States came to pass, and it made due impact on the American public mind. For those who may be further interested in what lay behind Mao's carefully staged propaganda stunt, there is a revealing article in the June 1967 issue of *Reader's Digest*. Entitled "I Fought in Red China's Sports War," it is the memoir of Shi Pen-shan, a young man of tremendous bravery and stamina who escaped from his regimented role as one of Communist China's top international competitors in its major sport, ping pong. His article describes the extreme lengths to which the Maoists have gone to establishing their superiority in the game of table tennis.

Confirming some of the observations on mainland conditions made by the ping pong players were the dispatches of the veteran Tillman Durden to the *New York Times*. His report from Canton, for example, told of a border official who protested loudly when Durden presented his passport containing a visa of the Republic of China. The Maoist would not acknowledge the existence of "Two Chinas," and Durden's entry permit was stamped on a separate piece of paper rather than in his passport. He described Canton as drab, with nothing more mechanical than bicycles to be seen. At Peking he found all the "antique charm" gone, and at Shanghai the roadways were choked with "frumpy blue-clad millions" while at night there was little illumination. Shanghai was "obviously full of energy and drive," but it had "little of the ebullience and sparkle of old." The bright lights on Nanking Road were few, the shops "dowdy" and all the merchandise "utilitarian." The buildings in Shanghai were notable for "dirt-encrusted windows, sagging doors, and trash under staircases."

A young female doctor living in a commune fifteen miles out of Peking told Durden that she had no way of getting to the city. There was indeed much new construction in Peking, but hardly any at nearby Tientsin. Debris clogged the side streets at Tientsin, Durden wrote, and "factory chimneys belch uncontrolled coal smoke." Education was totally oriented; all courses at the secondary level were taught in terms of Mao's thought, with quotations from the Red Book taking the place of the western classics. Students were compelled to work in school shops, and during their "vacations" they received military training, worked in factories, and spent weeks in rural communes. Work periods of two years, Durden noted, were required before approved senior middle-school graduates were allowed to go on to college.

Reporting on the life of foreigners in Peking, Durden found their movements definitely restricted though perhaps less so than at

194

the height of the 1966 cultural revolution. Foreigners were barred from some parts of the city and could go no more than a few miles outside the limits without a special permit. Innocent transgression of regulations might mean a jail sentence or hours of lecturing from a police official. It was impossible for a foreigner even to meet a Chinese socially except by special arrangements. "There is no such thing," Durden wrote, "as having a casual chat on the street or making a call without official approval." The Chinese who dared to speak casually to a foreigner usually faced police interrogation afterward. American newsmen gaining entry to the mainland were questioned at length about other Americans applying for entry permits. They also were required to describe the editorial viewpoint of their respective newspapers and magazines toward Chairman Mao's government. Such questioning gave the impression that journalists representing those publications with friendly attitudes would be favored in the granting of visas. So far, Durden noted, preference was going to correspondents who had been in China before the Communist takeover.

According to five newsmen returning from the mainland, most of the reporting on Communist China would still have to be carried on from the vantage points of Hong Kong and Tokyo. "You simply do not know what is going on in the government when you are in Peiping," said John Roderick of the Associated Press. Agreeing were Gregory Clark of the Sydney *Australian*, Max Suich of the Sydney *Morning Herald*, and John Rich and Jack Reynolds of NBC. Roderick, who covered China in the late 1940s, reported that the streets of Canton were virtually empty of vehicles and the airport had a single Soviet airliner. On the subject of women's life on the mainland, Roderick reported that he had not seen a single skirt or a single beauty parlor. Hairdos were bobs, pigtails or buns; jewelry was rare, shoes were flat, and make-up was seen only on the stage.

New York Times correspondent James Reston reported from Hong Kong on the great differences between life in that metropolis and life on the mainland. "Coming out of Red China into this recklessly beautiful city," he wrote, "is almost more of a shock than going the other way. Suddenly everything is different, everything is speeded up, as if somebody had flicked a switch on a gigantic movie camera and all the sights and sounds of life began to race and scream." On the mainland side Reston saw no commercial advertisements and very few cars or trucks. He heard "a different kind of noise" there—"not the quick beat of jazz or the sad yearning of regrets of unrequited love of Western music, but the incessant sound of modern Chinese martial music and the glorification of Mao Tse-tung." Reston's summation was in basic accord with the 1971 assessment of *Komsomolskaya Pravda*, the newspaper of the Young Communist League in the Soviet Union. Economic conditions were worsening on the mainland, that newspaper had reported, because so much money was now being spent for military purposes. The meager food rations fixed in 1957-59 had been cut by another twenty percent; there was an acute shortage in consumer goods, and industries had been sacrificed to the military build-up. About one-third of the national budget was being used for nuclear research and the manufacture of missiles.

None of this information, however, had much adverse effect on the drift of developments. The door to the mainland was opening. Pleased as Chairman Mao must have been with the publicity his "ping pong diplomacy" was receiving by way of the mass media in America, the practical results were even more auspicious. The White House now announced a long list of items which American firms would now be permitted to sell to the Chinese Communists. The list included wheat and roadbuilding equipment, and Chinese requests for jet transports and diesel locomotives would also be considered. Secretary of State Rogers then announced that the United States was prepared to exchange "non-secret" scientific and technical information with the Peoples Republic of China and other governments with which the United States did not have diplomatic relations.

These decisions, however "official," were not unanimously cheered in the administration. Defense Secretary Laird frankly opposed the lifting of restrictions on trade with the Chinese Communists. The lower level of technology on the Chinese mainland, he said, should preclude placing trade with Peking on the same basis as that with Russia. Adding up all the obvious moves by the President to loosen trade restrictions, some officials were wondering how Washington could ask Americans to open economic lines of contact with Red China at the same time that the government continued to refuse trade with Rhodesia, where Americans owned property and produced goods? In another context the assistant secretary of state for East Asian affairs, Marshall Green, has said that there was no plan to court Peking "at the expense of our friends on Taiwan, the Republic of China." And the New York *Daily News,* with the largest circulation of any newspaper in the United States, urged the Washington government to announce its determination to stand by "its oldest and firmest friend in Asia." "If we don't," said the paper, "we might as well write off that whole area."

In Taipei, of course, the possibility of detente between Washington and Peking was viewed with increasing alarm. Yet the

Chinese Nationalist leaders had overcome many difficulties and dangers before, and they were undaunted.

But the cruellest blow was yet to come. Even before the April ping pong episode the late Edgar Snow, that long-time admirer of Chinese Communism, was hinting that Chairman Mao had indicated to him that the President would be warmly welcomed at Peking if he wished to pay a visit. Then, in an intricately executed secret mission to the Chinese mainland early in July, Dr. Kissinger made preparations for the most dramatic pronouncement in Richard M. Nixon's long career. Speaking on television on July 15, the President astounded the world with the following statement:

I sent Dr. Kissinger, my Assistant for National Security Affairs, to Peking during his recent world tour for the purpose of having talks with Premier Chou En-lai. The announcement I shall now read is being issued simultaneously in Peking and in the United States. Premier Chou En-lai, and Dr. Henry Kissinger, President Nixon's Assistant for National Security Affairs, held talks in Peking from July 9 to 11, 1971. Knowing of President Nixon's expressed desire to visit the People's Republic of China, Premier Chou En-lai, on behalf of the Government of the People's Republic of China, has extended an invitation to President Nixon to visit China at an appropriate date before May, 1972. President Nixon has accepted the invitation with pleasure. The meeting between the leaders of China and the United States is to seek the normalization of relations between the two countries and also to exchange views on questions of concern to the two sides. In anticipation of the inevitable speculation which will follow this announcement, I want to put our policy in the clearest possible context. Our action in seeking a new relationship with the People's Republic of China will not be at the expense of our old friends. It is not directed against any other nation. We seek friendly relations with all nations. Any nation can be our friend without being any other nation's enemy. I have taken this action because of my profound conviction that all nations will gain from a reduction of tensions and a better relationship between the United States and the People's Republic of China.[9]

To make the announcement, the President and Dr. Kissinger came in by helicopter from the Western White House at San Clemente to the Burbank televesion studio where the slapstick *Laugh-In* show was taped. They knew that their understated declaration would startle the world. Afterward they went off in high spirits to Perino's, a fashionable Los Angeles restaurant, where the President jubilantly shook hands with bystanders on the sidewalk while Kissinger and four aides celebrated inside

[9] *U.S. Information Service*, London, Press Release July 16, 1971.

with a $40 bottle of Chateau Laffite Rothschild. At the apex of his own career, the good doctor was basking in the spotlight and enjoying a degree of power that professors only read about in their libraries.

The President's announcement was a bombshell that had global repercussions indeed. As one veteran diplomat put it, there had been "nothing like this" since the announcement of the Nazi-Soviet Non-Aggression Pact in 1939. The planning behind Dr. Kissinger's mission to mainland China actually began in the opening weeks of the Nixon Presidency. As soon as he was in office Mr. Nixon quietly but methodically started a systematic reversal of diplomatic signals that was intended to demonstrate to Mao Tse-tung's regime that the United States now wanted to "normalize" relations. The President had evidently been thinking about this for some time. As long ago as a year before his election, he had dropped a hint or two that he might be willing to depart from his earlier anti-Peking stand. A major problem, however, was how to get Dr. Kissinger into Chinese territory without letting his mission become public knowledge. The decision was made for Kissinger and his aides to slip in through Pakistan, a country on China's border that had the confidence of both Peking and Washington.

From the moment of departure Dr. Kissinger's "world tour" was understated, underpublicized, and played out so casually that newsmen and other observers were all but lulled to sleep. As he moved from South Vietnam to Thailand to India, the reporters who greeted him came away with little to write home about. So seemingly routine was Kissinger's trip that the two and a half days he was missing, and presumed ill in Pakistan, raised scarcely an eyebrow. The Pakistanis were asked in advance to participate in the deception and President Agha Mohammed Yahya Khan was apparently in on the secret. Kissinger's plane landed in Islamabad on the afternoon of July 8. After a ninety-minute chat with President Yahya Khan, he announced a sudden change of schedule. Word was put out that he was going to the mountain resort of Nathia Gali for a brief "working holiday." That was the last that the world knew of Dr. Kissinger's whereabouts for sixty-four hours.

On July 9 the Pakistan government announced that Dr. Kissinger had been forced to stay at Nathia Gali for another day because of slight indisposition, which was presumed by correspondents to be a case of common dysentery or "Delhi Belly." When pressed hard, a U.S. embassy official said that a physician had been sent to the mountain resort to handle the case. Why, asked a reporter, had not Dr. Kissinger been lodged in an air-conditioned room in Islamabad? The studied reply was that Dr. Kissinger did not want to "embarrass anyone in the capital" by his illness. At that point some of the newsmen grew skeptical, but their hunch was that Dr. Kissinger had gone off to meet a group of East Pakistan officials.

Instead of going to the mountains or to East Pakistan, Dr. Kissinger was spirited to the airport at Rawalpindi, seven miles from Islamabad, where he boarded a Pakistan International Airlines Boeing 707 and left non-stop for Peking. It was the best possible ruse: a secret is easy to keep in the rigidly controlled state of Pakistan. Even if the crew members had been curious, it is doubtful whether they even knew whom they were transporting. The nondescript doctor could easily pass for just another European businessman. And the fact that a Pakistani plane was flying to the capital of China was nothing out of the ordinary, since the Chinese did not have long-range jets for the nonstop flight between Rawalpindi and Peking. Under a bilateral agreement, Pakistan International Airlines had been carrying passengers and freight between the two capitals on both regular and unscheduled runs. Thus Kissinger's aircraft created no stir when it took off for Peking. Accompanying him on the flight were three aides: John Holdridge, a member of his staff who spoke Chinese; Winston Lord, a special assistant; and Richard Smyser, a Foreign Service officer specializing in Southeast Asian affairs. The rest of his staff remained behind in Rawalpindi, as much in the dark as anybody else and no doubt hoping that their chief would soon recover from his bout with Delhi Belly.

At noon on July 9 Dr. Kissinger's plane landed at a deserted airfield on the outskirts of Peking. It was met by Marshal Yeh Chien-ying, a high-ranking Politburo member, and three Foreign Office officials. One of these was Huang Hua, a leading expert on U.S. affairs whose assignment as ambassador to Canada had been delayed because of the Kissinger visit. The group drove to a handsome villa on a small lake outside Peking and sat down to a sumptuous Chinese lunch. While his aides attacked their food with chopsticks, Dr. Kissinger stuck to knife and fork. At four in the afternoon Premier Chou En-lai arrived, and the serious talking got underway. Chou and Kissinger, sitting at opposite sides of a table covered with green felt, exchanged views on into the night.

Dr. Kissinger had with him a bulky portfolio containing prepared statements and position papers drafted by President Nixon, Secretary Rogers, and himself. There was no prepared agenda.

The President's proposed visit was only one of many items discussed. Kissinger chose his words with even more care than usual while two interpreters—one born in the United States and the other a former Harvard student—translated them for Premier Chou. But it was largely an exercise in "face," since Chou's fluent English allowed him occasionally to correct the translators. Typically he used the charade of translation to give himself time to frame his replies, which he made without once consulting his notes.

The following morning, Saturday the 10th, Dr. Kissinger and his aides were treated to a tour of the Forbidden City. That afternoon Kissinger resumed his conversation with Chou in the large public building called the Great Hall of the People. This second session lasted as long as the first—about eight hours—and the Chinese, according to a White House spokesman, were "enormously gracious and polite." Kissinger's official statement was exuberant: "On the human level, we were treated extraordinarily well. The mood of the session was precise and businesslike. There was no rhetoric on either side. We spoke frankly, directly, and I believe usefully. It was not a conversation in which either side was trying to hold the other one up."

After dining by themselves that evening, the Americans rejoined the Chinese in a late session to work out the language of the joint communique. On Sunday there was a final meeting and a farewell lunch before Dr. Kissinger and his aides boarded their plane at one o'clock. His mission an unqualified success, Kissinger returned to his point of departure in the mood of a Wall Street broker. The man who was supposedly suffering from a stomach ailment in Pakistan had put on five pounds in China. According to White House wits, Kissinger was so impressed by the meals served him in Peking that he jested, "A guest of the state must have starved to death 3,000 years ago and the Chinese are determined that it will not happen again."

In his television announcement on July 15, President Nixon pointedly assured the American people his scheduled visit to the Chinese mainland would in no way be "at the expense of our old friends." This was his only allusion to the Republic of China, but he sent a personal letter to President Chiang Kai-shek which reiterated that the American government would continue to honor all its military commitments as formally expressed by treaty. The fifteen million people of Free China, and some twenty million overseas Chinese, reacted with remarkable calm to the President's bombshell. The announcement naturally gave cause for grave concern, but the people on Taiwan were buoyed by the recent words of President Chiang. A month earlier he had said:

If all of us stand firm in our conviction of what is right and just in accordance with our principles, we shall have peace of mind and find solace. We shall be free from anxiety and fear. Moreover, danger and doubt will give us opportunity to manifest our convictions of righteourness and justice, and anxiety and pain will provide our nation with opportunity for rebirth. . . . Some countries of today are myopic and lured by immediate advantage to the point of irrationality and the ignoring of righteousness. These nations talk of peace but actually are engaging in actions which destroy peace. Should we be angered, discouraged or even intimidated by these nations and thereby depart from our faith and lose our temper, this would be tantamount to failure. . . . If all of us can respect and reinvigorate ourselves, if we can be cautious enough to make sure that our judgement is sound and that we are holding firm to the independent and persevering spirit of our nation and people, if we can fight in terms of will, and not in terms of passionate nature, then there will be no test that we cannot pass, no difficutly that cannot be defeated.[10]

The effect of President Nixon's announcement was multiplied by the fact that it came without any prior diplomatic consultation whatever in Asia. Such secrecy was bought at a high price. In Japan, for instance, Prime Minister Eisaku Sato was bitterly resentful of the President's failure to give the slightest hint of his intentions. For more than two decades the United States government had pressed the Japanese to invest capital in Taiwan and to give moral support to Chiang's government. At the same time the Japanese had been cautioned not to attempt excessive trade with the mainland Chinese or to toy with notions of a close political relationship with Peking. In the face of an ever-present interest among certain powerful Japanese businessmen for closer contacts with the mainland, a succession of cabinets in Tokyo had faithfully followed the American lead. President Nixon's announcement now shook Japanese confidence in the durability of the U.S. stance in Asia. The frank consultations which Sato thought he was having with the United States were exposed as a sham, and his ministry was soon falling from power.

In Saigon the reaction of President Thieu was polite and guarded, for the obvious reason that South Vietnam was depending on President Nixon's continued support. But President Park Chung Hee of South Korea expressed great shock, and officials in both Malaysia and Singapore were so surprised at first they even doubted the accuracy of the news of the President's announcement. Similar shock was registered in the Philippines, where President Marcos

[10]*Asian Outlook* (June, 1971), Vol. VI, 4.

was profoundly disturbed, as well as in Indonesia, Australia, and New Zealand.

Only a Republican president of the impeccable anti-Communist credentials of Richard M. Nixon could have gotten by with such an announcement. A Democratic president would have heard cries of appeasement and voices of doubt, and these surely would have compromised his efforts. Certain members of Congress did raise questions about the projected trip. Some of these, of course, were strictly partisan. The ultra-liberal Senator J. William Fulbright of Arkansas, long an ardent advocate of rapport with Peking, thought that prospects might be worse than ever if something went amiss.

On the other hand, conservative Democrats and faithful Republicans who had held off on attacking the President on many of his domestic maneuvers now lashed out at the proposed journey. "It is the most human thing in the world," said Senator Ernest Hollings of South Carolina, "to turn away from difficult situations by indulging in wishful thinking. And the more difficult and threatening the circumstances, the greater the temptation to delude oneself into believing that all the dangers threatening us can be dissipated by a few simple devices." Senator John Tower of Texas declared that he was disturbed because of the "irrational attitudes . . . international banditry, and dogmatic, virulent, bellicose brand of Communism" to be found in Peking. Senator James Buckley of New York said bluntly that the President's visit would "strengthen the hands of those seeking accommodation with the Communists at any price," while Senator J. Strom Thurmond of South Carolina insisted on further reassurances to such old and trusted allies as the governments in Taipei and Seoul. Senator Peter Dominick of Colorado, one of the best posted and least quoted Asian specialists in Congress, expressed fear of "adverse effects . . . around the world." He was wary of such summitry: "Other presidents have tried this type of personal diplomacy. President Roosevelt did, and he ended up with Yalta and Potsdam. President Kennedy did, and he ended up with the Rose Garden in Vienna and subsequently the Berlin Wall and Cuban crisis. I, for one, hope we won't fall into similar quagmires as a result of the President's move." Congressman John Ashbrook of Ohio told the House of Representatives that the President's visit could only encourage the aggressive intentions of the Chinese Communists and their "client regimes" in North Vietnam and North Korea. Representatives John Rousselot of California, Otto Passman of Louisiana, and Philip Crane of Illinois expressed alarm that the President might make concessions which would undermine the American relationship with the Republic of China.

Other congressional leaders, of course, were ebullient. "I'm astonished, delighted and happy," said the usually taciturn majority leader, Senator Mike Mansfield of Montana. "I applaud the President's imagination and judgment," declared Democratic presidential hopeful George McGovern of South Dakota. The Senate Republican whip, Robert P. Griffin of Michigan, called the plan "a stunning and hopeful development," and Senator Hugh Scott of Pennsylvania, the minority leader, added a prediction that Hanoi would be "shocked and stunned," by the President's move.

Other reaction was perhaps more interesting. Thomas G. Corcoran, a political veteran who had been President Roosevelt's confidant and adviser, said that the effective bargaining power of the White House had been lost by the announcement of the forthcoming trip to Peking. "Tommy the Cork" expressed his fear that the incumbent, with an election in the offing, would be tempted to make too many concessions in return for "some kind of victory" on paper. Twelve conservative leaders, including publisher William A. Rusher of *National Review,* announced immediate "suspension" of their support of the administration because of the President's overtures to Red China and other foreign policy "failures." "F.D.R. would have hesitated to go to Berlin to wine and dine with Adolf Hitler," wrote columnist William F. Buckley, "but we are about to do that, and all the liberals who can't stand the Greek colonels are jumping for joy." Two other "old China hands" warned the President against trying to match wits with Chou En-lai. Bruno Shaw, who had lived in Hankow for ten years and published an English-language paper there, thought that the President "risks going down in history as the Neville Chamberlain of our time." Taiwan, he said, would become "the disposable Sudetenland of the East, no matter what fine words are uttered by the politicians who are presently in charge of our destiny." The perceptive Freda Utley, who understood Communism from the inside, noted that General Marshall had once been "charmed" by Chou En-lai and implied that now it was Mr. Nixon's turn. "It is almost as if," she said, "we were determined to repeat the errors of the past." So it seemed to other conservatives around the country who now asked themselves if U.S. officials would now make the same mistake, expecting a genuine detente with Mao Tse-tung, that was made with Soviet Russia in the early 1920's when Lenin needed capitalist help. They recalled the words of an old Chinese proverb: "Fool me once, your fault; fool me twice, my fault."

Criticism was by no means confined to conservatives. George Ball, the Democratic former undersecretary of state and a notable liberal, was deeply aggravated by the July 15 announcement. The only possible explanation for not consulting our allies, he declared in an article in the *New York Times,* was that such consultation would have increased the "chances of a leak." But a leak, though annoying, would scarcely have been disastrous, and no leak could have created anything like the "breakage" caused by the President's failure to consult. Unless the White House considered it clever and tactically advantageous to "heighten the drama by exploiting the maximum shock effect from what the President proudly described as the biggest surprise in history." Ball objected to the very manner of the President's dramatic *fait accompli.* We should neither wish, he said, nor can we afford to "indulge in the practice of astonishing our friends." Rather, our greatest need was to "establish confidence by conducting our affairs in a logical and predictable way, avoiding the unexpected and shocking." This meant that we should first make sure that "the way is carefully prepared" so that our allies were not "caught off balance." Ball, pulling no punches, made several more significant observations:

> First, the President has invited himself to visit a government with which we have no diplomatic relations, with which we have never concluded a treaty of peace ending the Korean War, and which continues to mount propaganda attacks against us in the most strident and virulent terms. Second, in spite of the fact that there seems no possibility of serious substantive accomplishment, the President is planning to stay in that country as a guest of the Government for at least a week—a longer bilateral visit than any American President has made to the government of any foreign nation in our entire national history. Under the established American practice, visits of heads of state or chiefs of government last two, or at the most, three days.[11]

It was only natural that our allies should take this to mean that the U.S. government "impliedly recognizes China's dominant position throughout the whole of the Far East" and thereby regarded it as "the wave of Asia's future." This action "strongly stimulates their impulse to climb quickly on the Chinese bandwagon." As Dean Acheson used to say, "When the President fumbles, the whole goal line is wide open."

"What do we have?" asked Richard F. Starr, associate director of the Hoover Institution. He answered his own question: "The President of the No. 1 power in the world going to Peking to pay tribute in the eyes of Mao Tse-tung." A former State Department official and a world traveler, Starr cautioned against basing a new China policy on hope alone. Labor columnist Victor Riesel reported that George Meany, president of the AFL-CIO, strongly

[11]*New York Times Magazine,* Feb. 13, 1972, 52.

disapproved of the President's proposed trip. Meany had told a convention of the International Longshoreman's Association in very blunt terms that "Red China" was "still a slave state where human freedom is nonexistent." President Nixon's plan to visit the Chinese mainland, he added, was "the No. 1 stunt of the No. 1 stuntman of our times," out of which there was "no indication that anything good can come. . . ."

The famous British pamphleteer Lord Halifax once quipped that the best qualification of a prophet was to have a good memory. Certainly, throughout the cold war, summit meetings between American presidents and Communist leaders have been marked by persistent failure. To be sure, President Eisenhower's ventures into summitry evoked momentary spasms of journalistic euphoria, as with the "Spirit of Geneva" in 1955 and the "Spirit of Camp David" in 1959, just as the impromptu Johnson-Kosygin meeting conjured up the "Spirit of Glassboro" in 1967. But each of these "spirits" quickly evaporated in the clear, dry air of reality. The sad but significant fact is that there has been scarcely an instance in the entire postwar period where a top-level conference with Communists produced any real diplomatic breakthrough. In giving excessive play to the quicksilver element of personal compatibility, the summit conference has usually created an illusion of understanding that was false and therefore dangerous. It is true that leaders with a common heritage of language, ideas, and national experience—as was the case in the Churchill-Roosevelt summits— have sometimes been able to appraise one another with fair precision, and true understanding has often been advanced by such face-to-face discussion. But when leaders have been of basically different ideology and background—to say nothing of language—summitry has proven more likely to produce mistaken and misleading impressions than any real meeting of the minds.

It is instructive to recall, for example, how Prime Minister Chamberlain was tragically taken in by Adolf Hitler at their Munich meeting in 1938. Not doubt Chamberlain spoke from conviction when he told the British people on his return to London: "After my visits to Germany I realized vividly how Herr Hitler feels that he must champion other Germans. He told me privately, and last night repeated publicly, that after the Sudeten-German question is settled that it is the end of Germany's territorial claims in Europe." Thus Chamberlain had brought back, he said, "peace in our time." Why was Chamberlain so easily deceived by so crude and brutal a liar as Hitler? Because he so deeply *wanted* to believe, and because his face-to-face encounter was with a man whose background and standards he could not possibly understand. Chamberlain had accepted the word of a Nazi rabble-rouser as readily as he would that of an English gentleman. Had the Prime Minister stayed in London, dealing impersonally with the Germans through his diplomatic agents, the mystique of personal contact would not have worked its malign spell—and the squalid betrayal of Czechoslovakia might never have occurred. Moreover, from what we now know about Hitler's incomplete preparedness and the plotting of his own generals against him, the European war might have been avoided altogether.

When Roderick Farquhar, one of Britain's foremost authorities on mainland China, was asked what the men in control of Peking could hope to gain by President Nixon's visit, he replied: "The immediate objective, I believe, is to soften us up—both America and Britain—so that they can get a favorable vote on their entry into the United Nations this autumn. They are trying to undermine America's willingness to support Chiang Kai-shek in a last-ditch endeavor to keep the Nationalists in the United Nations." Farquhar was right. After the shock effect of the President's announcement began to wear off, the immediate question looming on the horizon was whether the Chinese Communists would knock loudly at the door of the United Nations and, if so, should they be admitted? Should a regime which in seven years had fueled five foreign civil wars—in Korea, Indochina, Tibet, the Philippines, and Malaya—and which itself had used its armies against U.S. forces and consequently was condemned by the United Nations as an aggressor; which defied the U.N. decision to reunify Korea, and which openly proclaimed its continuing purpose to use force as an instrument of national policy—should that ruthless, irresponsible regime be given a permanent seat, with veto power, in the body which under its charter has "primary responsibility for the maintenance of international peace and security?" Apparently many Americans, or at least those with short memories, now thought so. A Louis Harris poll indicated that 48 percent of the American people favored the admission of Peking, 27 percent opposed it, and 25 percent were undecided.

On April 25, 1971—in the very month of ping pong diplomacy—a special presidential commission had formally recommended that Communist China join Nationalist China as a full-fledged member of the United Nations. This was an official endorsement of the "Two China" idea. The American people, already tired of the unreliable "findings" and biased mouthings of Presidential commissions, paid scant attention to the report. Yet it was the work of a blue-ribbon, fifty-member team headed by a distinguished ex-senator and former ambassador, Henry Cabot Lodge, and including such familiar names as Senators Aiken and Fulbright, Congressman

Cornelius E. Gallagher and Sherman P. Lloyd, ex-Senator Bourke B. Hickenlooper, Terence Cardinal Cooke, Dr. Norman Vincent Peale, Rabbi Bertram B. Korn, Erwin D. Canham of the *Christian Science Monitor*, James C. Hagerty, and the television personality Art Linkletter.

The Republic of China, of course, had been one of the original sponsors of the United Nations. It was conspicuously represented at San Francisco in the spring of 1945, and was given one of the five permanent seats on the Security Council. Now this nation was faced with a series of maneuvers by American officials. On August 2, 1971 Secretary of State Rogers announced the United States would favor the seating of the Chinese Communists in the General Assembly in the fall, but would oppose any move to expel the Republic of China. This was the public stance of President Nixon's "new" China policy. Rogers neatly avoided taking a position on the future of the "China seat" in the Security Council; he said only that the Security Council itself would make that decision, as provided by the charter. "We, for our part," he said, "are prepared to have this question resolved on the basis of a decision of the members of the United Nations." Rogers acknowledged that the Republic of China had "played a loyal and conscientious role . . . since the organization was founded" and had "lived up to all of its Charter obligations." He added that the Republic of China had made "remarkable progress in developing its own economy" and had "cooperated internationally by providing valuable technical assistance to a number of less developed countries, particularly in Africa."

The message that the United States was about to drop its long-standing opposition to U.N. membership for the Chinese Communists, but would fight any effort to expel the Nationalists, was reported to have been carried to President Chiang Kai-shek by a retired career diplomat and former under-secretary of state, Robert D. Murphy. He appears to have notified Chiang in April of what was emerging as the administration's official policy of dual Chinese representation in the United Nations. Murphy, then chairman of the board of the Corning Glass Company, was visiting Taipei in connection with his firm's plans to build a plant to produce television parts. He has confirmed that he was received by President Chiang and his wife, whom he had first met in Cairo in 1943, but has declined to comment on the conversation during this audience. Other sources have indicated, however, that Murphy had been asked to notify the Chinese Nationalists, on President Nixon's behalf, that the American administration was changing its policy on the matter of Chinese representation in the United Nations. If so, the announcement by Secretary Rogers in August that the United

States would now support the seating of Peking could have come as no surprise in Taipei.

After President Nixon's July 15 announcement of his intended visit to Peking, Chiang Kai-shek issued a call to "all forces of justice" to resist the effort of the Maoists to "smuggle" themselves into the United Nations so as to use the world body as a platform and "base" for a new international assault. This call was contained in a written message to the mass rally in Taipei commemorating Captive Nations Week. These were his ringing words:

> The rampancy of Communist enslavement and violence and the spreading counter-current of international appeasement constitute serious threats to the freedom of mankind. Nevertheless we have not the slightest doubt that enslavement and violence are like the flames of a fire which will soon be extinguished. The current smiling diplomatic offensive of the Maoists seeks to divide and confuse the free world, to smuggle the regime into the United Nations, and to use the international organization as the base for the regime's international united front. If this conspiracy should succeed, the United Nations Charter would be emptied of worth and the noble spirit and great objectives of the United Nations would sink into decadence. We must urge the parliamentary organs, the governments, the civic bodies, and the mass communications media of all countries to repeat and amplify our summons so that a great tide of the times will surge forward to oppose the enslavement and aggression of the Chinese Communists and prevent their admission to the United Nations. In so doing, we shall achieve the noble objective of safeguarding the United Nations and world peace. Humankind will be assured of immunity to Communist enslavement and guaranteed the enjoyment of freedom in perpetuity.[12]

The worst, as was expected, came on Tuesday, October 25, 1971. In an intense and emotion-filled meeting of more than eight hours, the General Assembly voted overwhelmingly to admit the Chinese Communist regime and to expel the Nationalist government. The vote, which brought "Third World" delegates to their feet in wild applause, was 76 in favor, 35 opposed, and 17 abstentions on a resolution sponsored by Albania and twenty other members. It called for the seating of Peking as the only legitimate representative of China and, concurrently, for the expulsion of "the representatives of Chiang Kai-shek." Thus it appeared that the United States finally lost, after twenty-two years, its fight to keep Nationalist China in the United Nations; the expulsion, which came with such apparent suddenness, was denounced by the chief American delegate, Ambassador George Bush, as a "moment of infamy." Actually, however, the expulsion was no surprise. The signal was flashed an hour and a half earlier when the Assembly voted 55 to 50, with 15 abstentions, to reject an American resolution

[12]*Free China Review* (August, 1971), 69.

that would automatically have made the expulsion of a charter member an "important question" requiring a majority of two-thirds to pass.

An analysis of the voting on the "important question" resolution shows that the abstention of eight nations, which had been thought almost to the last to be leaning toward the U.S. position, had been fatal to the American cause. Had these abstainers voted with the United States, the "important question" resolution would have been adopted by a count of 63 to 59. It has been argued that the 76 members who voted for the Albanian resolution to admit Peking and expel the Nationalists did in fact constitute to a two-thirds majority—and that therefore the matter is academic. Yet it can scarcely be denied that the vote on the Albanian resolution had been swelled by the pattern of the earlier voting. Meeting with newsmen shortly before midnight at his office across the street from the United Nations, Ambassador Bush was apologetic. The United Nations, he said, "crossed a very dangerous bridge tonight. I thought we would win. . . . It's hard to believe that a few hours ago we didn't think we had anything to worry about."

After the failure of the American resolution by the narrow margin of five votes, Foreign Minister Chow Shu-kai dramatically led his delegation out of the General Assembly meeting room. His departing words were terse: "The expulsion of a member state is an 'important question' under Article 18 of the Charter. The rejection of [the American] draft resolution . . . is a flagrant violation of the Charter. We have therefore decided not to take part in any further proceedings of the General Assembly." With this gesture the Republic of China formally withdrew from the United Nations before it could be technically expelled. Mr. Chow then called a press conference and released a full and very strong statement. The Republic of China, he said, "cannot let the majestic headquarters of the United Nations become the place where justice and law yield place to lawlessness and injustice. Responsibility for this state of affairs must be borne by those who have sacrificed the lofty principles of the Charter on altar of expediency. They will have to answer to the judgement of history and posterity."

Asserting again that his government had faithfully discharged all its charter obligations over a period of twenty-five years, Mr. Chow continued: "To deny the Republic of China its rightful position in the United Nations is to violate the Charter and negate the noble and sacred principles and purposes upon which the United Nations was founded." On the other hand, he said, the Maoist regime had committed innumerable crimes against the Chinese people since seizing power in 1949. Such a regime was "the enemy of the Chinese people, the enemy of international peace," and could never properly represent the nation of China in the international community. Once it had been seated in both the General Assembly and the Security Council, he warned," it will surely transform the United Nations into a Maoist front and a battlefield for international subversion."

In response to questions which followed, Mr. Chow expressed his conviction that Taipei's bilateral relations with her friends would not be seriously affected. For years his government has worked hard in conjunction with the United States, Japan, and others to preserve stability in the world. It would continue to do so, but on the other hand it was also prepared for contingencies—including the worst. Speaking eloquently and philosophically, the Foreign Minister said: "Now that the tempest is over, we see tranquility ahead and sincerely pray that our like-minded friends in the United Nations would continue the struggle against injustice. . . . I take this opportunity to express the profound gratitude of my government to the friendly delegations which have lent us their unstinted support throughout the years. . . . We shall continue to struggle with like-minded governments for the realization of the ideals upon which the United Nations was founded but which the General Assembly has now betrayed. We are confident that the cause for which we have been fighting for more than a quarter of a century will in the end prevail." That cause was still to liberate the mainland from Maoism and restore freedom to the Chinese people.

The Chinese Communists had not really expected to be admitted into the United Nations in 1971. President Nixon's announcement of July 15 proved the decisive factor in the matter. This was acknowledged by Premier Chou En-lai himself. In a five-hour interview with Neville Maxwell of the *London Times* the Red premier gave credit where it was due. "As soon as he [Nixon] said he would come," Chou mused, "many countries followed suit, and this affected the outcome of the voting. . . ." He pointed out that ten nations which voted against the American resolution had no diplomatic relations with Peking, and if these men had supported the U.S. position it would have been upheld. But these ten were not convinced that the American position was sincere. After all, the President of the United States had announced his intention to pay an official visit to a capital where he had no embassy. Chou continued: "Why should we talk with President Nixon? Because Nixon is the President of the United States of America. . . . Since he wants to come, we will talk with him. . . . At the beginning we talked with his representatives, but matters could not be cleared up and they did not dare to shoulder the responsibility. . . . Finally President Nixon himself knocked on the door, saying that he wished to come to Peking for talks. So well and good, we invited him to come for talks.

The *New York Times*, though clearly sympathetic to the seating of Peking, editorialized that "the people of Taiwan" deserved better of the world organization than expulsion. The Los Angeles *Herald Examiner*, carrying the syndicated column of Bob Considine, told its readers: "The scene in the UN Assembly was right out of the jungle. The delegates of the mendicant little nations clapped and jigged not so much because they were happy to see Nationalist China bounced, or even Red China admitted. They were ecstatic because their numbers had defeated the United States." To William F. Buckley the scene was grotesque. "The general elation over at the United Nations," he wrote in this column, "was most graphically expressed when, after the vote defeating the United States on the important procedural point, the delegate of Tanzania stepped forward to the podium and danced a jig. The jig expressed that special delight one feels on beating a giant."

In Washington the reaction was naturally mixed, but among members of Congress there was discernible disgust with the United Nations. Senator James Allen declared that the world body had been "flawed and incapacitated" by the admission of the Chinese Communist regime. The senator from Alabama made this assessment in a commentary on Chiao Kuan-hua's maiden speech at the UN on November 15, 1971. After reading this inflammatory address, Senator Allen concluded that the Chinese Communists meant to use their voice and their veto to promote revolutionary activities throughout the world. The Red Chinese objectives, he said, differed only slightly from those of Soviet Russia, and were differences of means rather than ends. The time was at hand, he insisted, to reevaluate the UN as a viable institution. Its prestige was at an all-time low, according to recent polls, and the Senator wished his colleagues to question "its intentions, its ends, its utility" and to examine dispassionately the consequences of continued American participation and support.

On the House side, Representative Mario Biaggi of New York warned that the presence of Communist China, with its well-known hostility toward Israel, could jeopardize settlement of the Arab-Israeli conflict. He stressed that Peking's ties with the so-called Third World posed "a formidable threat" to all peace efforts in the United Nations. Alarmed by Chiao Kuan-hua's vehement assault on Israel in his first speech to the world body, Congressman Biaggi voiced his fear that the Chinese Communists might work to expel Israel and seat the Palestine guerillas. For a long time Peking had given encouragement to the Palestinian "liberation" movement as a double-edged weapon against both the United States and the Soviet Union. Now that Peking had gained admission, the rapport between the Chinese Communists and the Palestinian guerillas was bound to grow even closer.

211

In his General Assembly speech of November 15, Chiao Kuan-hua had indeed made an overt pitch for the Palestinians. "The essence of the Middle East question," he said, "is aggression against the Palestinian and other Arab peoples by Israeli Zionism with the support and connivance of the superpowers." The Chinese "government and people," he went on, as though the words were snynonymous, "resolutely support the Palestinian and other Arab peoples in their just struggle against aggression and believe that, persevering in struggle and upholding unity, the heroic Palestinian and other Arab peoples will surely be able to recover territories of the Arab countries and restore to the Palestinian people their national rights." Again on December 8 Chiao Kuan-hua told the General Assembly that both superpowers were "taking advantage" of the temporary troubles of the Palestinians and other Arabs to work "dirty political deals" in their jockeying for oil resources, strategic points, and "spheres of influence." His two speeches made it abundantly clear that Peking had no intention of seeking a solution in the Middle East on the basis of the 1967 Security Council resolution.

In supporting the Palestinians the Maoist regime took the line that Israel was unilaterally responsible, to date at least, for the failure of all Middle Eastern negotiations. But a spokesman of the Israeli foreign ministry, Gideon Rafael, remarked in a radio interview that it was Communist China, rather than the Soviet Union, which held the key to peace or war in the Middle East. The Peking regime sought "an American-Soviet confrontation" in his part of the world, Rafael said, and "that is why she incited the Arab governments to war."

Chou En-lai himself had pledged support for the "liberation" of the Palestinians in May, 1971, during a "Palestinian International Week" in Peking. As reported in the *Peking Review,* a "grand rally" in the Great Hall of the People was attended by some 10,000 people including such notables as Vice Premier Li Hsien-nien, Acting Foreign Minister Chi Peng-fei, and a visiting delegation of the Palestinian Liberation Organization. The leader of the delegation, Abu Ammar Sa'ad, and five others were personally received by Chou En-lai. Speaking at the rally, Abu Ammar Sa'ad declared that the "Palestinian revolution" was linked inseparably with "Arab liberation" and "world national liberation" movements. It was "an important and basic conviction of ours," he said, that "the Zionist movement will not be able to save the Jews." Answering for the Chinese, Liu Hsi-chang of the local revolutionary committee pledged continuing support: "The Palestinian people have waged tit-for-tat struggles against U.S. imperialism's counter-revolutionary dual tactics, and the Palestinian guerrillas have victoriously stood stern tests. The workers, peasants, and PLA men in

Peking firmly support the Palestinian people in their struggle to liberate their homeland and firmly support the Arab peoples in their struggles against the U.S. imperialism and Israeli Zionism."

At the end of March, 1972—one month after President Nixon's pilgrimage—another delegation of Palestinians visited Peking. The *Peking Review* reported on April 7: "Shouting slogans of 'Salute to the heroic Palestinian people!' 'Long live the militant unity of the people of China and Palestine!' and 'Long live the great unity of the people of the world!', more than 2,000 people in Peking warmly welcomed the Delegation of the Palestine Liberation Organization at the airport on March 30. They expressed their firm support for the Palestinian people's just struggle against U.S.-Israeli aggression." In response to a pledge of support reiterated by the acting foreign minister, Chi Peng-fei, the head of the Arab delegation defined "our Arab liberation movement" as part of "a common struggle waged together with the liberation movements of the rest of the world, the progressive forces, and the anti-imperialist forces in all countries." He added his opinion that "the trend of history" was "irresistible" and that "the people want to make revolution."

The same issue of the *Peking Review* reported that Chou En-lai and Chi Peng-fei had engaged the Arab leaders in "cordial and friendly conversations." Then, on April 6, Chou wired his greetings to the executive committee of the Palestine Liberation Organization on the occasion of the opening of the Palestinian congress. His warm words were reported in the April 14 issue of *Peking Review*:

> Dear friends, I wish to take this opportunity to reaffirm to you: The Chinese Government and people will unfailingly and resolutely support your just struggle. We will forever stand together with the Palestinian and other Arab peoples. We are convinced that, by persevering in the great unity against imperialism, persisting in a protracted armed struggle and guarding against all sorts of schemes of the enemy, the Palestinian and other Arab peoples will be able to overcome the temporary difficulties along their roads of advance and win final victory.[13]

Temporarily housed in the Roosevelt Hotel in New York City, the Communist delegation to the United Nations soon decided that larger and more secure quarters were needed. The first choice for their permanent headquarters was a mansion once owned by the late theatrical entrepreneur Billy Rose. When a deal failed to materialize on this property, negotiations began for the Lincoln Square Motor Inn, at 155 W. 66th Street. This eleven-story structure, adjacent to the New Lincoln Center, was finally purchased by the Chinese Communists for $4.8 million. In contrast with the Republic of China dele-

[13]*Peking Review*, April 7, 1972, 23.

gation, which scattered their living quarters around Manhattan, the Communists housed themselves in one large building closely guarded by security agents. An expensive wall around the entire building further demonstrated the paranoia and suspicions of its inhabitants. Out of this stronghold the Chinese Communists now began to send their intelligence people scurrying about the city, to the consternation of the FBI and the New York Police Department.

In evaluating the American responsibility for the UN debacle of October, 1971, one fact is central. It is essential to understand that on the very day the China question was being decided, Henry Kissinger was in Peking for the second time. Ostensibly he was there to make final arrangements for the President's forthcoming visit. But the fact that he chose this very moment to call again upon the Chinese Communists was important if not decisive in the swing of the voting. Ambassador Bush, of course, categorically denied that the United States was in any way insincere in its maneuver to keep the Republic of China in the international organization. He was personally confident that the American policy of "Two Chinas" would succeed. He considered the Peking delegate's inaugural address to be a mere firing of "empty cannons of rhetoric." The intemperate language of that speech, he said, contained nothing new. Perhaps it did not, but in Peking's official response to fifty-seven messages of welcome the deputy foreign minister, Chiao Kuan-hua, flatly demanded that the United States get out of Asia; and Huang Hua, who had once screamed obscenities at the Americans in the Korean peace talks at Panmunjom, vehemently attacked the superpowers in his maiden address to the Security Council.

It is worth noting that the same Huang Hua, one of Peking's most experienced and shrewdest agents, was busy on a special project in the weeks preceding the October 25 vote at the UN. From his office in Ottawa, where he was conveniently placed as Mao Tsetung's ambassador to neighboring Canada, Huang was working out the details for a visit to the mainland by none other than John Stewart Service. The "young China hand" of World War II days was now on the library staff of the University of California, Berkeley, as curator of the Chinese collection. The university press had just published his labored defense of himself in the notorious "Amerasia" case of 1945, and he was preparing a volume of memoirs to sit on library shelves alongside those of his wartime diplomatic colleagues, John P. Davies and O. Edmund Clubb. Mr. Service's monograph, entitled *The Amerasia Paper*, was a direct attempt to refute my own two-volume publication, *The Amerasia Papers: A Clue to the Catastrophe of China*, released through the United States Senate Judiciary Committee in 1970. The burden of the argument by Mr.

Service in this bitter apologia is that he, Davies, Clubb, and other young diplomats in China during World War II were correct in their prophecy that the social programs of Mao Tse-tung's "agrarian reformers" presented a brighter future for the Chinese people than did the "reactionary" projections of Chiang Kai-shek's "inefficient" and "corrupt" Kuomintang. The same theme, with embellishments, is broadcast yet more boldly in Mr. Service's second and larger work, *Lost Chance in China*.[14] Noticing this book in his review column in *Esquire*, Malcolm Muggeridge writes:

> As for John S. Service's dispatches explaining how Mao, though a Marxist, had no intention of establishing a dictatorship, but was a democrat at heart who asked nothing better than to live in peace and amity with the United States, I can only say that anyone who can believe they represent a lost chance in China will, like the man who took the Duke of Wellington for a Mr. Smith, believe anything.[15]

[14]John S. Service, *Lost Chance in China* (New York: Random House, 1974).
[15]April, 1974, 24.

7

Nixon's "Journey for Peace" [1972]

AFTER THE SHOCK of the China vote in the United Nations, the American people began to look forward with anxious curiosity to President Nixon's forthcoming visit to Peking. Preparations promptly got underway for what was to be the stellar spectacular of the decade. The White House announced that the President's party would be on the mainland for a week—from February 21 to the 28th—with stops in Shanghai and Hangchow as well as Peking. When questioned by newsmen, Dr. Kissinger stated categorically that no opening of formal diplomatic relations would result from the chief executive's visit. Treaty commitments to the Republic of China, he said, would not be affected. When asked, however, about the possibility of a future meeting between President Nixon and President Chiang Kai-shek, he declared coldly: "We are well aware of the views of the government of the Republic of China."

The unstated American attitude on the "Taiwan question" was already clear. The United States was now prepared to leave this matter to "direct negotiation" between Taipei and Peking. Yet there was some indication that Dr. Kissinger had already given certain assurances to the Chinese Communist leadership. One of these had to do with the size of the U.S. military presence on Taiwan. Professor Ross Terrill of Harvard, after a quick trip to Peking, wrote in the *Atlantic Monthly* that he was told that Dr. Kissinger had intimated that the U.S. forces on Taiwan would be reduced before the President's trip. Writing from Peking, James Reston of the *New York Times* felt that Mr. Nixon should anticipate "no concessions on Taiwan" from the Chinese Communist leaders, and "only violent opposition to a stronger military role for Japan." Reston wondered whether the United States could afford the real price of rapprochement with the Peking regime. The question being asked by Western diplomats in Peking, he said, was "what Mr. Nixon hoped to get out of all this, except a relaxation of tensions as an argument for re-election."

Premier Chou En-lai sounded a similar note. Speaking to a Yugoslav newsman, he said that the "first requirement" in his negotiation with President Nixon would be not merely a termination of the war in Vietnam but also the withdrawal of American forces from "the area"—by which Chou may well have meant the whole of East Asia rather than Indo-China alone. And he told a British visitor: "President Nixon himself knocked on the door saying that he wished to come to Peking for talks. So well and good—we invited him." This reminds one of Dean Acheson's acute comment: "In all bargaining, the side more eager for agreement will pay more to get it." President Nixon himself was cautious. In his September 16 press conference, he had used these words:

> I think that one of the reasons that these talks may be productive is that Chou En-lai, both publicly and privately, doesn't take the usual naïve, sentimental idea—and neither do I. Well, if we just get to know each other all of our differences are going to evaporate. He recognizes and I recognize that there are very great differences between the People's Republic of China and the U.S. We both realize that at this point it might serve our mutual interests to discuss those differences.[1]

Such remarks are reminiscent of what Mao Tse-tung said in 1945: "There are no straight roads in the world. We must be prepared to follow twists and turns and not try to get things on the cheap." The Maoists would never have invited Mr. Nixon "for talks" without a prior decision to give him something, or at least pretend to, in return for what they wanted most. And, as James Reston put it, what they wanted above all was Taiwan.

Dr. Kissinger had worked out all the details for the President's visit on his second meeting with the Chinese Communists in October. "I believe," he then said to newsmen, "that the Chinese, in their long and distinguished history, have never encountered anything like the presidential party. This is something that will take a little getting used to." Previously he had told other reporters: "What we are doing now with China is so great, so historic, that the word 'Vietnam' will be only a footnote when it is written in history." Taking seven assistants with him, Dr. Kissinger was given a low-level welcome by Yeh Chien-ying,

[1] *U.S. News and World Report*, Sept. 27, 1971. 81.

deputy chairman of the Central Military Affairs Commission, and acting Foreign Minister Chi Peng-fei. When his plane landed at Shanghai to pick up a group of Chinese officials for the short flight to Peking, foreign correspondents and some diplomats were allowed to watch from a distance of about one kilometer. Kissinger spent six days in Peking planning the itinerary of the President's visit.

Despite warnings from Vice President Agnew and some other advisers, Mr. Nixon was determined to carry out his dramatic plan. One day, in the midst of a foreign policy discussion in the Oval Office, the President leaned back in his chair, picked up a paperweight, and thumped the top of his desk for emphasis. "Russia," he said, "isn't going to make any effort to get China into the family of nations. It is up to the United States. We have got to start the dialogue. Maybe it won't happen in five years, maybe not even in ten years. But in twenty years it had better be, or the world is in mortal danger. If there is anything I want to do before I die, it is to go to China. If I don't, I want my children to."

The President hoped to discuss both practical and philosophical issues with Chairman Mao and Premier Chou. "Because of a lack of communications," he said, "we are a mystery to them as they are a mystery to us. It would be useful on the part of both sides to discuss our philosophical backgrounds, differences, and some similarities." Both Mao and Chou were men of a philosophical turn of mind, the President added, and "my approach to problems of the world is not tactical." To him it was essential to "take the long view" that U.S. foreign policy be based on "a well-developed, well-understood philosophy, a framework for our international relations."

Speaking with Congressional leaders on the South Lawn of the White House just before his departure, the President described his trip as "the beginning of a process," to which the Senate Majority, Mike Mansfield of Montana, responded: "We wish you well on this voyage of discovery." With the applause of Congressional leaders of both parties ringing in his ears, the President threw in this word of caution: "We, of course, are under no illusions that twenty years of hostility between the People's Republic of China and the United States of America are going to be swept away by one week of talks that we will have there."

As the President and his wife walked past their guests in this unusual red-carpet send-off, Mr. Nixon poked some Congressmen and cabinet officials jovially in the ribs and bent close to whisper remarks that newsmen could not overhear. Yet he was restrained as he outlined the goals of his journey to the impressive crowd that had assembled to bid him bon voyage. He said:

We must recognize that the government of the People's Republic of

China and the Government of the United States have had great differences. We will have differences in the future. But what we must do is to find a way to see that we can have differences without being enemies in war. . . . I would simply say in conclusion that if there was a postscript that I hope might be written with regard to this trip, it would be the words on the plaque which was left on the moon by our first astronauts when they landed there: "We came in peace for all mankind.[2]

In addition to the President and Mrs. Nixon, the official U.S. delegation included Dr. Kissinger and a dozen senior advisers and aides. Backing up these officials were about a hundred staff people, Secret Service agents, and assorted technicians. Some advance government men, representing both the government and the media, were already in China making preparations. Two chartered jets, flying ahead of the President, had brought almost a hundred press correspondents, braodcasters, and communications engineers.

The air distance from Washington to Peking is approximately 11,500 miles. As the President boarded his blue and white Boeing 707, formerly called "Air Force One" but recently renamed the "Spirit of '76," his mood was ebullient. The first stop was the Marine Corps air station at Kaneohe Bay for a layover of a day and a half in Hawaii. To the crowd that assembled to see him off, the President declared dramatically that tomorrow he would be in China. He thought it appropriate, he said, that his journey was beginning in Hawaii "where East and West really do meet."

The President's aides had paced his journey with the hope of adjusting to the physiological effects of crossing many time zones and the international date line at jet speed. The next stop was on Guam, for an overnight rest. Four more hours in the air the next morning brought the big plane to Shanghai's Hung Chiao Airport. After taking tea at the terminal during the hour's refueling, the Americans were joined by six Chinese crewmen and three interpreters for the short hop to Peking. These Chinese were supposed to be fluent in English, but the navigator had to rely on earthbound air controllers to translate his flight-deck conversations with the American pilot and co-pilot.

President Nixon got his first glimpse of the capital of Communist China about 11:25 on Monday morning, February 21, when the "Spirit of '76" broke through the smog from a million coal-burning chimneys and began its final approach into Peking's wind-swept airport. The chief security agent on board, a Secret Service Officer, radioed to an agent on the ground: "What about the crowd?" Back came the answer: "There is no crowd." Incredulous, the Secret Service

[2]New York Times, Feb. 18, 1972.

219

man in the plane tried again: "Did you say no crowd?" "That is affirmative—no crowd." In a second plane carrying the American press corps, Peter Lisagor of the *Chicago Daily News* cracked: "When Nixon sees the size of this crowd he's going to come out for busing." This evoked laughter, but the interpreter Fu Fung-kuei rebuked the Americans. "In China, we love our leaders," he said sternly, "and would never think of making a joke about them."

Awaiting the President's plane were forty-two Chinese officials headed by Premier Chou En-lai, a military band, and honor guard of 500 soldiers, sailors, and airmen in brown fur hats and greatcoats. Also on hand were the American journalists and advance men—but no foreign diplomats, as would have been the case for the chief executive of a nation with which diplomatic relations were in effect. Except for a handful of curious airport employees, bus drivers, and limousine chauffeurs, there were no ordinary folk at all to greet the President of the United States. "I was outraged," wrote James Michener in the *Reader's Digest*, "at the ghastly silence and cool reception that greeted our President."

The physical arrangements were equally depressing. A single American flag fluttered inconspicuously from a tall staff, opposite another displaying the scarlet banner of the People's Republic of China. Between them, superimposed on the bleak stone front of the terminal building, was a gigantic color portrait of Chairman Mao. On all sides of the airfield were huge signs bearing the strident slogans of Chinese Communism: "People of oppressed nations the world over, Unite!"—"Long live the great Chinese Communist Party and long live our great leader Chairman Mao"—and "The theoretical basis governing our thinking is Marxism-Leninism."

Such was the scene as the "Spirit of '76" rolled to a stop, the door opened, and President Nixon emerged hatless and smiling from the cabin. It will long be regarded as one of the great ironies of history that Richard M. Nixon, the fearsome Red fighter of an earlier time, should be the first American president to shake the hand of Chou En-lai. Twenty years earlier Mr. Nixon was saying that if Taiwan fell, "the next frontier is the coast of California." And ten years back he was still insisting that any gesture of concilliation with Communism would prove "detrimental to the cause of freedom and peace."

In a few minutes the airport amenities were over, and the President's motorcade was sweeping along the fifteen miles of open road into the capital city of Communist China. Here and there along the road were knots of people, held back at the intersections by unarmed police or heavily armed soldiers of the People's Liberation Army. All along the route were giant pictures of Mao Tse-tung.

The Chairman's round countenance smiled down from portraits twenty stories high on government buildings and apartment houses.

The streets of Peking, wide and lined with bare winter trees, were almost free of motor traffic despite the noon hour. About the only powered vehicles to be seen were trolley buses and an occasional government automobile, built in Shanghai and painted green. Hugh A. Mulligan, in an Associated Press dispatch, noted that in Peking "you seldom see a television antenna, a flock of sparrows, a girl wearing makeup or a dress." According to Mulligan, jukeboxes were unknown and pianos were almost as rare, for Mao Tse-tung had decreed: "In our world the piano is not required." Anti-American posters were nowhere to be seen. Robert E. Gomperts of Atherton, California, who traveled 3,000 miles in China as one of twelve members of the so-called "Committee for a New China Policy," observed that when his group arrived in January a common poster in the streets read: "We must defeat the U.S. aggressors and all their running dogs wherever they may be." In the next few weeks, however, most posters referring specifically to the United States had been removed from sight. A few remained in Tien An Men Square in the center of the city. One read, "We warmly hail the great victories of the three Indochinese peoples in their war against U.S. imperialism". Another read, "All peace-loving countries and peoples should unite and oppose aggression, interference, and bullying by U.S. imperialism."

At the same time the Chinese people were being politically prepared for the President's visit by way of special education in their communes, factories, and cadre schools. There were still plenty of Maoist slogans and sayings in plain view. The President's motorcade passed a billboard carrying this slogan: "Make trouble fail. Make trouble again and fail again until its doom. This is the logic of imperialism and all reactionaries in the world in dealing with the people's cause. They will never run counter to this logic. This is Marxist law." Another large red signboard read: "Proletariat of oppressed peoples and oppressed nations, Unite!"

Since the people of Peking had not been ordered to appear along the roads leading into the city, the President's party found the countryside curiously devoid of human life. Had their masters ordered it, the airport would have swarmed and the roads would have been lined. Great crowds would have been assembled, instructed, and carefully rehearsed. Instead, the Communists presented a scene that was stark and cold.

On the western outskirts of Peking was the compound where the American party would be housed. For the use of the Nixons was a guest cottage of nondescript architecture called Tiao Yu Tai, "Angling Terrace," a yellowish brick structure distinguished mainly by empty gardens and barren willow trees framing a small frozen lake. Quarters nearby had been prepared for the President's principal aides, Dr. Kissinger and Secretary of State Rogers.

President Nixon had barely arrived at his guest house when the telephone rang. "Chairman Mao Tse-tung would be pleased," said a polite voice, "to receive the President of the United States at his residence, at Mr. Nixon's convenience." Only Dr. Kissinger accompanied the President on his one-hour visit to the Chairman's book-lined room. Allowing for the time taken for translation, the Nixon-Mao meeting provided at the most a half-hour of conversation. In Taiwan the meeting was interpreted as an audience. The Chinese Nationalists regarded it, in the words of one Taipei newspaper, as "kow tow diplomacy" of the most obvious sort. Chairman Mao had virtually summoned the American chief executive into his presence, much like some bygone emperor receiving the envoy of a tributary state.

That night Premier Chou En-lai hosted a banquet in the President's honor at the gilded Great Hall of the People. President and Mrs. Nixon ate Peking Duck with chopsticks, or tried to, while Chou tapped his foot to a rendition of "Turkey in the Straw" by the People's Liberation Army band. Throughout the three-hour meal Chou's musicians mingled Chinese folk songs with such American favorites as "Home on the Range," "America the Beautiful," and "The Star Spangled Banner." Mr. Nixon was so impressed by the performance that he remarked in a toast: "Never have I heard American music played better in a foreign land." Then, after the last toast, the President dramatically left the head table and strode to the bandstand to congratulate the startled leader.

Premier Chou was not to be outdone. In one toast he remarked that the ideological differences between the Chinese and American governments should not hinder the two peoples from establishing "normal" relations on the basis of five principles. These were, in order, a mutual respect for sovereignty and territorial integrity, mutual nonaggression, noninterference in each other's internal affairs, equality and mutual benefit, and peaceful coexistence. In other toasts President Nixon waxed even more eloquent:

There is no reason for us to be enemies. Neither of us seeks the territory of the other; neither of us seeks domination over the other; neither of us seeks to stretch out our hands and rule the world. Chairman Mao has written: "So many deeds cry out to be done, and always urgently. The world rolls on. Time passes. Ten thousand years are too long. Seize the day, seize the hour." This is the hour. This is the day for our two peoples to rise to the heights of greatness which can build a new and a better world.[3]

On the 25th the President gave a banquet honoring Chou En-lai. In his opening toast Mr. Nixon seized on the symbolism of the Great Wall of China, which he had just visited. The Peking talks, he said, had begun to remove the "wall" of misunderstanding which had separated the two nations. He referred to "the hope of our children" that peace might be "the legacy of our generation to them." It all depended on a shared interest in building "a new world order." Mr. Nixon closed with a line from George Washington's famous valedictory: "Observe good faith and justice toward all nations; cultivate peace and harmony with all."

Finishing his toast, the President stepped back from the table as a waiter handed him a glass of Mao Tai, a colorless liquor distilled from sorghum. He raised his glass to Chou, then circled four nearby tables and toasted each Chinese dignitary in turn with a small sip of Mao Tai and an ever-so-slight bow. Each official got Mr. Nixon's practiced stare in the best Chinese custom while Premier Chou grinned so broadly that it appeared to American reporters that he might burst into laughter at any moment.

Once again Premier Chou was not to be outdone. After describing his discussions with President Nixon as "honest and frank" and therefore "beneficial" to both sides, he offered this elliptical vision of the future: "The times are advancing and the world changes . . . the strength of the people is powerful and that whatever zigzags and reverses there will be in the development of history, the general trend of the world is definitely toward light and not darkness." As might be expected, Chou thus aligned the Chinese Communist cause as usual with the inexorable tides of history.

Just as some ease was beginning to be established, there was a tense experience for President and Mrs. Nixon. It came at the performance of an elaborate ballet entitled "The Red Detachment of Women" in the Great Hall of the People. Sitting between the Nixons was Madame Mao Tse-tung, the old Shanghai actress who had emerged from obscurity a few years earlier as the fire-breathing dragon lady of the cultural revolution. She led the applause as the drama unfolded and the peasants turned on the wicked land-lord who has abused them. The climax came as women soldiers in ballet slippers did target practice on a crude caricature of Chiang Kai shek. The Nixons clapped politely at the close, and the President

[3]*Department of State Bulletin*, March 20, 1972, 421.

remarked cautiously the next day that he loved the dancing and the music. He called it a play with a powerful message, as indeed it was; the ballet extolled party doctrine, and that was its prime reason for being. The Nixons had to sit through a propagandistic portrayal of the triumph of communism over capitalism. After it was done, they were taken to the sports stadium to be treated to a gymnastic exhibition that was superb.

Everything about China, in fact, seemed superb—the food, the hospitality, the rich civilization of the past, the promise of the future. But the President was most impressed, quite naturally, by the Great Wall. It was worth a presidential allegory: No more walls, he said, let us have an "open world." American television crews had seized the Wall atop the mountains that once sealed off Peking from the barbarians. President Nixon preened before the cameras, never tiring of repeating that his Chinese hosts had made it possible for "the story of this historic visit to be read, seen, and heard by more people all over the world than on any previous occasion in history." Later, as the Nixons toured the old imperial palace in the "Forbidden City," the President philosophized on the ways of the ancient emperors. Walking bareheaded in the snow, he reported to his hosts that his daughter Julie had said by telephone that the television pictures were coming over beautifully.

Millions of Americans, watching the televised satellite reports, got the correct impression that in China it was routine to treat people as useful robots rather than as human beings. The network cameras were especially revealing in what they could not show. Hence the newsmen assigned to cover the President's visit were forced to present endless small talk about the least important things imaginable while the cameras spanned such vacuous scenes as a military band tuning up. While the Presidential party was visiting the Great Wall, however, the cameras picked up a crowd of Chinese workers— the type once called coolies—who suddenly appeared with transistor radios and cameras in their hands or hanging from their shoulders. They snapped pictures, played their radios, and smiled on cue. "For the most part," wrote Stanley Karnow for the *Washington Post*, "the Chinese being displayed to the U.S. presidential party and the foreign press have apparently been selected and programmed to behave according to a scenario prepared in advance. . . . The 'average' citizens being encountered by Mr. and Mrs. Nixon on the sightseeing tours have evidently been stationed at their positions beforehand."

There were strange aspects to some other scenes. During the snowstorm which hit on the fourth day of the President's stay in Peking, thousands upon thousands of Chinese swarmed into the streets to shovel and sweep them clean. This was perhaps the biggest street throng Mr. Nixon saw on his entire trip. One liberal American publication called the street-sweeping operation "a startling lesson in social cooperation," adding that the President must have "detected a civic spirit and camaraderie that are spectacularly lacking in the present-day U.S."

On another occasion the TV eye picked up a crowd of Chinese strollers with cameras and radios, apparently enjoying the sights of historic Peking. But one American newsman, who happened to linger behind after the President had gone, saw the Red Guards quickly come and take up the cameras and radios which the "tourists" had displayed in front of the TV crews. It is beyond question that what the American people saw on television was exactly what the Chinese Communist regime wanted them to see.

American journalists learned quickly there was only one God in China—and his name was Mao Tse-tung. All answers to their questions began with "Before the Liberation" or "Since the Liberation." What this really meant, of course, was "Before Mao" and "After Mao." The impression was conveyed that the Chinese people were generally in excellent spirits, laughing and singing most of the time. Some journalists may have believed this, but others were not so naïve. Barbara Walters of NBC observed that Chinese "accomplishments" under Mao have been made only at a stiff price. "At every level," she reported, "there is no room for individual thought or expression. Are the people happy? Who knows? I'm not even certain *they* do." Continuing, she noted there was "a drabness, a grayness" with "no beauty, no texture, no creative art." Everything was "the same, mass-produced, and mass-induced." Although the Chinese were courteous and cooperative, she was able to make no friends. "After one week in Romania, also a Communist country, I had made several friends among interpreters. In China, I never got beyond small talk or Mao talk."

An item in *Time* told of two ace reporters who visited a school in Peking. They first went into a chemistry classroom which had a large picture of Chairman Mao looking down at the students. When the reporters entered, not a single head turned to glance at them. The English class was even more austere. On the blackboard was written: "I love Chairman Mao" and other such sayings. When the teacher asked who could recite the day's lesson from memory, every hand went up. The students were learning by rote, as Chinese have learned for centuries. Like the old McGuffey Readers, the test stressed "virtues"—except that in today's China the only virtues were the thoughts of Mao Tse-tung. On the front wall, flanking the inevitable picture of Mao, were two slogans from his writings: "Education must serve the proletarian politics and be combined with productive labor" and "The force at the core, leading our cause forward, is the Chinese Communist party; the theoretical basis guiding our thinking is Marxism-Leninism." Li Shu-ying, a girl of 15, was asked by the reporters what she wanted to do in adulthood. "I wish," she replied, "to be the successor to the revolutionary cause of the proletariat. I will do what will be beneficial to the people." What exactly would she like to do if she could choose anything at all? Her choice, she said, would be "what the party needs."

An elderly professor of physics at Peking University, Chou Pei-quam, confessed to a group of American reporters that he had harbored revisionist and bourgeois thoughts before the Cultural Revolution of 1966. But then he re-studied the works of Chairman Mao and came around to "the correct theoretical line." Professor Chou's account of how he altered his thinking was enough to chill his American listeners, and Eric Sevareid was particularly saddened by it. The university in China, said the senior CBS commentator, had become "an inferior junior college"—a condition which could not continue for long because "any society needs educated men and women." Sevareid's view of the situation was akin to that of the "old China hand" Theodore White, an ultra-liberal Harvard classmate of John F. Kennedy, and author of the popular series on recent presidential elections. At Harvard, White noted, "we give more courses in Chinese culture and history than they give at Peking University. And we teach them at a higher level."

The Peking phase of the "Journey for Peace" ended on February 25 when, accompanied by Premier Chou, the presidential party left for the ancient city of Hangchow in two Soviet-built Ilyushin-18-turboprop airliners. The Chekiang Province revolutionary committee met the planes, applauding as Mr. Nixon walked down the red-carpeted ramp. The President, smiling broadly, applauded back in the best Chinese style. In less than a week in China, he had learned his manners well.

The resort of Hangchow was the storybook Chinese city of pagodas and lotus blossoms. Marco Polo, who visited the place at the end of the thirteenth century, called it "the greatest city which may be found in the world, where so many pleasures may be found that one fancies himself to be in paradise." President Nixon must have found it almost as fascinating. The Americans were given a tour in a yellow and blue pleasure boat that proceeded in leisurely fashion past the great bridges and gardens that were first described by Polo. When Premier Chou caught the sight of author-correspondent Theodore White, he remarked: "He

226

has not been here since liberation." Smiling, White replied, "That's not my fault." The Premier laughed and said: "We, too, are to blame." When Barbara Walters of NBC asked the President what he thought of Hangchow, Mr. Nixon replied: "This is like the hors d'oeuvres. You want to come back for more."

After this sojourn the President's party flew to Shanghai, a metropolis of more than ten million, now wired for sound and color by the Radio Corporation of America and Comsat. From Shanghai an 1,800-word "Joint Communique" was issued on February 27 to the deeply curious world. It came after two nights of intensive bargaining which, it may be assumed, centered on the question of the future of Taiwan. The most important part of the Chinese statement read:

> The government of the People's Republic of China is the sole legal government of China; Taiwan is a province of China . . . the liberation of Taiwan is China's internal affair in which no other country has the right to interfere; and all U.S. forces and military installations must be withdrawn from Taiwan. . . .

The American reply was this:

> The United States acknowledges that all Chinese on either side of the Taiwan Strait maintain there is but one China and that Taiwan is a part of China. The United States Government does not challenge that position. It reaffirms its interest in a peaceful settlement of the Taiwan question by the Chinese themselves. With this prospect in mind, it affirms the ultimate objective of the withdrawal of all U.S. forces and military installations from Taiwan. In the meantime, it will progressively reduce its forces and military installations on Taiwan as the tension in the area diminishes.[4]

This was the official product of the President's "Journey for Peace." Certain questions need to be posed that, unfortunately, have not yet been seriously asked by very many Americans. What "peaceful settlement" might be expected between a nuclear-armed totalitarian state of about 800 million voiceless robots and an island sanctuary of 15 million people, of whom only two million had come as refugees from the mainland? What could such a tiny minority really "negotiate"? What indeed was there to "settle"—except the ultimate question of the life or death for the Chinese Nationalists? Can it be reasonably doubted that a reign of terror would be unleashed on the people of Taiwan if their island were surrendered to the Red Chinese?

The United States is, of course, bound by formal treaty to the pro-

---

[4] *The New York Times*, February 28, 1972.

tection of Taiwan. A treaty must be regarded as more than an "interest"; it is a binding international obligation. Yet the Chinese Communists are permitted to declare arrogantly that "all U.S. forces and military installations must be withdrawn from Taiwan," and in response the Americans say that their "ultimate objective" is indeed to withdraw all U.S. forces and military installations from Taiwan. Such an objective was never before enunciated or even implied. The slender reservation of leaving open the deadline for withdrawal is virtually undercut, needless to say, by the promise that American forces "in the meantime" would be progressively reduced "as the tension in the area diminishes."

The language is hopelessly vague. In precisely what "area," and "tension" upon whom? Who exactly would define these terms? Would it be Dr. Kissinger and President Nixon, on the one hand, or Premier Chou and Chairman Mao on the other? When Dr. Kissinger was asked in a news conference at Shanghai why the American government had failed to take official note of its treaty commitment to Taiwan, he ducked the question altogether. His bland reply was that it was always "extraordinarily difficult" to discuss such a thing "on the territory of a country with which we do not maintain formal diplomatic relations." But the niceties of diplomatic etiquette had in no way restrained the Red Chinese, and the American President was not inhibited from making an official response. Somewhat lamely Dr. Kissinger added that the issue of Taiwan was "a matter of profound principle" in the eyes of the Chinese Communists. Was Taiwan less a matter of principle to the Americans?

The Shanghai communique included a statement by the Peking regime that it "firmly supports the struggle of all oppressed people and nations." Communists traditionally define oppression, of course, as a condition existing solely because of the existence of a "class society," i.e., any non-communist society. In the communique, therefore, the Chinese Communists explicitly committed themselves to continuing revolutionary warfare against all non-communist governments. While they were telling this to the Americans, President Nixon and Dr. Kissinger were assuring them that the United States government was no longer particularly interested in the fate of their next potential victims on Taiwan who have held out against Communism for more than twenty years. This part of the communique might also be interpreted as a declaration of war on the United States since it asserts Peking's intent to support a "people's revolution" everywhere—not excluding this country. But Chou En-lai was safe in declaring it; he knew that the American side had no intellectual defense against it, no philosophical ground to stand on except pragmatism.

Into the communique Chou En-lai neatly inserted a reference to his long bankrupted "Five Principles of Peaceful Co-existence" first enunciated at the Bandung Conference of 1955. Since that time, events have proven that these "principles" were nothing more than a thick smokescreen put up by the Peking regime to facilitate their infiltration, subversion, and armed aggression on a global scale. Some of the nations that participated in the Bandung Conference have already tasted its bitter fruits.

The Shanghai communique was indeed so lopsided that Mr. Nixon's defenders have taken to claiming, without a shred of evidence, that the President must have obtained from Premier Chou some special concessions or advantages not even hinted at in the joint statement. If so, what are we to make of the President's unequivocal public declaration on his return that he made no secret deals in China? If Mr. Nixon was telling the truth, then he sacrificed the American commitment to Taiwan for nothing. If he was not telling the truth, then his word in the field of foreign affairs can no longer be trusted. It is obviously one or the other; there can be no third alternative.

In no way did the Shanghai communique contain the slightest renunciation of the possible use of force against Taiwan. The American statement readily confirmed the contention of both the Communists and the Nationalists that Taiwan was "part of China." It emphasized, however, that since the Taiwan question was "internal," this remained "the crucial question" obstructing normal relations between Communist China and the United States. It reported Washington's desire for a peaceful settlement "by the Chinese themselves," and with that "prospect" in mind it asserted the President's "ultimate objective of the withdrawal of all United States forces and military installations" from the island. In the meantime, but without timetable, Mr. Nixon promised progressively to reduce the 8,000-man American contingent in Taiwan "as the tension in the area diminishes."

The Shanghai communique stated the Nixon-Kissinger belief that the effort to reduce "the tension in the area" would be served by improving communications between nations with different ideologies so as to lessen the risks of confrontation through accident, miscalculation or misunderstanding. Neither Washington nor Peking should claim infallibility, and each should be prepared to reexamine its own attitudes for the common good. On his part, Dr. Kissinger observed tersely to newsmen that the Chinese Communists could hardly be expected to send official representatives to Washington as long as the Chinese Nationalists maintained diplomatic status there. The Peking government, he said, would probably choose to move slowly and indirectly on all matters of Sino-American exchange. He thought a "contact point" between Washington and Peking might be established in the "reasonably near future," though not in the United States. He cited the precedent of the occasional and slow-paced ambassadorial talks between the United States and China in Warsaw over the past fifteen years. Officials going to Peking "from time to time" could have ambassadorial or even cabinet rank, he said, now that the President and the Secretary of State had both been there. Dr. Kissinger was not modest in describing his own role. The opening of China, he said, was "an important event in the mechanics of my success," the "main point" of which "comes from the fact that I have acted alone."

President Nixon was explicit in declaring that the new American approach to China would not be "at the expense of old friends." This was an unmistakable allusion to the Nationalist Chinese government on Taiwan. He appeared to be saying that the United States would maintain its defense commitment to Taiwan under the 1954 treaty even though this commitment was nowhere mentioned in the Shanghai communique. Yet the communique expressed an American acknowledgement that there was but one China, and the island province of Taiwan was a part of it. Would not the Chinese Communists then be entitled, at any time they saw fit, to claim that the United States was violating the spirit of the communique by continuing to extend military aid to the Republic of China? Would not such aid be "interference," from Peking's viewpoint, in the internal affairs of China? Eight times in the communique the Chinese Communist regime pledged "firm support" to its own allies. Yet Peking insisted that the United States declare an "ultimate objective" of withdrawing all American forces and military installations from Taiwan. "After a week of hard negotiations," the syndicated columnist Joseph Kraft wrote, "the Chinese stood firm. It was the Americans who 'caved in'."

From Taipei came the strongest disapproval of "the so-called joint communique." An 850-word statement from the foreign ministry predicted diametrically the opposite of "the generation of peace" forecast by President Nixon. The free nations of the Western Pacific, this statement read, would be the first to suffer from the aftermath of the President's visit if they entertained the "slightest delusion of coexisting peacefully" with the Chinese Communists. As for the Nationalists, they would simply consider null and void any agreement between Washington and Peking involving their rights and interests: "The destruction of the tyranny of the Chinese Communist regime is a sacred responsibility of the government and people of the Republic of China, which will never waver or change under any circumstances." At the same time the 1,374-member National Assembly passed by acclamation a resolution condemning President Nixon's trip to the mainland. "Not only will it fail to contribute to world peace," the resolution read, "but it will make the Free World countries lose their faith in the United States."

While the President was still in China, the American press indulged in an orgy of speculation on the possible long-term consequences of the epochal "Journey for Peace." Predictions varied in details, but on the whole they were cautiously optimistic. On the East Coast the outlook was generally bright. The *Concord Monitor* declared Mr. Nixon's trip "one of greatest diplomatic and political coups of the century," while the *New Haven Register* regarded it as "an attempt to take a first step" and the *Boston Globe* as a "good start." The liberal Atlanta *Constitution* looked forward to "an agreement for some kind of American presence in Peking and concommitant arrangements for the Chinese in Washington," but its local rival, the *Journal,* warned Georgians that it was "far too early to wax euphoric" on the outcome. "Yet the risks are well worth taking," said the *Charlotte News,* "even if the only result is a crack in the isolation that was partly China's own choosing, and partly the choosing of the West."

In mid-continent the mood was mixed. Glowingly optimistic was the *St. Louis Post-Dispatch:* "Many Americans may be viewing Communist China in a favorable light for the first time. This of itself is a notable advance in international amity and a heartening portent." The *Detroit Free Press,* on the other hand, warned of "great difficulty" ahead and noted caustically: "We hope Mr. Nixon's reference to 'a long march together' was lost in translation, but the thought is worth remembering."

The prognosis on the West Coast was perhaps least optimistic. The *Seattle Times* distinguished between "the euphoria reported from Peking" and "the specifics of agreements," and the *Portland Evening Express* predicted the "concrete results" of the President's trip would be "small at this time." In Los Angeles both major newspapers were skeptical. "What we have seen so far out of China," the *Times* said, "have only been images, two-dimensional, without depth, and ultimately without much real meaning." The *Herald-Examiner* was even more pointed: "What is going on can be viewed as a carefully considered major move by Peking to help accomplish its continuing aim of emergence as an active world power. A smiling dragon is a big improvement over one spitting—but it is still a dragon. We better not forget, even for a moment." The *Sacramento Union* went so far as to instruct the President on what specific assurances to obtain: "We would expect the Chinese leaders to assure him that they will stop menacing their neighbors, stop supporting guerrilla subversion in other countries, stop polluting the atmosphere with nuclear tests, and stop vilifying the United States at every turn."

It hardly needs repeating that President Nixon's spectacular "Journey for Peace" yielded no such assurances. Instead, the American chief executive left in China his own implied assurance that the United States would no longer regard the Peking regime as a menace to its neighbors or an exporter of subversion. More even than this, the President left his solemn promise at Shanghai that the Chinese Communists would be allowed to settle their "Taiwan question" with no further imposition on the part of the United States. This, in a word, was the tragedy of Mr. Nixon's trip to China.

8

Repercussions
[1972-1974]

ONE OF THE first products of President Nixon's journey to the Asian mainland was the flowering of an old dream long cherished by admirers of the Peking regime. This was the dream of inevitable collaboration between the mainland Chinese and the Chinese of Taiwan. For years the admirers of Mao Tse-tung's "social revolution" had predicted, in their learned papers and books and press statements, that the day would come when all the Chinese peoples of Asia would know the blessings of the new system. In advancing this version of the "One China" concept, Mao's sycophants around the world were merely italicizing the Peking party-line as authored by Premier Chou En-lai and his controlled press. Now that so consecrated an anti-Communist as Richard M. Nixon had eaten Peking duck at Chou's banquet table, the great day seemed just around the corner. Prior to Mr. Nixon's trip, the prediction was always that the inevitable collaboration would occur, after the passing of the aged rivals Chairman Mao and President Chiang. But now no further delay seemed necessary; the old enemies might still be alive, but the "new China policy" of the United States had made this fact obsolete.

What Mao Tse-tung's foreign friends conveniently overlooked in their idyllic speculations, however, was another fact—the actual attitude and response of the people of Taiwan. In their reveries Mao's admirers had always imagined that a native revolution of some sort was boiling beneath the surface in Taiwan. The eruption of this volcano, they predicted, would finally blow apart the "corrupt" Nationalist government at Taipei and allow the oppressed Taiwanese to welcome the liberators from across the Formosa Strait. The twin ideas of "oppression" and "corruption" on Taiwan were, of course, central and integral to the whole dream of inevitable collaboration; the people of Taiwan were supposed to respond accordingly when the moment was ripe. The moment was now ripe, but the response was not as advertised. The people of Taiwan reacted to President Nixon's trip in reverse: they united behind their leaders as never before.

On May 15, 1972, the central committee of the Kuomintang admitted three native Taiwanese to full membership, and at the same time many younger Taiwanese officials declared their unswerving loyalty to the National government. If a native revolt was brewing on Taiwan, responsible Taiwanese either know nothing of it or refused to sully isolated examples of legitimate democratic dissent by labelling these "rebellion." Instead they joined the old mainlanders in enthusiastic endorsement of the position of the National government as enunciated by Premier Chiang Ching-kuo. The Republic of China, he declared in a speech to the Legislative Yuan, would never compromise with the Chinese Communists and would never adopt the view of any other government toward the Chinese mainland.

Chiang Ching-Kuo's words were clear as bugle notes. Democracy and dictatorship, he said, were antithetical and irreconcilable; the fundamental contradictions between them could not be surmounted by any so-called detente because the fundamental struggle was still between freedom and slavery. Premier Chiang acknowledged that the Chinese Communists might alter their tactics because of ideological contradictions within their own camp, but superficial relaxation on their part would bring no relaxation on the part of the Free Chinese. In the past six months, he said, the world has witnessed "many perverse changes" that appeared "deceptive and treacherous" in the eyes of a people dedicated to principles of justice, but in the end such reverses would only strengthen the national determination of the Free Chinese.

On June 27, 1972, the central committee of the Kuomintang reaffirmed the premier's position with the following resolution:

After the conclusion of the Russo-American summit conference, we will never accept any influence of multipolar international politics. To recover the mainland of China is the primary target of the current struggle. The [Central] Committee unanimously supports the firm stand Premier Chiang Ching-kuo has expressed that the Administration adheres to the anti-Communist national policy under which no contract will be sought with the Chinese or Russian Communists and seeks consummation of the faith in national recovery and reconstruction.

This stand was reiterated in a strong speech by Dr. Chang Pao-shu, secretary-general of the Kuomintang. Every KMT member knew, he said, that Peking was again spreading the "peace talk" rumor, but "none of us will be daunted or affected in any way" by the new tactic. The Communists always resort to force when convinced they can win on the battle field; they will "talk peace" only when realizing they cannot win militarily. The Peking regime had suffered serious internal problems since Mao Tse-tung decided to purge Lin Piao, Dr. Chang noted, and its leaders now had no choice but to hide behind the facade of detente with an old foe.

From Taipei's point of view, any real "normalization of relations" between Peking and Washington was a practical impossibility. For more than twenty years the Chinese Communists had relentlessly preached an anti-American gospel to their subjects; it was therefore simply unrealistic to expect a whole generation of mainland Chinese suddenly to believe that effective detente was at hand. Officials in Taipei, better equipped than "experts" elsewhere to understand the intricacies of the mainland mentality, predicted that there would now emerge an internal as well as an external foreign policy at Peking. Externally, detente with the United States would be the great goal and the Soviet Union the great threat; internally, however, the Americans would still be regarded the "Running dogs of imperialism," and the only feasible diplomatic arrangement would be a new bridge of understanding between Peking and Moscow.

In the leading commercial nation of Asia, Japan, the implications of President Nixon's journey were profound. Should the Tokyo government follow suit and open a flirtation with the Chinese Communists? The Taiwan trade was suddenly at stake. Japan had already displaced the United States as Taiwan's chief trading partner. Their two-way commerce in 1971, for instance, exceeded one billion dollars—a third more than Japan's trade that year with mainland China—and was showing a consistent rise of about twenty percent per annum. Moreover, the Japanese investment on Taiwan, which had grown to almost a hundred million dollars, stood in jeopardy.

Less than six months after President Nixon's pilgrimage, the conservative Sato government fell in Tokyo. On July 7, 1972, Kakuei Tanaka took over as premier at the head of the Democrat-Liberal party. Quickly, as might be expected, Chou En-lai invited the new

Japanese leader to Peking for a summit meeting to begin on September 25. More than forty years of enmity between Japan and the Chinese mainland appeared to be ending with dramatic swiftness, and to many Asians this prospect was as electric as the American president's announcement of a year earlier. A Japanese newspaper editor had then written that President Nixon was "running the risk of sacrificing a partnership" for the sake of courting an old adversary. The same might now be said of Tanaka.

Anticipating an adverse effect, a former ambassador to the United States expressed his fears publicly. The same apprehension was reflected by a retired admiral who, as head of the Japanese National Defense League, observed that the atmosphere in Tokyo since President Nixon's trip had degenerated into a "China mood." Other elder statesmen were advising Tanaka not to cut ties with the Nationalist Chinese, but it was difficult for the new premier to withstand pressures building up on the part of both ambitious businessmen and the ultra-leftist wing of his party.

According to another naval officer, Admiral Hoshino, the new premier could not long oppose the "China mood" because he simply had to win the election which would take place before the end of the year. When announcing his decision to accept Chou En-lai's invitation to the summit, Tanaka took pains to point out that the Japanese-American security treaty had not changed and that the "Taiwan clause" was still in effect. (Under this clause Tokyo had acknowledged that the Chinese Nationalist defense system was important to Japanese security in East Asia.) It was the Soviet military build-up along the Chinese border, said Admiral Hoshino, that caused Chou to "quicken the pace" and steal a march, diplomatically over the shaky new government in Tokyo. An example of the Peking technique was clear in the abusive handling of Tanaka's personal representative at Peking, Zentaro Kosaka, when summoned to Chou's office one evening at ten. Referring angrily to a recent report from Taipei suggesting that Tokyo was not ready to cut diplomatic ties, Chou pounded the table and insisted that it must be done at once. Kosaka meekly conveyed Chou's demand to his superiors.

Meanwhile, Tanaka was busy taking the popular pulse. A cabinet-sponsored poll in September showed that 73 percent of the Japanese people felt that the government should not cut ties with Taipei. This heavy majority evidently believed that Japan owed an old obligation to Chiang Kai-shek's Nationalists dating back to the end of the Pacific war. (It was the Generalissimo who had then insisted that Hirohito be allowed to remain as emperor; moreover, he had demanded no reparations, had sent no occupation police to Japan, and had allowed some 2,000,000 captured Japanese soldiers to return to their homeland.) But late in September, despite assorted advice from experienced sources and in the face of much public sentiment against a basic departure in policy, Premier Tanaka did visit Peking for five days of summitry with the Chinese Communists. In the subsequent communique Japan recognized the People's Republic of China as the "sole legal government of China," and that Taiwan was an "inalienable part" of its territory; and diplomatic relations between the two countries would be established immediately.

Reaction in Taipei was immediate and vigorous. On October 2 the national Assembly formally declared "null and void" the September 29 joint statement of Tanaka and Chou En-lai. Many other offices promptly condemned Tanaka's move—the Taiwan Provincial Assembly, the Federation of Labor, the Chamber of Commerce, and the Chinese Language Society—and a student demonstration in front of the city hall brought forth placards reading "Down with Japan" and Boycott Japanese Goods." The students burned Japanese commodities and Tanaka's effigy, pledged full support for whatever action the government might take against Japan, and paraded through Taipei's main throughfares in ten groups.

The individual voices of protest were unusually strong. Dr. Ku Cheng-kang, honorary chairman of the World Anti-Communist League, urged "freedom-loving peoples" the world over to guard against the Tanaka-Chou collusion. The establishment of relations between Tokyo and Peking, Dr. Ku predicted, would bring "scourges" of Communist infiltrators into Japan and would endanger the peace of the whole Pacific region. The traditional Double Tenth message of President Chiang Kai-shek on October 10, 1972, contained a sharp indictment of the Tokyo government for its "abnormal relations" with the Chinese Communists. President Chiang declared that the Japanese premier had publicly ignored "justice, law and reason" by disregarding the opinions of experienced persons in Japan and the international community. Tanaka, he said, had brazenly attempted to distort "the unlawful into the lawful and the abnormal into the normal" by "opening the door for the thief."

Editorial reaction was equally explicit. The English-language *China News* of October 2 termed Tanaka's move a classic example of old-style Japanese treachery. While the Republic of China continued to have thousands of supporters in Japan, the Tokyo government had "plunged the dagger into the back of its friend in September of 1972 just as in September of 1931, July of 1937, and December of 1941." According to the *Chung Yang Jih Pao* (Central Daily News), the Tanaka-Chou joint statement would evoke the anger of all justice-motivated peoples once they understood its implications.

There may have been just cause for Taipei's attitude in this instance, but the fact is that the Tanaka government was forced into its new relationship with the Peking regime primarily as a result of the Nixon-Kissinger accommodation. To the Japanese, territorial propinquity created a special situation: they could not permit American businessmen a chance to capture the mainland market without also putting one foot in the door. As one realistic Japanese official said, "Our honeymoon with Communist China may last one year at the most. Then you can watch for Peking to gradually tighten the screws."

The President's trip caused eyebrows to arch throughout East Asia. In the city-state of Singapore, the world's fourth largest port and the crossroads of the Pacific, many leaders were profoundly concerned. Singapore had hitherto been little influenced by pressure from its neighbors. Approximately one-fourth of its people are Malay, Indian, Pakistani, Ceylonese, or Eurasian; three-fourths are Chinese. With tax-free, strike-free inducements and an abundance of skilled labor, the city-state had more than 200 international businesses. Traditional values were respected. No pornography shops or drug dens were allowed to operate, and no pill-popping hippies were permitted to land. The ministry of education, disapproving hair below the shirt collar, had instructed school principals to dismiss male teachers and students who ignore its standards. Signs in the shops warned customers: "Man with long hair will be waited on last."

The Cambridge-trained prime minister, Lee Kuan Yew, was a skillful administrator who wanted no part of Communism, domestic or imported. He had impressed many American visitors. Spiro Agnew found in Singapore "one of the most advanced societies on earth," and John Connolly called the city-state "the best-run country in the world." Prime Minister Yew's formula was simple: "Nothing is free." The twin ingredients of Singapore's progress, he often said, were the people's will to work and their willingness to pay a fair price.

Some pundits have said that Yew should have been engaged as a public-relations consultant by the last three American presidents because he did so superior a job in explaining what the United States was doing in Indo-China. "However history may judge the American intervention in Vietnam," he liked to tell visitors, "it has broken the hypnotic spell on the other Southeast Asians that Communism is irresistible, that it is the wave of history." But now he was not so optimistic. President Nixon's trip had discouraged him. He predicted that some of his neighbors would now "go neutral" and others would become overtly pro-communist. He went on to suggest that a buffer zone against Communist infiltration be established in Thailand. Once, when complimented on his grasp of the world scene, he replied: "Well, I have to have it. When the elephants are on the rampage and you are a mouse, it can be a painful business."

Next door in Malaysia, the effects of the "Journey for Peace" were quickly felt. The Malaysian government suddenly withdrew from ASEAN (Association of Southeast Asia Nations) and began moving toward accommodation with Peking. Officials in Kuala Lumpur evidently hoped that a visible gravitation toward Maoist ideology would result in diminishment of Communist guerrilla activity in the northern sectors of the country. A reconciliation with Peking, they now believed, might also slow down the open revolt by the Malaysian Communists entrenched in Sarawak, Northern Borneo.

In Indonesia, on the other hand, an influx of 15,000 Chinese Communist agents trained in espionage has caused great concern to President Suharto's government. The attorney-general reported that these subversive agents had been smuggled in by way of Hong Kong, Malaysia, and the Philippines. Moreover, a large number of Indonesian-born Chinese have recently expressed a desire to visit their homeland. This request was rejected by authorities who had vivid memories of the abortive summer coup of 1965 which caused the Indonesian government to break relations with Peking.

In South Korea the situation was equally serious as internal squabbles now began among leading officials. When President Park Chung-hee clearly indicated his negative reaction to the new posture of the United States government, some members of parliament started to agitate for a gesture of conciliation toward the Communists of North Korea. University students joined in, and soon the issue was constitutional revision.

Of all the nations of southeast Asia, the Philippines have felt the shock of the new China policy perhaps more drastically than any other. When President Ferdinand E. Marcos was first informed of the text of the Shanghai joint communique, he cried out: "If this can happen to Nationalist China, there is no assurance that it won't happen to us." President Marcos has good reason to be worried. Over the last few years Communist-inspired insurgency has been a major problem in the Islands. An index to the depth of the trouble is the continual plotting against the life of Marcos himself. At least six assassination attempts were made on the life of the President since 1972.

What brought on this tendency to violence? After World War II the revolutionary movement in the islands consisted chiefly of the Huks, a force of 10,000 directed by experienced Communist agents, but by 1964 the government had reduced Huk strength to practically zero. Recently, however, insurgency has been on the rise, and the most important of three leftist groups, the "New People's Army," is believed to be receiving both guidance and weapons from the Chinese mainland.

Part of the political appeal of the left in the Philippines is, of course, anti-Americanism. The United States is naturally unpopular in some quarters because of its military presence at such large bases as Clark Field and Subic Bay. But a more important factor lies in the residual bitterness of some Filipinos against the harsh realities of economic life in the islands. After a generation of independence the Philippines continue to suffer from crippling unemployment, soaring inflation, and a great gap between the tiny rich minority and the impoverished majority—as well as obvious political corruption and lawlessness ranging from extortion to piracy. President Marcos, now in his second term, had spent several years wrestling unsuccessfully with such problems as these, problems which, according to the insurgents, were of the President's making. Then came the dramatic American gesture in China and the corresponding acceleration of insurgency in the Philippines.

The imposition of martial law in the Philippines, along with the imposition of censorship of the press, restriction of travel abroad, and the commandeering of airlines and other utilities, which was President Marcos' response to the insurgency, when viewed as an admission of breakdown in constitutional government, inevitably threatens the U.S. stake in the islands. The American stake is both military and economic. On the military side, there are the five bases considered by strategic experts to be the most important American installations in the Western Pacific. On the economic side, some 800 American companies have a total investment in the Philippines of at least two billion dollars. President Marcos is now saying that his government must "renegotiate" not only the military-bases agreement but also all its other agreements with the United States. This pronouncement marks the most definite move yet by the Filipinos to wean themselves from American influence. Marcos made the statement following a three-hour meeting of his National Security Council in which the foreign minister, Carlos P. Romulo, offered an assessment of President Nixon's Peking and Moscow summitry and its possible long-range effects on Southeast Asia.

In Australia the reaction to President Nixon's summit diplomacy was perhaps less dramatic but no less forboding. Changes were quick and stunning. The socialistic Labor Party now took control of the government and the new prime minister, Gough Whitlam, wasted no time in moving away from the pro-American stance of his predecessors. He immediately established formal relations with both mainland China and East Germany, and then solemnly warned the French to cease their missile-testing in the Pacific. (France and Israel, incidentally, seem to be the only Western nations which are not intimidated by the nebulous specter of "world opinion." Paying no attention to such contrived clamor, France went blandly ahead with her nuclear tests in the Pacific. The French nuclear deterrent may be small, but by no means is it negligible. The British government then refused to join Australia in condemning the Pacific tests—a refusal which angered not only Prime Minister Whitlam but also England's own band of nuclear disarmers, most of whom were Laborites.)

Anti-Americanism soon became open and even vociferous in Prime Minister Whitlam's cabinet. The labor unions, which generally set the political coloration of the party, were strongly influenced by Australian Communists whose particular target was the presence of American military bases in northern Australia. Their hatred of the United States was reflected throughout the party and even influenced the political climate in neighboring New Zealand.

After a private tour of five weeks throughout southeast Asia, a former Australian defense minister, Malcolm Fraser, expressed his conviction that his nation was now an unreliable neighbor. Fraser felt that Prime Minister Whitlam had seriously damaged Australia's reputation. The various heads of state, he said in a newspaper interview, could not understand Whitlam's abruptness in recognizing Peking and were surprised that Australian officials did not discuss the matter with them first. The Thai government, for example, resented the fact that Whitlam had called for the removal of U.S. troops from Thailand and the withdrawal of Australian troops from exercises of SEATO (Southeast Asia Treaty Organization).

A desire to please the Chinese Communists has characterized the Whitlam government from the beginning. The new prime minister hoped thereby to gain an economic advantage from trade with the Chinese mainland; he also hoped to add to his political prestige by playing a pivotal role in regional affairs. Instead, he has tarnished Australia's reputation among her neighbors. Whitlam's early decision not to participate in the work of the Asian and Pacific Council has paralyzed that body, and his withdrawal of troops from the SEATO exercises has dealt a severe blow to collective security in the Pacific.

In the spring of 1973, just a year after the President's trip to Peking, the new American ambassador to Australia, Marshall Green, foresaw "flexibility" as the coming U.S. policy in East Asia. Using Japan as an analogy, Green said the United States was now willing to accept the reality that allies may sometimes find it necessary to "take a different path" toward common goals.

What then was the immediate aftermath of President Nixon's visit to Communist China? Throughout Southeast Asia there was a feeling that America had chartered a new Asian course that spelled uncertainty. Skepticism began to flow into the capitols of our Asian allies that America may not "stay the course" regarding its present commitments, economic and military. A psychological turn toward more self-reliance and less dependency upon Washington became common. Like a pebble in a stream, waves of gravitations towards Peking by our allies have already begun and the end is yet not in sight nor are consequences which may affect our national security. The danger lies in a policy that may placate Peking too far at the expense of our friends in Asia.

9

Forecasts

As THESE PAGES go to the printer in the fall of 1974, the global situation remains touchy and tentative. Two and a half turbulent years have passed since President Nixon made his "Journey for Peace" to Peking. Since then the United States government has gambled continuously on the Nixon-Kissinger doctrine that a "just and lasting peace" could be achieved, and a quarter-century of Cold War finally terminated by smiles, toasts, and promises at the summit with the leading Communists of the world. To advance his concept of detente, President Nixon met spectacularly three times at the summit with the current masters of the Soviet Union; and Dr. Kissinger's shuttle diplomacy has produced highly touted results in both Indo-China and the Middle East. The "peace with honor" objective of the administration was the former President's best credit with the American people. And on taking office President Ford promised continuity in foreign policy. Many Americans are optimistic that the age of armed confrontation is passing into history. Others are not so certain. Among the unconvinced are some members of Congress who happen to regard former President Nixon's new China policy with a measure of skepticism.

During the month of May, 1973, more than fifty members of the

U.S. House of Representatives went on record with their current views of Chinese-American relations. The theme of their remarks was that the United States government, while easing tensions with the Chinese Communists, must do nothing to lessen its endorsement of the freedom of the people of the Republic of China on the island of Taiwan. This position was bipartisan. "Few allies in our history have proven as reliable and resolute as the Republic of China," said Congressman J. Kenneth Robinson, a Republican from Virginia, adding that the people of this "brave and industrious island merit fully a profession of our enduring friendship and help in the advancement of their national identity, freedom from aggression and continued economic progress." Congressman William Dorn, a Democrat from South Carolina, declared that the people of Taiwan "deserve the highest commendation and accolades of the free world for the leadership they have exercised, and the burdens they have borne with equanimity, in the ongoing struggle to see that free men do not forget the real nature—the real face—of their common enemy."

Other House members added words of praise. Clement Zablocki, a Wisconsin Democrat, noted that while some Americans had obviously been impressed by Mao's mainland "model" for so-called progress in Asia, there was "an even more impressive model" of true Asian progress to be seen on Taiwan. Robert Leggett, Democrat of California, stated unequivocally that the Republic of China represented what the United States has been trying to achieve in Asia since 1945: a dynamic society that is constantly building and improving upon the foundations of a prosperous life for its people.

Trent Lott of Mississippi, recalling President Nixon's pledge that his moves toward lessening tensions with the Chinese Communists would never be "at the expense of our old friends," insisted that nothing be done which might "compromise the freedom" of the Chinese on Taiwan. Edward Derwinski of Illinois stressed the same point. "To abandon strong and dependable friends to obtain a few concessions," he said, ". . . would indeed be a very questionable move." Robert Sikes of Florida emphasized the moral obligation of Americans to maintain their support of the Republic of China. "Today," he added, "the free Chinese probably are stronger than they ever have been. . . . The country is so strong economically that it gives foreign assistance to less fortunate nations."

Extensive remarks on this point were offered by an Indiana Republican, John Myers, who just returned from a trip to Taiwan. He reviewed the island's economic achievements, noting that the Republic of China was one of the very few nations that had outgrown the need for direct American aid. Even more to its credit was the fact that the Republic of China was now furnishing "substantial technical assistance and even some economic aid to other under-developed nations around the world." Myers proposed that the United States government encourage the free Chinese to take the lead in providing technical aid to the developing nations. Such a program, he argued, would contribute "in a solid, measurable degree" to international stability.

Myers' proposal was warmly supported by his Indiana colleague, Earl Landgrebe, who stressed that the Republic of China was ready, willing, and able to extend such assistance to other countries. Richard Ichord of Missouri added that in 1972 Taiwan showed a growth in gross national product of eleven percent, the highest in all Asia. But the "most miraculous statistic," Ichord said, was that a small island with a population of scarcely fifteen million should surpass the immense Chinese mainland in total foreign trade. James Martin of North Carolina seconded Ichord's views.

According to William Randall of Missouri, Taiwan was unique in that it presented "the only Chinese alternative to the fundamental evils of a Communist world." In the Republic of China, he noted, the people actually particpate in elections and are permitted to discuss public affairs! Carlos Moorhead of California urged that the 1954 mutual defense treaty be newly empahsized, and that the American people be made newly aware of the "wise policy" of Presidents Eisenhower, Kennedy, and Johnson. An outspoken freshman Republican, Steven Symms of Idaho, observed: "We might consider moving the headquarters of the United Nations to Peking and let them pay for the forty per cent share that we have been paying for the past twenty-five years!"

Bill Chappell of Florida, a member of the important House Appropriations Committee, remarked that the Republic of China was a fine example of what free people could do on their own. Across the Taiwan Strait, on the other hand, was a classic example of what enslaved people could never do! Dan Daniel of Virginia, a member of the House Armed Services Committee, thought it absolutely necessary for members of Congress to remind their constituents of the continuing importance of the symbolism of Free China. Those nations that the United States may need as its allies at some future time, he said, are now "watching closely our attitude and our actions toward this staunch friend of earlier days." Another member of the Armed Services Committee, Samuel Stratton of New York, warned the administration against getting "carried away" with its new romance with the Peking regime. The Republic of China, he said, had shown that it could "stand strong and tall on its own two feet," and its future would never be determined by any "smoke-filled room" agreement among diplomats of other nations. Stratton's fellow New Yorker, John Murphy, invoked old Wilsonian ideals when he warned President Nixon not to betray "the very principles and ideals upon which we were created and for which we have pledged to struggle."

Eleven members of the House of Representatives formally introduced a resolution calling on the administration to do nothing which might "compromise the freedom of our friend and ally, the Republic of China, and its people." Proposing the resolution on the floor, Trent Lott of Mississippi warned that if the United States did not periodically reaffirm its basic commitment to principles and friends, there was a danger that some nations might mistake such official silence for abandonment. "Let the world make no mistake," he said, "that there are many in the Congress who will never sanction any such abandonment of our free Chinese allies." The young congressman noted that more than fifty members of the House had spoken up on the necessity of keeping close relations with the Republic of China. "While different viewpoints were expressed on the wisdom of our current policy to mainland China," he added, "there was complete agreement that the United States government should make no declarations, come to no agreements, or take no actions which would compromise the position or the existence of our free Chinese friends on Taiwan and the other islands." Joining Lott in the resolution were Sikes, Derwinski, Zablocki, Robinson, Leggett, Joe Waggonner of Louisiana, James Hanley and Jack Kemp of New York, and Don Clausen and Del Clawson of California.

Congressman Jack Kemp of New York came strongly to the support of the Lott resolution. The status of the Republic of China was simply not negotiable, he said, because the freedom of the Chinese people was itself not negotiable. Speaking on the house floor soon after his return from a visit to Taipei, Kemp declared his total rejection of the nation that the Republic of China could be "used as a bargaining counter in any negotiations between major powers". He called upon his House colleagues to get firmly behind this resolution because it would provide encouragement to a nation which was "one of the most important and inspiring symbols of freedom in the world today and a symbol of man's indomitable will and desire for freedom. . . . The real revolution in Asia is taking place on Taiwan where free people are accomplishing miracles despite recent adversity."

Elaborating on the burgeoning economy of Taiwan, Congressman Kemp noted that since the U.N. debacle of 1971 the Republic of China "has presented a picture of calm, resolute and determined self-confidence in the face of the injustice it has suffered." He was skeptical of many of the glowing reports of those Americans who had recently visited the Chinese mainland. These people, he said, praised what they saw to be achievements "while neglecting to consider the terrible human costs of these accomplishments in terms of both physical suffering and in the stifling of the individual creative spirit." No one could understand the mainland, he added, without also visiting Taiwan and talking with some of the Chinese who risked their lives to escape the tyranny that prevailed there.

What these congressmen said in the spring of 1973 can correctly be interpreted as representing the actual views of a substantial percentage of the American people. If the question of whether the U.S. Government should continue to support the Republic of China were to be brought up for major debate in the Congress, a great flood of letters and telegrams would substantiate this. For fifty years the American people and the Free Chinese have cherished the same lofty ideals of peace and justice, and together they have resisted all enemies of these ideals and the Free Chinese urgently need American sympathy and assistance in resisting the subversion and aggressiveness of the masters of the Mainland, and, conversely, many Americans still recognize Taiwan as an aircraft carrier which is indispensable to the future stability of East Asia.

When all has been said, two vital questions remain to be resolved. What is the true purpose of the Washington-Peking detente from the viewpoint of the Chinese Communist leadership, and what is the real intention of the Chinese Communists toward the Chinese Nationalists on Taiwan? A confidential directive from the Central Committee of the Chinese Communist Party released by the Kunming Military Region under date of March 30, 1973, provides some definite answers. This authenticated document is so revealing that extensive extracts from its pages are reprinted here:

> The visit of Nixon to China led to the announcement of a Sino-U.S. joint communique, in which both sides agreed to expand understanding between the two countries, to establish people-to-people contacts and exchanges in science, technology culture, sports, and the press. This is a matter of profound significance in going one step further to open up the gate of contacts between the people of China and the United States. . . . When Marxism-Leninism is integrated with the revolutionary practices of China, the Chinese revolution puts on a new look. Now our influences have reached the United States. If only we work with patience and enthusiasm, Marxism-Leninism and Mao Tse-tung's thought will definitely be integrated with the practices of the revolutionary movement in the United States, thereby speeding up the process of revolution in the United States. . . . Our invitation to Nixon to visit China proceeds precisely from Chairman Mao's tactical

247

thinking: "exploring contradiction, winning over the majority, opposing the minority, and destroying them one by one." And this by no means indicated a change in our diplomatic line. . . . We agreed to Nixon's tour of China in order that on the one hand we could curb the collusion between the United States and the Soviet Union, weaken their strength, and keep them from taking reckless and impetuous actions to start a war. On the other hand, we use peace talks as a means of forcing U.S. imperialism, now beset with difficulties, at home and abroad, to withdraw its forces from Indochina, Taiwan, the Taiwan Strait, of propelling a peaceful settlement of the questions of Taiwan, Indochina, Vietnam, and of alleviating the tension in Asia and other parts of the world. . . . The visit of Nixon to China was bitterly condemned by the Chiang gang as a "perfidious and unrighteous act" of U.S. imperialism. A meeting was held to discuss the question of neutralization of Southeast Asia by the foreign ministers of Malaysia, Indonesia, the Philippines, Singapore and Thailand. . . . Contradictions between Japan and the United States · were unprecedently sharpened. . . . This state of affairs benefits our work and the people's revolution. . . . The Shanghai Communique released during the visit of Nixon to China has forced U.S. imperialism to take cognizance of the fact that Taiwan is a part of Chinese territory and that the ultimate objective is the withdrawal of all U.S. forces and military installations from Taiwan. This keeps U.S. imperialism from making a further intervention in Taiwan. Simultaneously with improvement in the Sino-U.S. relations, there will arise a gradual alienation in the relations between the United States and the Chiang gang. This is beneficial to our settlement of the Taiwan question without foreign intervention. . . . Comrades, the present improvement in the Sino-U.S. relations does not mean that the Taiwan question can be settled immediately. We must see that the liberation of Taiwan is a complex struggle. On the question of liberating Taiwan there exist two possibilities: liberation by peaceful means and liberation by force of arms. At present, U.S. imperialism has not yet withdrawn its forces from Taiwan and the Taiwan Strait, and the Chiang gang is still doing its utmost to repress the demands of those advocating peace talks with us. We definitely must not pin out hope on a peaceful liberation. Our Army must particularly step up preparations for war and be ready at all times to liberate Taiwan by force of arms.[1]

From their own recent words, the intention of the Chinese Communists regarding Taiwan is unmistakable. They mean to "liberate" the island in one way or the other, either peacefully by subversion or by sheer military power. But the United States remains formally committed, despite all Nixon-Kissinger designs of detente, to the protection of Taiwan from any external attack.

[1]Full text of this document in *Issues and Studies*, Vol. X, No. 9 (June, 1974) and No. 10 (July 1974).

The concept, expressed in the Shanghai statement, that Taiwan is an internal Chinese problem does not alter the treaty commitment of the United States to defend the island. This fact remains central to every weighing of the China question in the future.

The Cold War has been declared at an end, but in the Forbidden City of Peking it is still being waged. Americans should take to heart, now more than ever, the famous inscription engraved on the National Archives Building in Washington, D.C., "What is Past is Prologue." Americans have before them today the full record of Asian history—a record in which appeasement of one sort or another invariably encouraged aggression. Irresolution is still the precursor of war.

Winston Churchill was once asked if the United States could continue to hold the dominating world position. He answered, out of his deep wisdom, "It can do so, if it will stay the course." What Churchill said can certainly be applicable today. What America needs is "staying power" if she is to carry on the leadership of the free world. This is what the Communists seem to have over us—they are dedicated to "stay the course" regardless of the defeats they may experience, and that is why, in the opinion of many, they are winning. In his book, *War and Peace,* the late Secretary of State, John Foster Dulles expressed the problem of America cogently: "What we lack today are not material things. Our material production has broken world records time and again. What we are truly short of is the commitment of justice and motive power. Without such a conviction all other things will have little value. Our material power is enormous," he wrote, "but our moral power is growing increasingly weaker." The greatness of the American nation does not lie in its wealth, high living standard or number of nuclear weapons, but rather in its sincere dedication to the idea of freedom and democracy.

Selected Readings

THE FOLLOWING LIST of fourteen books includes some of this author's favorite readings on Modern East Asian Affairs. Not in the list is his own book, *How The Far East Was Lost: American Policy and the Creation of Communist China, 1941-1949* (Chicago: Regnery Co. 1963), and in paperback (New York: Twin Circle: 1973). This book, as well as most of those listed below, seldom appear today in the footnotes or bibliographies of Far Eastern publications. The reason, of course, is that their decidedly anti-Communist point of view is not in current fashion.

Beezley, P.C., *They Have Sown the Wind* (Mattoon, Ill., Munson Books)

Bouscaren, Anthony T., Daniel Lyons, *Left of Liberal* (New York: Twin Circle, 1969)

Chennault, Claire Lee, *Way Of a Fighter* (New York: Putnam's, 1949)

de Jaegher, Raymond J., and Irene Corbally Kuhn, *The Enemy Within* (New York: Doubleday, 1952)

Hunter, Edward, *The Black Book on Red China* (New York: Bookmailer, 1958)

Liang, Ching-Tung, *General Stilwell in China: The Full Story* (New York: St. John's U. Press, 1972)

Lohbek, Don, *Patrick J. Hurley* (Chicago: Regnery, 1956)

Miles, Milton E., *A Different Kind of War* (New York: Doubleday, 1967)

Morris, Robert, *No Wonder We Are Losing* (New York: Bookmailer, 1958)

Rowe, David Nelson, *Modern China: A Brief History* (Van Nostrand Reinhold, 1959)

Shih, Paul K.T., *Decision for China* (Chicago: Regnery, 1959)

Tansill, Charles C., *Back Door to War* (Chicago: Regnery, 1952)

Utley, Freda, *The China Story* (Chicago: Regnery, 1951)

Vinacke, Harold M., *The United States and the Far East, 1945-1951* (Stanford, 1952)

Index

251

military officer in China, 98ff.; defeated in Burma, 99; opposes Chennault, 100; loses authority, 102, and Mao, 105

Stimson, Henry L., on Kellogg-Briand treaty, 68; on Japanese in Manchuria, 69ff.; and embargoes on Japan, 79f.; on lend-lease to China, 96

Stuart, John L., 130, 136, 141

Sun Yat-sen, 19, 24; as revolutionary leader, 21f.; as president of China, 22; resigns, 23; Lansing denigrates, 27; deals with Communists, 30; and Borodin, 31f.; dies, 33

Taft, William Howard, and Dollar Diplomacy, 64

Taiping uprising, 16f., 56

Taiwan, importance of, 145; Acheson and Truman abandon, 146; U. S. treaty to defend, 150ff.; Communists threaten, 154; success of order on, 172ff.; Nixon changes attitude toward, 227; as uniting against merger with Mao, 234; Congressional support of, 244; Red China threatens, 248

Tientsin, Treaty of, 16, 54

Truman, Harry S., and fall of China, 119, 138, 140; abandons Taiwan, 146; defends Korea, 148; on MacArthur, 149

Tsai Yuan-pei, 25

Tuchman, Barbara, as critic of Chiang Kai-shek, 92

Tzu Hsi, Empress, 17, 19; supports Boxers, 20; dies, 21

United Nations, Communist China and, 154ff., 169, 206; Nixon welcomes Red China to, 182; Red China admitted to and Nationalist China expelled, 208; reaction to admission, 211

United States, and Open Door, 20, recognizes Republic of China, 38; aids Stalin in WW II; a Century of Relations with, 52; treatment of Chinese in, 57f.; imperialism, 59f.; supports China on Manchuria, 68; loses peace in WW II, 115; summary of position in China war, 143f.; Congressional support of Taiwan in, 244

Vandenberg, Arthur R., 137f.

Vietnam, 176, 238

Voitinski, Gregori, founds Chinese Communist Party, 27

Wallace, Henry A., 106f.

Wang Ching-wei, 22

Wedemeyer, Gen. Albert C., 116, 118, 142f.; assesses Chinese war effort, 110f., 118, 127., 132; on Formosa, 139

Whampoa Military Academy, 32

White, Harry Dexter, on aid to China, 78; on U.S.-Japanese detente, 85; as author of ultimatum of Japanese, 85f.; as partisan of USSR, 86, 97; as holding up money for Chinese war effort, 97

White, Theodore H., 46, 226

Wilson, Woodrow, 25; Chinese policy of, 65f.; Japanese policy of, 65f.

Yalta, 127, 138; Roosevelt at, 113

Yuan Shih-kai, 19, 21, 22; as president of China, 23; monarchic aspirations of, 23f.; dies, 24, 27